What readers have to say about CodeNotes

"I bought two of your CodeNotes books and I'm a true believer—well written and concise, and I will quickly snatch up the rest as they become available."—DAN, California

"First, I must say I'm so impressed with this book (and, by extension, with the series). [The information] tends to be delivered in the form of concise, accurate writing by experts who don't dumb down the material but rather . . . give a high-level overview. Thanks for such a wonderful series and please keep them coming!"—ARTHUR, Maryland

"CodeNotes offers a good general overview of the .NET platform and the technologies. In short, I believe Random House has hit the bull's eye with the CodeNotes' tight and coherent format."—PRIIT, New York

"I just picked up two of the books in the CodeNotes series and am I ever pleased! Well written, helpful, and to the point. Even better is the fact you can hold them in your hand, take them on a plane, and generally enjoy them. No more of the bloated tomes filled with useless code and explanations, or CDs that are simply advertising vehicles. Can't wait to pick up a few more! Congrats on a great concept, well executed and delivered."—MARK, Canada

"I will be using [CodeNotes] quite often while on engagements as they are compact, concise, and something that I can hand to a developer who I need to get up to speed on a technology, and they can read it by the next day and get to work. And they are nice, small references to have around that don't weigh 9 pounds (with 8.5 pounds of useless information)." —LEE, Oklahoma

"I've recently discovered the CodeNotes series and have become a big fan. The admirable goal of these books is to give you a practical understanding of the subject in 200 pages or less. I've got three of these books and find them all to be well written, appropriately concise, yet filled with what's necessary to get you up to speed on the subject matter. . . . I applaud these sorts of books making an inroad into the technical shelves. More often than not, I don't need a 1,000-page technical epic that is a chore to both carry around and actually read."—TOM, Illinois

"This is a great little book. If you are like me—not a programmer, but [someone who] ends up doing lots of the Web front-end development tasks because the real developers 'don't do scripting'—then this book is for you. It gives real-life examples that can be used to get you started on that dynamically cascading menu or that regular expression to validate your data-entry field."—TUDOR, Australia

"I've been developing software for thirty years and have often read big fat technology intro/overview books that mostly miss the mark. I need to get up to speed quickly on the .NET technologies, and recently purchased three CodeNotes for my Palm handheld. These are the most fantastic technical overviews I have ever read! They assume an intelligent reader, yet explain core concepts in a very straightforward manner. The pointers to the Code Gallery are an excellent solution to reducing book size/reading time, while providing access to more details for those who want it. The samples in the books are terse and informative. The writing style is very comfortable. I could go on and on. Great job, folks!" —DAVID, Wisconsin

OTHER TITLES IN THE CODENOTES SERIES

CodeNotes for J2EE: EJB, JDBC, JSP, and Servlets

CodeNotes for .NET

CodeNotes for Java: Intermediate and Advanced Language Features

CodeNotes for VB.NET

CodeNotes for Web-Based UI

CodeNotes for Oracle 9i

CodeNotes for ASP.NET

CodeNotes for XML

CodeNotes for Web Services in Java and .NET

CodeNotes® for C#

Edited by GREGORY BRILL

CodeNotes® for C#

RANDOM HOUSE TRADE PAPERBACKS
NEW YORK

As of press time, the URLs displayed in this book link or refer to existing websites on the Internet. Random House, Inc., is not responsible for the content available on any such site (including, without limitation, outdated, inaccurate, or incomplete information).

No part of this document may be reproduced or transmitted in any form or by any means, electronic or mechanical, for any purpose, without the express written permission of Random House, Inc. Information in this document is subject to change without notice. While every effort has been made to make this book as accurate as possible, the authors and the publisher assume no responsibility for errors or omissions or otherwise for the use of the information contained herein.

A Random House Trade Paperback Original

Copyright © 2002 by Infusion Development Corporation

All rights reserved under International and Pan-American Copyright Conventions. Published in the United States by Random House Trade Paperbacks, a division of Random House, Inc., New York, and simultaneously in Canada by Random House of Canada Limited, Toronto.

RANDOM HOUSE TRADE PAPERBACKS and colophon are trademarks of Random House, Inc.

CodeNotes® is a registered trademark of Infusion Development Corporation.

Sun, Sun Microsystems, Solaris, Java, JavaBeans, and all Java-based trademarks are trademarks or registered trademarks of Sun Microsystems.

Microsoft, Windows, Windows 2000, Windows XP, Internet Explorer, .NET, ASP.NET, C#, J#, VS.NET, and VB.NET are trademarks of Microsoft Corporation.

Library of Congress Cataloging-in-Publication Data
CodeNotes for C# / edited by Gregory Brill.
p. cm.
Includes index.
ISBN 0-8129-6646-5
1. C# (Computer program language) I. Brill, Gregory.
QA76.73.C154 C63 2002   005.13'3—dc21   2002026583

Printed in the United States of America

Random House website address: www.atrandom.com

246897531

Using CodeNotes

PHILOSOPHY

The CodeNotes philosophy is that the core concepts of any technology can be presented succinctly. The product of many years of consulting and training experience, the CodeNotes series is designed to make you productive in a technology in as short a time as possible.

CODENOTES POINTERS

Throughout the book, you will encounter CodeNotes pointers such as ◦⁽ᶜᴺ⁾CS010101. Notice that the first two letters are C and S (as in C-Sharp) and the remaining characters are numbers. These pointers are links to additional content available on-line at the CodeNotes website. To use a CodeNotes pointer, simply point a web browser to www.codenotes.com and enter the pointer number. The website will direct you to an article or an example that provides additional information about the topic.

CODENOTES STYLE

The CodeNotes series follows certain style guidelines:

- Code objects and code keywords are highlighted using a special font. For example, `array[3]`.

- Code blocks, screen output, and command lines are placed in individual blocks with a special font:

```
//This is an example of code block
```

Listing 1.1   Listing ChapterNumber.ListingNumber Some code

What You Need to Know Before Continuing

This installment of CodeNotes is for developers of all skill levels. As long as you understand basic programming and OOP concepts, you should be able to follow the examples in this book. However, several of the advanced topics require more background than can be compressed into this format. For these topics you can usually find more material on the CodeNotes website.

If you are familiar with at least one modern programming language, such as C++, Java, or Visual Basic, then you should be able to follow the ideas presented in this book. This book does not assume any knowledge of the .NET Framework in which C# applications execute. However, if you want an introduction to the .NET Framework, please see *CodeNotes for .NET*.

About the Authors

SHELDON FERNANDEZ is a senior developer at Infusion Development Canada located in Toronto, Canada. He has developed software for Silicon Valley startups as well as financial and medical institutions in the United States and Canada. He has worked with Microsoft technology for many years and has taught numerous aspects of the .NET Framework (including C#) to a variety of companies, including financial institutions in New York City and software companies in California.

Sheldon, who possesses a computer engineering degree from the University of Waterloo, was also the primary author on *CodeNotes for .NET, CodeNotes for VB.NET,* and *CodeNotes for ASP.NET.* Thankfully, the time he spent authoring this latest CodeNotes was counterbalanced by his intense following of the 2002 World Cup.

CONTRIBUTING AUTHOR

BRENT WILLIAMS is director of training for Infusion Development Corporation. Brent has worked in a variety of product development, training, and consulting positions for corporations in New York, Tokyo, and various cities in Canada. Brent spends his free time canoeing, mountain biking, sailing, and otherwise enjoying the great outdoors. Brent lives in a quiet farmhouse in Chatham, New Jersey.

ABOUT THE EDITOR

GREGORY BRILL is the founder and president of Infusion Development Corporation, a firm specializing in architecting global securities trading and analytic systems for some of the world's largest investment banks. Author of *Applying COM+* and creator of the Infusion Antenna for BlackBerry™, Gregory has written and been quoted in a variety of technology user and business articles. He lives in the New York metropolitan area with his wife and young daughter.

ABOUT INFUSION DEVELOPMENT

Infusion Development Corporation, www.infusiondev.com, is a technology training, software development, and consulting company specializing in the financial services industry. Based in Lower Manhattan, with a second office in Toronto, Infusion developed the Infusion Antenna for BlackBerry™ and formulated the CodeNotes book series with Random House.

More information about the authors and Infusion Development Corporation can be found at http://www.codenotes.com/do/aboutus.

Acknowledgments

First, thanks to John Gomez, who saw the potential of the CodeNotes idea before anyone else and introduced me to Random House. Without John, there would be no CodeNotes. I'd also like to thank Annik LaFarge, who fearlessly championed the series and whose creativity, enthusiasm, and publishing savvy have been instrumental in its creation. Thank you to Mary Bahr, our unflappable editor at Random House, who paved the way and crafted the marketing. Thank you to Ann Godoff, whose strength, decisiveness, and wisdom gave CodeNotes just the momentum it needed. And of, course, the production, sales, and business teams at Random House, with particular thanks to Howard Weill, Jean Cody, and Richard Elman.

On the Infusion Development side, thank you to Tom Nicholson and Rob McGovern for their patient editing. And thank you to the entire cast and crew of Infusion Development, who have supported and encouraged this venture throughout, with special gratitude to Irene Wilk-Dominique, Jessica Pollack, and DeBorah Johnson, who helped administrate and manage so much of this process. I know CodeNotes was extremely trying and tough to do, and involved an awesome amount of research, writing, and editing. But here it is . . . exactly as we envisioned it.

—Gregory Brill

Contents

Using CodeNotes	*vii*
What You Need to Know Before Continuing	*viii*
About the Authors	*ix*
Acknowledgments	*xi*
Chapter 1: Introduction	*3*
Orientation: Why Switch to C#?	*11*
Book Contents	*16*
Core Concepts	*17*
Some Simple Examples	*23*
Chapter Summary	*33*
Chapter 2: .NET Installation	*35*
Requirements	*35*
Installing .NET	*36*
Chapter 3: The .NET Framework	*40*
Topic: The Common Language Runtime	*41*
Topic: The Base Class Libraries	*49*
Topic: Assemblies	*56*

Topic: C# Interoperability with Other Languages	66
Chapter Summary	72
Chapter 4: Syntax and Concepts	**73**
Topic: Data Types and Operators	74
Topic: Controlling Program Flow	101
Topic: Strings, Arrays, and Collections	118
Chapter Summary	131
Chapter 5: .NET Language Features	**132**
Topic: Attributes	133
Topic: Reflection	141
Topic: Delegates	149
Topic: Garbage Collection	161
Chapter Summary	172
Chapter 6: Object-Oriented Programming (OOP)	**174**
Topic: Classes and Objects	175
Topic: Class Inheritance	188
Topic: Interfaces and Structures	201
Topic: Class Infrastructure	211
Chapter Summary	221
Chapter 7: Native and Unsafe Code	**222**
Topic: PInvoke and DllImport	224
Topic: COM Interop	230
Topic: Unsafe Code	236
Chapter Summary	245
Index	**247**

CodeNotes® for C#

Chapter 1

INTRODUCTION

Innovation is the hallmark of the software industry. Like clockwork, the widespread adoption of a particular standard is frequently accompanied by the introduction of a new one. Programming languages are no exception. Drawing upon both theory and practice, a new language will often address the shortcomings and limitations of its predecessors while boasting innovations to boot. So it is with C#.

As you have likely heard, C# (pronounced "C-Sharp") is a new programming language designed by Microsoft. Although the spectrum of existing documentation on C# can give varying impressions as to its place within the software development community, a diagnosis of the language is prone to the following two distinct observations:

1. Formally, C# is a specification for a computer language that Microsoft announced in June 2000. Syntactically, the language is similar to C++ and Java, eliminating (or obscuring) many of the complexities of the former while improving on some of the conventions of the latter. The C# specification was recently ratified by the European Computer Manufacturers Association (ECMA), which means that other vendors can provide their own implementations of the language. Therefore, writing C# applications for operating systems other than Windows will be possible (in fact, as we will see, it is already possible).
2. Practically, C# is the "native" language of the .NET Frame-

work, which is Microsoft's new strategy for the development and deployment of software. As we will see throughout this book, in addition to revamping significant portions of Windows architecture, .NET improves upon existing Microsoft technologies such as ActiveX Data Objects (ADO, for database access) and Active Server Pages (ASP, for web development). Furthermore, .NET introduces some fundamentally new concepts into the realm of software development, such as cross-language inheritance and component versioning through public-key cryptography.

In this regard, C# is not so much a new creature as an improved form of older languages that has been adapted to the .NET environment. For developers C# can serve as an excellent entry point into the .NET world (although, as we will see, other languages are also supported by the framework). By using C# to leverage the .NET Framework you can develop a variety of applications, including traditional Windows desktop applications, web-based applications, and software components that communicate over the open standards of the Internet (web services).

In this book we will examine both the theory and practice behind C#. Whereas theory encompasses the syntactical conventions of the language (such as supported variable types, loop constructs, and object-oriented features), practice incorporates the surrounding .NET Framework on which a C# application executes. Remember, however, that technically C# is nothing more than language specification, and while in practice it is intrinsically tied to .NET, there is no stipulation that it remain so. (An open source effort to port the language to Linux is already in progress; see ᴄɴ⇨CS010001 for details.) Nevertheless, a portion of this book is dedicated to exploring the natural habitat of C#, which is .NET.

C# Is Just Another Language . . .
While it is easy to become buried in the marketing hyperbole, remember that C# is just another language. Although there are some noteworthy innovations with Microsoft's latest creature, the language merely builds on concepts with which you are likely familiar. Memory allocation, array usage, and class inheritance are all-important aspects of C#, though they may be used with slightly different conventions and assumptions than the language you are currently using.

What is special about C# is that it was designed specifically with component development in mind. This means that authoring classes in C# is extremely straightforward because of the language's intrinsic support for component-based features such as properties and events (in contrast to existing languages that obscure the process to varying degrees).

From a syntax perspective, C# is a derivative of the "C" language family, which means that C++ and Java developers will be able to pick it up with relative ease. The language will pose more of a challenge to Visual Basic developers because its syntax is not as rich or "English-like." In addition, C# is built on object-oriented (OO) features such as inheritance, polymorphism, and interfaces, which were either absent or obscured in Visual Basic 6. In the upcoming orientation section we will expand on some of the challenges that developers will face as they migrate from a particular language to C#.

. . . and a Completely New Framework

C# may be just another language, but it is built on a fundamentally new framework. It can be argued that .NET represents the most significant architectural change in Microsoft technology since the introduction of 32-bit Windows 95. Many of the concepts and technologies that you may be familiar with, such as DLLs, COM, and ActiveX, have been overhauled or deprecated by .NET. (As we will see, however, they have not been rendered obsolete because there is still a place for legacy technologies within the framework.) In addition, .NET applications are not run directly by the operating system but instead execute through an intermediary called the Common Language Runtime (CLR), which in some ways is similar to a Java Virtual Machine (VM).

Two Steps

Given these two aspects of Microsoft's new development tool, the requirements for becoming a productive C# developer are twofold:

1. You must familiarize yourself with the conventions of the language. This includes understanding how C# syntax elements (classes, functions, loops, etc.) are utilized as well as learning how programmatic tasks (such as the manipulation of strings) are carried out.
2. You must understand the intricacies of the .NET Framework. To this end let us now examine exactly what the .NET Framework is.

THE .NET FRAMEWORK

C# is simply a piece of a larger and more encompassing entity: Microsoft's new .NET Framework. Depending on your interests and development background, you may already have a number of ideas as to what the .NET Framework entails. As we will see in this book:

- .NET fundamentally changes the manner in which applications execute under the Windows Operating System. With .NET, Microsoft is in effect abandoning its traditional stance, which favors compiled components, and is embracing Virtual Machine (VM) technology (similar in many ways to the Java paradigm).
- In addition to introducing C#, .NET brings about significant changes to both Visual Basic and Visual C++. .NET also provides a common library for all languages (discussed shortly).
- .NET is built from the ground up with the Internet in mind and embraces open Internet standards such as XML and HTTP. XML is also used throughout the framework as a messaging instrument, for file storage configuration, and for documentation purposes in C#.

These are all noteworthy features of the .NET Framework, which consists of the platform and tools needed to develop and deploy .NET applications. We will take a closer look at the .NET Framework in Chapter 3, but its essential components are summarized here. For a thorough introduction, however, please see *CodeNotes for .NET*.

The Common Language Runtime

The Common Language Runtime (CLR) is the execution engine for all programs in the .NET Framework. The CLR is similar to a Java Virtual Machine (VM) in that it executes byte code on the fly while simultaneously providing services such as garbage collection and exception handling. Unlike a Java VM, which is limited to the Java language, the CLR is accessible from any compiler that produces Microsoft Intermediate Language (IL) code, which is similar to Java byte code. Code that executes within the CLR is referred to as "managed" code. Code that executes outside its boundaries (such as VB6 and Win32 applications) is called "unmanaged" code. The C# compiler does not translate source code into native machine code but converts it into IL code, which is, in turn, run by the CLR. Therefore, C# applications are said to be "managed" by the CLR.

The Base Class Libraries

In C# (and in .NET), functionality is exposed through a collection of classes called the Base Class Libraries (BCL). The BCL provides thousands of prewritten classes that you can leverage for services such as File I/O, database access, and common operations such as sorting. Consider, for example, how you currently manipulate a string. The approach depends, of course, on the language you use:

- Visual Basic users would leverage built-in language functions such as `Mid$()`, `InStr$()`, etc.
- C++ developers could manipulate the string directly in memory (using pointers) or, more likely, leverage prewritten libraries such as the C-Runtime Library, the Standard Template Library (STL), or the Microsoft Foundation Classes (MFC).
- Those using Java would utilize the `String` or `StringBuffer` class of the Java Class Libraries (JCL). (Java users will find the BCL very similar to the JCL.)

In C# you manipulate strings by using the `System.String` and `System.StringBuilder` classes found in the BCL. The BCL is significant because it is accessible to *any* language that targets the CLR (not just C#). This is in contrast to pre-.NET technology where every language has its own supporting libraries that are accessible only from that particular language (the MFC, for example, is only accessible from C++). Thus, once you understand how to use the `System.String` class, you can leverage it not only from C# but from *any* of the .NET languages discussed below.

C# Compiler Tools

Writing .NET applications requires a compiler that translates source code into IL code. There are two ways to perform the compilation process in C#:

1. Using the C# command-line compiler (csc.exe) that ships with the .NET Framework. The command-line compiler allows you to write C# code in a text editor (Notepad, for example) and then produce a .NET program from the command prompt.
2. Using Microsoft's latest Integrated Development Environment (IDE)—Visual Studio .NET (VS.NET for short). Visual Studio .NET is an amalgamation of the Visual Studio 6 environment that was used for Visual C++ and the intuitive VB Forms editor that was used for Visual Basic development. VS.NET offers many sophisticated features such as automatic code generation, powerful debugging capabilities, and Rapid Application Development (RAD) facilities.

We will illustrate both compilation approaches at the end of this chapter, but in general you will want to use VS.NET for C# development. As we will see, for certain operations the IDE generates a considerable amount of boilerplate code behind the scenes, which you would have to write manually if you developed outside the tool's confines. However, unlike the command-line compiler that ships with the .NET Framework (which is available from Microsoft for free), Visual Studio .NET must be purchased separately.

In addition to language compilers, the .NET Framework contains a large assortment of command-line utilities. Some of these utilities are incorporated directly in VS.NET's development environment, whereas others are exclusively stand-alone. We will examine some of these utilities throughout this book.

The .NET Languages

In addition to C#, Microsoft provides four other language compilers for the .NET Framework:

1. Visual Basic.NET, the new version of Visual Basic
2. JScript.NET, an evolved version of the popular scripting tool
3. Managed C++, a modified version of C++
4. J#, Microsoft's offering of the Java syntax for the .NET Framework

The first two compilers ship as part of the framework itself (and thus are free), the third is included with VS.NET, and the fourth must be purchased separately. Other companies are in the process of porting additional languages to the .NET Framework. Two noteworthy efforts are NetCOBOL by Fujitsu Software and Visual Perl by Active State. For more information see ☞CS010002.

Although the focus of this book is obviously C#, it helps to understand the other languages in the .NET Framework because language interoperability is a cornerstone of .NET development.

Visual Basic.NET

When Visual Basic was first released in 1992, its approach to application design was remarkably straightforward. Instead of the C++ technique, which required many lines of complicated code, VB allowed developers to "paint" their applications within a comfortable design environment. This approach was not only more intuitive than C++ but much faster as well. Even C++ purists had to concede that what was arduous in C++ was easier in VB. Although Visual Basic's capabilities now transcend GUI design, it is still a popular choice for creating desktop applications for the Windows Operating System.

As its name suggests, Visual Basic.NET is the latest version of Visual

Basic for the .NET Framework. Under this new version of the product (which was once known as Visual Basic 7), the language has undergone a significant face-lift. In addition to introducing new features into the language (such as true object inheritance and structured exception handling), VB.NET has removed some cumbersome and unusual aspects of its predecessor (e.g., default properties, optional parentheses, etc.). As a result, VB.NET brings about some syntax changes that break compatibility with old VB source code. For example, procedure parameters are now passed by value (ByVal) by default, and not by reference (ByRef). Certain syntax elements such as GoSub, IsNull, and IsMissing have been removed from the language altogether. For a thorough introduction to VB.NET, see *CodeNotes for VB.NET*.

One of the most notable aspects of .NET from a Visual Basic perspective is that the VB Forms engine that drove GUI design in Visual Basic 6 has been overhauled and integrated into Visual Studio .NET. This means that you can now "paint" desktop applications using non-VB languages such as C#. The third example at the end of this chapter demonstrates this approach.

Managed C++

C++ does not "clean up" after the developer. When you allocate memory in C++, there is no entity such as the CLR that ensures it is properly released. As a result, C++ developers have always been responsible for managing memory manually. In addition, C++ allows the use of "low-level" memory manipulation techniques such as pointers and unbounded arrays. Although such latitudes can be dangerous when used incorrectly, they are invaluable for computationally intense operations such as image manipulation and numerical calculations.

Moving C++ to the .NET Framework is problematic because of two competing principles:

1. The latitude that C++ affords developers (direct memory access via pointers, manual memory management, etc.)
2. The CLR's responsibilities for automatic memory management (garbage collection) and code sanity checks (which are difficult to perform in a pointer-ridden language such as C++)

Managed C++ is a set of extensions added to the C++ language that enables it to run within the CLR. The most notable extension is the introduction of "managed types," which shift the burden of memory management from the C++ programmer to the CLR. Placing the __gc extension in front of the declaration of a class, for example, allows instances of the class to be accessed by other .NET languages and garbage collected by the CLR. Another extension is that of managed arrays, which allows these data structures to be managed by the CLR. Managed exception handling is another modification, which differs from C++ exception handling in both syntax and behavior. Additional information on managed C++ can be found at ⊶CS010003.

JScript.NET
A common misconception is that JScript, Microsoft's equivalent of Netscape's JavaScript, is somehow related to the Java programming language. In fact, JavaScript was misleadingly named by Netscape for marketing purposes. Neither JScript nor JavaScript is based on or have any direct relationship to Java. In fact, both JScript and JavaScript are implementations of ECMA-262 script, a specification defined by the European Computer Manufacturers Association (ECMA). Prior to .NET, JScript was used primarily as a tool for client-side script code. For a closer look at JScript and JavaScript, see *CodeNotes for Web-Based UI*.

With the .NET Framework, JScript has evolved into a mature language that offers many improvements over its predecessor. First-class language elements such as classes, inheritance, and compiled code have all been added to this new incarnation of the scripting tool. In addition, JScript.NET can optionally contain typed variables (you can still use JScript in a typeless manner, and it will "infer" a variable's type at runtime). For a closer look at JScript.NET, see ⊶CS010004.

J#
J#, pronounced "J-Sharp," is a Microsoft product for developers who wish to use the Java syntax in the .NET Framework. It is incorrect to think of J# as a product for writing Java applications since J# programs do not run within the confines of a Java Virtual Machine. As you might expect, J# applications are instead executed by the CLR (J# converts Java syntax into IL code). As of this writing, J# is in its beta stage. The Java Class Libraries (version 1.1.4) have been converted to BCL equivalents, and the product contains many of the proprietary extensions found in Visual J++ (Microsoft's Java development tool before the days of .NET).

J# is part of Microsoft's Java User Migration Path (JUMP) initiative. The purpose of JUMP is to make it easier for developers familiar with the Java syntax to utilize the .NET Framework. Another part of the JUMP suite is the Java Language Conversion Assistant, which converts Java source code into C#. More information on the JUMP program and its associated products can be found at ⊶CS010005.

Orientation: Why Switch to C#?

Given that evolved versions of the languages you are currently using already exist, you may ask why you would want to move to C# in the first place. Although it is true that the languages previously discussed can produce .NET applications, switching to C# is beneficial for two important reasons:

1. C# is the "intrinsic" language of the CLR, which is to say that it was designed from the ground up with the .NET Framework in mind. This is in contrast to other languages that had to evolve into their present .NET manifestations, which in many cases take on additional features (structured exception handling, inheritance, etc.) that they did not previously support. As such, C# provides syntactical amenities specific to the framework that other languages do not supply. For example, as we will see in Chapter 5, C# exposes native syntax elements to deal with garbage collection complexities and .NET callback mechanisms (delegates). Although other .NET languages expose such features, their integration is sometimes awkward, leading to more verbose implementations when compared to C#. In short, when it comes to developing .NET applications, C# is often syntactically "cleaner" than VB.NET, JScript.NET, J#, or managed C++.
2. C# has "next-generation" support for the development and usage of components (i.e., native syntax elements for object properties, events, etc.). This is an important consideration because development in .NET is heavily component based (e.g., the Base Class Libraries, etc.).

Even if you intended to use other languages in .NET, it is worthwhile to at least familiarize yourself with C# since a large portion of .NET sample code on both the Internet and the MSDN is written in Microsoft's new language.

All Languages Are Equal?
A marketing line you will frequently encounter is the claim that *all languages in the .NET Framework are equal*. You have already been told that C# offers some innate syntax advantages over other languages such as VB.NET and managed C++, and so this claim may seem suspect.

Remember that functionality in the .NET Framework is exposed through the Base Class Libraries, which are accessible to *all* languages. The BCL exists as language-neutral IL code that is executed by the CLR. Therefore, regardless of the particular .NET language you use, at the end of the day an application is nothing but IL code executed by the CLR. This leads to a very important statement regarding language choice in .NET: *The performance of all languages in the .NET Framework is roughly equivalent since they all compile to IL code and are executed by the CLR. Your choice of language in .NET will be primarily a function of syntactical preference rather than any performance advantage of one language over another.*

Thus, in terms of performance, all .NET languages can be considered equal (give or take 5 percent). Syntactically, however, they may be very different, and your productivity in C# will depend on how comfortable you feel with the dialect. In addition, C# offers another advantage over managed C++ and JScript.NET, which is discussed in the next section.

Visual Studio .NET Support

In addition to providing a comfortable and powerful design environment, VS.NET allows you to design desktop and web-based applications in a VB6-like manner (i.e., by dragging and dropping controls onto a form). As of this writing, this process can be performed only with C#, VB.NET, or J#. As we will see in Chapter 3, this limitation exists because these are the only languages that plug into VS.NET's Web Forms Designer, which drives the automation process.

Therefore, if you wish to develop .NET desktop and web-based applications by using languages such as managed C++ or JScript.NET, you must do so programmatically without the benefit of VS.NET's intuitive design environment. This more laborious approach is demonstrated at ᶜᴺ►CS010005.

Thus, the overall advantages of using C# in .NET are twofold: (1) it is the native language of the CLR, and (2) it is natively supported by Visual Studio.NET.

WHAT DOES C# MEAN TO ME?

Your perspective of C# will be dependent largely on your development background. The following section details some issues that developers will face as they migrate from a particular language.

C++ Developers

C++ developers will have a relatively small learning curve to begin writing code in C#. Minor details notwithstanding, syntax elements such as variable declaration, flow and control statements (e.g., `do/while`, `for`, etc.) in C# are essentially identical to C++. And while certain features such as operators (bitwise, logic, etc.) and structure types (`structs`) behave somewhat differently in C#, they are easily understandable in light of previous C++ experience. In addition, C# does not contain some features that developers enjoyed in C++. Elements absent from Microsoft's newest language include templates, macros, and multiple class inheritance, as well as header files, which have been supplanted by C#'s in-line implementation syntax (meaning that code is declared and implemented in one location).

The biggest challenge for C++ developers moving to C# is not becoming familiar with syntax but, rather, adapting to the .NET Framework in which C# applications execute. Specifically, to account for the presence of the CLR, C++ developers must relinquish some of the latitude they previously enjoyed. For example, as we will learn, much like a Java VM, the CLR performs garbage collection and destroys objects once they are no longer being used. Such automatic memory management is in stark contrast to C++ where memory management is the responsibility of the programmer. Thus, in C# you do not `delete` or `free` objects, but simply let the CLR handle memory management. Furthermore, because .NET applications execute within the protective confines of the CLR, "low-level" techniques such as direct pointer manipulation and boundless arrays are accessible only through C#'s *unsafe* options, which we will examine in Chapter 7.

C++ developers moving to the .NET Framework have two obvious language paths: C# and managed C++. The on-line article at ᴄɴCS010006 discusses the merits of each approach.

Visual Basic Developers
The biggest hurdle Visual Basic developers will face as they move to C# is familiarizing themselves with the "C-style" syntax on which C# is based. The syntax differences between C# and VB are plentiful and will be illustrated throughout this book. Some fundamental changes include the following:

- Code blocks, loops, and control constructs are usually placed within curly brackets (`{}`). They are not terminated with keywords such as `Next`, `Loop Until`, `Wend`, etc.
- When a variable type is declared, the type precedes the variable name, e.g., `long count`. (There is no `Dim` or `As` in the declaration.)
- Statements are frequently terminated with semicolons (called a statement delimiter). This allows multi-line statements without the underscore marker.

- C# is a case-sensitive language. Thus, `myVar` and `MyVar` refer to two different variables.
- The names of some data types in C# are different from their VB counterparts. For example, in C# an `Integer` is declared as an `int` and a `Single` is declared as a `float`.
- Array elements are denoted using square brackets: `a[4]=7`.

There are numerous other syntax changes that we will illustrate throughout this book. An excellent way for VB developers to become familiar with C# is to utilize the Microsoft Development Network (MSDN). The MSDN contains a myriad of .NET examples in both VB.NET and C#. By comparing examples written in VB.NET with those written in C#, you will get a feeling for how source code in Visual Basic translates into Microsoft's newest language.

Visual Basic developers should keep in mind that VB.NET also exposes true OO features and native threading capabilities, as thoroughly discussed in *CodeNotes for VB.NET*. This being the case, VB.NET may seem like a better choice for VB developers migrating to .NET. A contrast between C# and VB.NET from a VB6 perspective can be found at ^{CN}CS010007.

Java Developers

It is fair to say that Java developers will have the easiest time migrating to C#. If you come originally from a C or C++ background, you will find C# quite similar to Java, but with cleaned-up versions of many of your old toys, such as the C++ preprocessor and operator overloading.

Features such as garbage collection, strong type checking, a root `object` class, namespaces (packages), reflection and serialization capabilities, and monitor-based thread support should already be familiar to most Java developers. Several Java language features have similar but different incarnations in C#, such as these:

- Object properties in Java are expressed using the Java Bean syntax (`get` and `set` methods) and are determined by means of introspection. As we will see in Chapter 6, properties in C# are in fact a first-class language construct.
- Java supports a set of primitive types (e.g., `int`) and a corresponding set of wrapper types (e.g., `java.lang.Integer`). In Java the conversion between these two types must be performed explicitly. For example, to add an integer to an `ArrayList` class you might use `al.add(new Integer(4))`.

In C# the conversion from a primitive (`int`) into an object (`System.Int32`) is implicit, allowing for `al.Add(4)`. This implicit conversion (from a primitive type to an object type) is a process known as *boxing*. The converse (from object type to primitive) is called *unboxing*. Boxing is covered in Chapter 4.

- C#'s documentation-generation approach is similar to JavaDoc, but it uses XML and is written using a single-line `///` instead of Java's multi-line `/** ... */`.
- There are several minor tweaks to control structures such as `switch`, `break`, and `continue`, and there is a new `foreach()` loop.
- Certain Java keywords for object-oriented design have different names or additional requirements. For example, the Java `final` keyword is replaced by the C# `sealed` keyword. These concepts are discussed in Chapter 6.

Other C# features that may be completely new to Java developers:

- A stripped-down C-style *preprocessor*, which is useful for writing test or debug code.
- Operator overloading. You might, for example, overload the addition operator for a `Matrix` class in order to facilitate `MatrixC = MatrixA + MatrixB`. Operator overloading also allows us to compare strings with `==` rather than `equals()`.
- Cast overloading, which allows you to prescribe what occurs when a class is implicitly or explicitly cast to another type. For example, you might write code for the casting of a class to a `bool`, which would allow it to be used in an `if` or `while` statement.
- *Indexers*, which permit classes to be referenced in an array-like fashion (e.g., `z =myClass[5]`). Essentially, indexers overload the array subscript characters (`[]`).
- Attributes, a powerful approach to decorating your code with rich type information. For example, rather than marking a class as serializable by *implementing* the `Serializable` marker interface, in C# you add a `[Serializable]` *attribute* just above the class definition. Attributes are covered in Chapter 5.
- C# supports the famous (or, arguably, infamous) `goto` statement.

Finally, there are a few features of Java that C# does not support:

- Checked exceptions. In C# you may throw an exception from any method without declaring the exception in the method signature.

- Inner classes. Event handling is performed using the general-purpose *delegates* and *events* (covered in Chapter 5). However, you will have to write separate classes for I/O filters, sorting algorithms, and many of the other tasks you would normally use an inner class for in Java.

C#: A FUSION OF EXISTING LANGUAGES

In light of these comparisons, you can see that C# is a syntactical blend of existing languages. In mathematical terms:

```
C# = (Java x C++)
- complex C++ features (multiple inheritance, templates)
+/- slight changes to C++/Java operators, conventions & constructs
+ hidden "unsafe" features (pointers, unbounded arrays)
+ high-level VB-style elements (foreach, is, as)
+ intrinsic support for components (properties, events)
+ native support for .NET elements (garbage collection, delegates)
+ other amenities (in-line XML documentation)
```

Book Contents

Chapter 1, Introduction: In this chapter we examine the fundamentals of C# and the .NET Framework on which C# applications are built. The Core Concepts section of this chapter lays the groundwork for the more advanced topics in later chapters. This chapter concludes with some simple C# examples.

Chapter 2, .NET Installation: This chapter provides installation instructions for .NET. Like many software products, new versions of the .NET Framework will be released in the form of service packs. In addition to this chapter, readers are encouraged to consult the on-line instructions at ᴄɴ⇒CS010008 for the most up-to-date installation instructions.

Chapter 3, The .NET Framework: In this chapter we examine the .NET Framework itself, emphasizing the portions that are relevant to C#. The .NET Framework is the foundation for all .NET applications, languages, and services.

Chapter 4, Syntax and Concepts: This chapter delves into the details of the C# syntax. Topics covered include data types, loop and control statements, and special collection classes in the BCL. For those unfamiliar with the conventions of C++ or Java, this chapter outlines many of the standard syntax constructs in C#.

Chapter 5, .NET Language Features: In this chapter we examine the new language features in the .NET Framework. Topics include attributes, which are nonprogrammatic code statements that can be used to influence application behavior, and delegates, the new type-safe callback mechanism in the managed environment. Garbage collection, the new way that memory is managed in .NET, is investigated, as is reflection, the ability to ascertain type information about an application at runtime.

Chapter 6, Object-Oriented Programming: This chapter investigates C#'s OOP features, such as classes, interfaces, and structures. As this chapter illustrates, C# exposes numerous techniques to write powerful classes for the .NET Framework.

Chapter 7, Native and Unsafe Code: The new execution environment of the .NET Framework raises integration issues with legacy technologies. In this chapter we examine the features .NET offers to leverage existing technologies, such as COM and Win32 DLLs, from C#. In addition, this chapter highlights C#'s special unsafe code features that allow the use of pointers.

Core Concepts

This section defines terms you may or may not be familiar with and is broken into two parts: *Windows Concepts,* which explains some of the Windows technologies that you may be currently leveraging, and *.NET Services,* which describes some of the new subtechnologies in the framework (such as ASP.NET and ADO.NET).

Windows Concepts

The switch to the protective environment of the CLR may trouble some experienced Windows developers. Microsoft landmark OS is a complex entity, and mastering its idiosyncrasies and nuances can take many years. A natural question for developers given the introduction to .NET is the status and usefulness of the underlying technologies that fuel the operating system. In this section we present some common Windows technologies from a .NET perspective. This section also serves as a good basis for developers without prior Windows experience.

Windows API (Win32)

In the early days of Windows, developers wrote applications in C using the Windows API. As its name suggests, the Windows API is the Applications Programming Interface for the Windows Operating System. Any service performed by the OS, be it memory management or File IO, can be accessed by using one of the thousands of functions in this library. If you peer inside the `%winroot%\system32` directory, you will find the hundreds of DLLs that expose these functions.

The problem with the Windows API is that it is a C-style library that is difficult to use. For example, to open a text file with the API you must use the Win32 `CreateFile()` function, which accepts seven parameters that prescribe the file name, access mode (read/write), whether the file is to be shared, and so on. In addition, there is no logical grouping of the Windows API; it is merely an assortment of thousands of functions. For this reason the Win32 API is usually spurned in favor of frameworks such as Microsoft Foundation Classes (MFC), Visual Basic, and, with .NET, the Base Class Libraries.

All these frameworks do, however, is wrap the Win32 API in a more intuitive manner. Any Windows application that attempts to open a file, regardless of the technology in which it is written, implicitly uses the Win32 `CreateFile()` function underneath. In fact, every program on the operating system, be it a device driver or a .NET application, eventually reduces to a collection of Win32 API calls. In other words, the Windows API is the most direct means of talking to the operating system.

In Chapter 7 we will illustrate how to invoke the Win32 API directly from C# using a technology called Platform Invoke (PInvoke). As we caution in that chapter, however, calling Win32 functions from C# incurs significant overhead. Furthermore, the BCL exposes an intuitive class framework that offers virtually all the functionality of the Win32 API, but in a managed and organized manner.

COM/ActiveX

Microsoft's Component Object Model (COM) is the standard architecture behind component communication on the Windows OS (if you are familiar with CORBA, you can think of COM as the Microsoft equivalent). For example, when you utilize ActiveX controls or components from VB6, COM serves as the communication mechanism between the application and the external service. Although COM components were originally written in C++, Visual Basic 5 allowed developers to write their own COM components through its ActiveX-DLL and ActiveX-EXE project options. Because COM components were authored before .NET, they are "unmanaged" as they execute outside the CLR.

Although the concept of a component has evolved into the "Assembly" in the .NET world (as Chapter 3 illustrates), Microsoft does not expect developers to abandon the large number of COM components in existence. Facilities exist to call these entities from .NET. In Chapter 7 we will examine the *COM* Interop technology, which allows you to call legacy COM/ActiveX components from C#.

COM+
Windows 2000 introduced COM+, which is a collection of services that COM components can utilize to better their performance in the enterprise application setting. Some of these services include transactions (used when a component communicates with a database), object pooling (increases performance by reusing objects to avoid initialization overhead), and queuing (allows a client to communicate with an object asynchronously). You can leverage COM+ from C# by writing a *serviced* .NET component, which is built by using special classes in the BCL. For more information on .NET and COM+, see ⌕CS010009.

.NET Service Concepts
In addition to a new execution environment for applications (the CLR), the .NET Framework includes evolved versions of existing Microsoft technologies as well as some entirely new ones. As we will see in Chapter 3, all these technologies are exposed through the Base Class Libraries and are thus accessible to C# and other .NET languages.

Although C# is simply a language, from a practical perspective it is grounded in the .NET Framework. The technologies discussed in this section are one of the primary reasons that you would want to switch to C# and .NET in the first place.

Windows Forms
Windows Forms is the name of the library that is used for desktop GUI development in the .NET Framework. What is noteworthy about this technology is that it allows developers to employ the "VB6-form" methodology when using C#. When you design desktop applications in Visual Studio.NET—by dragging and dropping controls onto a form—an entity called the Windows Form Designer (WFD) translates your actions into C# code that leverages the appropriate BCL classes. This code is placed in a special region of the code listing that is marked with special tags (as we will see in Chapter 3). The by-product of such automation is that you can develop Windows desktop applications in C# with the same ease and power as Visual Basic 6.

Although Windows Forms employs a Visual Basic approach toward application design, there are a number of changes from VB6. For example, intrinsic controls in VB6 (such as buttons, textboxes, and labels) are now classes exposed by the BCL. Thus, when you draw a button on a form in VS.NET, the environment leverages a special Button class behind the scenes. Because controls in .NET Framework exist as classes, they are subject to OO principles such as inheritance and polymorphism (class inheritance concepts are covered in Chapter 6). This capability gives rise to a very powerful technique called *Visual Inheritance,* which allows you to apply object inheritance principles to the GUI elements of a desktop application. You can, for instance, design a "base" form and then inherit its properties across multiple "derived" forms. As with standard class inheritance, changes to the base form propagate automatically to the derived ones.

GDI+
GDI+ is a powerful library that can be used to render graphics in your applications. These classes allow you to draw 2D graphics, perform image and font manipulation, and carry out sophisticated operations such as texture and gradient filling. GDI+ also includes native support for popular graphic formats such as JPGs and GIFs.

GDI+ is an evolved version of the Windows Graphics Device Interface (GDI), a Windows OS technology that is used to draw graphics and formatted text on video displays. GDI+ is considerably more intuitive than its predecessor. The entire technology is exposed through a straightforward class hierarchy that is easy to use from C#. Java developers will find that GDI+ supports functionality similar to that found in the Abstract Window Toolkit (AWT) graphics library and the Java2D APIs. More information on GDI+ can be found at ⚓CS010010.

ASP.NET
ASP.NET is Microsoft's new technology for developing web-based applications. The most significant feature of ASP.NET is that it allows one to develop web applications using the intuitive drag-and-drop methodology that popularized Visual Basic. Simply paint your application within the intuitive development environment of VS.NET, and it will look and behave identically when deployed on a client's browser. Thus, just as you can use C# to quickly design desktop applications via Windows Forms, you can utilize C# to rapidly design web-based applications by means of ASP.NET. In addition to this noteworthy capability, ASP.NET boasts a number of improvements over Microsoft's older Active Server Pages (ASP) web technology. These improvements include:

- Support for fully compiled and typed languages such as C#
- Improved execution speed because applications are compiled (not interpreted as with traditional ASP)
- Separation of code from content, which means that the presenta-

tion (HTML) and programming (code) aspects of an application are kept in separate files. This is in contrast to ASP where HTML is intermixed with script code.
- Seamless support for multiple browser types by means of the framework's web control technology. A web control resides entirely on the web server and generates client-side and server-side code to render itself appropriately in a browser.
- Numerous technology improvements to handle security, caching, state management, and debugging

A closer examination of these points can be found at ˢᴺ⟩CS010011, although for a thorough examination of Microsoft's new web platform, see *CodeNotes for ASP.NET*.

ADO.NET
ADO.NET is the new data access model for the .NET Framework. ADO.NET is not simply the migration of Microsoft's popular ActiveX Data Object (ADO) model to the managed environment, but a completely new paradigm for data access and manipulation. With ADO.NET you can communicate with any database from C# by using a paradigm that was designed specifically for distributed computing. Microsoft's new data access technology is built upon two major principles:

1. *Disconnected data:* In ADO.NET virtually all data manipulation is done outside the context of an open database connection. Data is read into an entity called a Dataset, after which the database connection is immediately closed. Operations such as updates, inserts, and deletes are performed against the Dataset as required. When the database is ready to be updated, it is reopened, and data is transferred from the Dataset. This model is appropriate for web applications since clients are not continually connected to their datastores.
2. *Universal data exchange via XML:* Datasets can converse in the universal data format of the web, namely XML. Specifically, a Dataset can save its contents in XML or import data in XML format. A significant limitation of traditional ADO was that it could be used only by COM-capable clients. ADO.NET, however, supports XML, allowing data to be transferred easily to non-Windows clients with no support for COM. This is especially important in the Internet's heterogeneous environment where one may want to cooperate with non-Windows machines running UNIX and the like.

As you might expect, ADO.NET is exposed through the BCL. The object model is divided into two layers: Managed Providers, which do the actual communication with the database, and the disconnected Dataset, which stores the data. Once you are familiar with the C# language, you can consult ⇨CS010012 for more information on ADO.NET and a C# example that utilizes the framework to communicate with a database.

Web Services

Web services are software components that can be accessed over the Internet. Applications running on remote machines, on potentially different platforms, can access these components in a language-independent manner. In the past several months, web services have received a tremendous amount of publicity. In fact, one of the major marketing points for the .NET Framework is that it was designed specifically with web services in mind.

Web services are advantageous because they can be accessed by any client that understands HTTP and XML. Because messages travel to and from a service over HTTP, web services are not hindered by firewalls. This is especially important for corporations that wish to expose extensive business logic to clients on the web, but do not wish to compromise the security of their network. In addition, by leveraging a new standard that converts method invocations and results into XML (the Simple Object Access Protocol, or SOAP), web services avoid the problem of cross-language barriers. As long as both the sending and receiving systems can understand XML and SOAP, it doesn't matter whether the code is Java or C#, or whether it is running on UNIX or Windows.

Writing a C# web service in the .NET Framework is made extremely easy through the wizards in Visual Studio. If you venture into the world of web services from a .NET perspective, you will come across terms such as Web Service Description Language (WSDL), Discovery Files (DISCO), and, of course, SOAP. A full treatment on the subject can also be found by consulting *CodeNotes for Web Services in Java and .Net*.

Despite the marketing force behind the concept, web services do have a couple of drawbacks when compared to standard software components. For example, because web services are usually HTTP entities, they must execute under the auspices of Microsoft Internet Information Server (IIS) when they are exposed from the .NET environment. Another by-product of being HTTP-enabled is that web services do not maintain the state in between method invocations (by default). This means that each call to the web service results in a new component being instantiated. A final limitation of web services is that their underlying communication mechanisms (HTTP and XML) are slow and verbose compared to other distributed standards such as COM, CORBA, or Java Remote Method Invocation (RMI).

Therefore, although web services are ubiquitously accessible, they may not be as versatile as the software components you've designed in the past. When universal accessibility is not essential, .NET Remoting (covered next) offers a worthwhile alternative to writing distributable components in .NET.

.NET Remoting

Conceptually, .NET Remoting is similar to the web service paradigm: Both technologies allow you to communicate with a remote object. The difference is the amount of flexibility at the hands of the developer. Whereas a .NET web service object must reside in IIS and must communicate by means of HTTP, a component exposed through Remoting is not so restricted. Instead, the component can be housed in a custom "host" of your own design, freeing it from the scrutiny of a bulky web server. Additionally, a Remote component can be accessed through fast communication protocols such as direct TCP/IP. If you are familiar with frameworks such as distributed COM (DCOM), CORBA, or Java RMI, you can think of Remoting as the .NET version of these technologies.

The added flexibility of Remoting, however, comes at the cost of complexity and limitation. In addition to not working easily with company firewalls, .NET Remoting can quickly plunge into the difficult concepts of channels, object lifetime, and leasing, which are beyond the scope of this book. A more extensive overview of Remoting can be found at ⁽ᶜᴺ⁾CS010013.

Some Simple Examples

In this section we will write the familiar Hello World program in C#. If you have not already done so, now would be a good time to consult Chapter 2 to ensure that you have properly installed the .NET Framework and VS.NET.

In order to illustrate the versatility of C# and the .NET Framework, we will write three versions of the Hello World program:

1. A console application that we compile from the command line
2. A console application that we develop from VS.NET
3. A Windows Forms application that we "paint" in a VB6-like manner using VS.NET

For those unfamiliar with the concept, a *console application* is a program that runs entirely within the command line (DOS prompt) with no graphical elements. For example, the XCOPY.EXE utility that ships with all versions of Windows is a console application because its output is contained within the command prompt. Also remember that C# ships with a stand-alone compiler (csc.exe), which allows us to compile programs from the command prompt. (csc.exe itself is another example of a console application.)

Hello World Application #1

Although developing applications outside an IDE such as Visual Studio will be new to many VB developers, it is a common operation performed with C++ and Java. Using your favorite text editor (such as Notepad), save the contents of Listing 1.1 in a file called HelloWorld.cs.

```
// VB developers, note how comments are written in C# (see Ch4)
// C# "Hello World" Program.

public class HelloWorld {
  public static void Main () {
    System.Console.WriteLine("Hello World!");
  }
}
```

Listing 1.1   HelloWorld application #1

Because a console application executes within the confines of the command prompt, there must be a designated point where the program begins its execution. This is in contrast to form-based applications developed in VB6 where you write code to respond to user actions (if they click a button, etc.).

If you are familiar with Java or C++, you are aware that a program's execution always begins at a method called `Main()`. Such is the case with C#—a console application starts automatically at the `Main()` method. If you try to write a console application without such a method, the compiler will generate an error. (Unlike Java, the `Main()` method does not have a specific signature. It can either be empty, as in Listing 1.1, or capture the command-line arguments, as in the second example later in this topic.)

Unlike C++ or Visual Basic, C# has no concepts of global functions. Instead, a function must always reside within a class (for this reason, functions in C# are properly referred to as *methods*). Thus, the console application in Listing 1.1 consists of a class named `HelloWorld`, which contains a single method named `Main()`. As in Java, the `Main()` method must be of the *static* type and is therefore declared with the `static` keyword in Listing 1.1. (C++ developers should also note that the declaration of a class is *not* terminated with a semicolon in C#.) Versions of Visual Basic prior to VB.NET did not have the concept of static methods, and thus a slight explanation is in order.

Static Members in C# (for VB Developers)
In Visual Basic 6, before you can access the methods of a class, you have to instantiate the class:

```
Dim s as New SomeClass    'instantiate the class
s.Foo                     'call Foo
```

Listing 1.2   VB method access

In C#, by designating a member *static,* you can access it without first instantiating the class. Consider the class C# in Listing 1.3.

```
public class SomeClass {
    static int size1;
    int size2;

    public static void Method1 () {}
    public void Method2(){}
}
```

Listing 1.3   Static and non-static members

As you can see from the listing, `SomeClass` contains two methods (`Method1` and `Method2`) and two member variables (`size1` and `size2`). Because `size1` and `Method` are declared with the `static` keyword, they can be accessed without instantiating the class (note that static member variables such as `size` will be shared by all instances of the class).

```
SomeClass.size = 45;      // Call static members directly
SomeClass.Method();       // on SomeClass
```

Listing 1.4   Calling static members

However, in order to access `size2` or `Method2`, we would have to first create an instance of `SomeClass`.

```
SomeClass s = new SomeClass()
s.size2 = 45;
s.MyMethod2;
```

```
// Note that you cannot call a static member on an
// instantiated class:
s.MyMethod; // WRONG!
```

Listing 1.5   Calling non-static members

The term *static member* may seem confusing. In object-oriented terminology a class's *methods* and *variables* are also referred to as the class's *members*. Thus, in Listing 1.3, Method is a static *method,* size is a static *variable,* and both are also static *members*. VB developers should also note the use of the void keyword in Listing 1.3. A method that is declared with void does not return a value (the equivalent of the Sub keyword in VB).

Source Analysis Continued
The concept of static class members is important because several classes in the BCL expose static members. One such example is the Console class that we used in Listing 1.1. This class exposes a static method named WriteLine(), which outputs a string to the console. Because WriteLine() is a static method, we must call it directly through the Console class (as opposed to first instantiating the class). Finally, we must prefix the Console class with the word System because it is located in the BCL (a consideration that is related to the concept of namespaces, which we will examine in Chapter 3).

Listing 1.1 is very straightforward. When the program is invoked, it begins its execution at the requisite Main() method, which in turn uses the BCL Console class to write "Hello World" on the screen.

Compiling and Running the Application
To compile the Hello World application, click on the VS.NET command prompt found in the VS.NET Tools folder (consult Chapter 2 for installation details). Save Listing 1.1 in a file called HelloWorld.cs and execute the following line at the command prompt (make sure you are in the same directory where HelloWorld.cs is located):

```
csc.exe HelloWorld.csc
```

You have just created your first C# application; the C# compiler will produce a file called HelloWorld.exe that displays "Hello World!" when it is executed. But just what type of executable did the C# compiler create?

.NET Executables

It is important to understand that the executable you just created will only run on those computers with the .NET Framework installed. Unlike applications produced with C++ or Visual Basic 6, a .NET executable is not a native Win32 program but a sequence of Intermediate Language (IL) code instructions. Without the CLR, the application is merely a dormant file on your hard drive because there is no entity to make sense of its contents. Thus, if you attempt to run the HelloWorld.exe application we created on a .NET-less machine, you will receive an error informing you that `mscoree.dll`—a system file that loads the CLR—cannot be found.

Recap

This example has illustrated some important aspects of C#:

- Methods must be placed within classes (there are no global functions).
- A `static` method can be invoked directly on a class, without first instantiating the class.
- A console application begins its execution at a static `Main()` method.
- C# applications can be produced outside a development environment by means of the C# compiler (csc.exe).
- Internally, .NET executables consist of IL code, which means that they will only run on a machine that has the .NET Framework installed.

Hello World Application #2

In this example we will re-create the application we wrote in Listing 1.1, but we will do it from the Visual Studio.NET environment. Start VS.NET by going to the *Microsoft Visual Studio.NET* folder in your Start menu. Next, start the IDE by clicking the *Microsoft Visual Studio.NET* icon. If you are running VS.NET for the first time, you will be asked to choose your preferred keyboard and window layouts; choose the keyboard and window schemes you are most comfortable with depending on the environment from which you are migrating. If you don't have a preference, choose the *Visual Studio Default*. Next, go to the File menu and select New → Project, which will bring up the dialog box in Figure 1.1.

As illustrated in Figure 1.1, choose Visual C# Projects under Project Types, and Console Application under Templates. Give your project a name and specify the directory where it will be stored. As a side note, you should be careful not to double-click on a template because it will

28 · *CodeNotes® for C#*

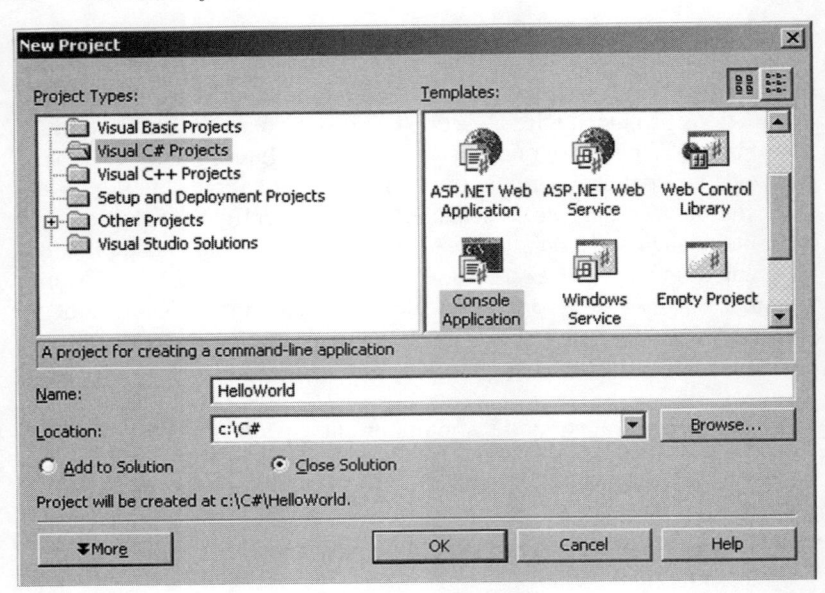

Figure 1.1   New project dialog box

automatically launch the project with the default name and location. You should always take the time to look at the project screen after selecting your template and make sure that you have a proper name and path before clicking the OK button.

Click OK, and in a moment VS.NET will create a C# console project for you. Because the environment knows that you are writing a console application, it automatically inserts some boilerplate code into the project. Specifically, it inserts a class with the same name as the project (HelloWorld, in our case) and gives the class a static Main() method. In fact, you only have to add the following highlighted line of code to the project to make it functional.

```
using System;

namespace HelloWorld
{
   class Class1
   {
     /// The main entry point for the application.
     [STAThread]
     static void Main(string[] args)
     {
```

```
        Console.WriteLine("Hello World!");
      }
    }
}
```

Listing 1.6   HelloWorld application #2

Unlike the previous example, the application is not compiled from the command line. Instead, you can compile and run the project directly from the VS.NET environment by going to the Debug menu and clicking Start (or you can simply press F5, which is the normal hotkey for the Start command).

If you compare this application with the one we created from the command line (Listing 1.1), you will notice a couple of differences. Most notably, we did not have to prefix the `Console` class with the `System` keyword. We can get away with this omission thanks to the first line in Listing 1.6 (`using System;`). This line saves us some typing by referencing the `System` namespace implicitly—an important technique that we will revisit in Chapter 3. Another difference between both applications is the declaration of the `Main()` statement. Whereas in the first application this method is declared as `static public void Main ()`, Listing 1.6 is somewhat different: `static void Main(`**`string[] args`**`)`. Although both variations of the `Main()` declaration are acceptable, the second is preferable because it allows you to capture command-line arguments that are passed into the application. For example, if you invoked the application in the following manner: `HelloWorld /someoption1 /someoption2`, then the second declaration of `Main()` would populate the `args` string array in Listing 1.6 with the command-line parameters `/someoption1` and `/someoption2`. By inspecting this array you could modify program behavior based on command-line options (as is often done with console utilities such as XCOPY). You should also note that projects created within VS.NET contain documentation that appears to be in XML format.

```
/// <summary>
/// The main entry point for the application.
/// </summary>
```

Listing 1.7   C#'s XML documentation

These insertions are related to C#'s XML documentation facilities that we will explain in Chapter 4.

A final difference between both applications is the `[STAThread]` line that precedes the `Main()` statement in the second listing. We will relegate a discussion of this line (which is called an *attribute*) to Chapter 7, but basically it has important implications for .NET applications that attempt to access COM objects.

There are numerous advantages to developing within Visual Studio.NET as opposed to a simple text editor such as Notepad. For one thing, you will notice that VS.NET provides syntax coloring for C# code, making it easier to read, and IntelliSense, making it easier to write. More important, the environment offers powerful debugging capabilities such as breakpoints, variable inspection, and code stepping, which you enjoyed in previous versions of Visual Studio and Visual Basic.

Hello World Application #3

In this example we will create yet a third version of the Hello World application. Unlike the previous two examples, this application will be a form-type application recognizable to Visual Basic developers. Close the console project you created in the previous example, go to the File menu, and select New → Project. You will once again be greeted with the dialog box in Figure 1.1. This time select Window Application under the project template, set your project name to HelloWorld3, choose a file path, and click OK. Wait a minute, and VS.NET will manifest itself in the graphical design environment illustrated in Figure 1.2.

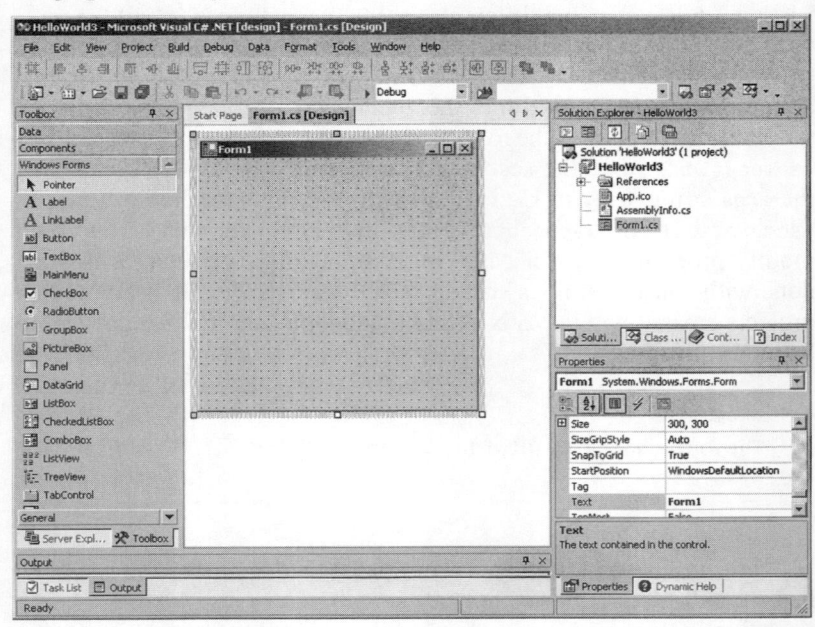

Figure 1.2   VS.NET desktop design environment

Take a moment to explore the VS.NET IDE, and if you are familiar with Visual Basic, you will find several recognizable design elements: the Toolbox that contains controls such as buttons and textboxes; the Property Inspector that details the characteristics of a given control; the Project Explorer (now called the Solution Explorer); and the Form design window that allows you to resize the form and place controls on it.

Developing desktop applications in C# proceeds along the same intuitive lines as VB6. All you need to do is drag the appropriate controls onto the form and then write the event logic behind the controls. To this end, drag a button from the toolbox onto the form, double-click it, and insert the following highlighted line into the project:

```
private void button1_Click(object sender, System.EventArgs e)
{
    MessageBox.Show("Hello World!");
}
```

Listing 1.8 Windows form code

Run the application by pressing F5, and with only one added line of C# code, you have created a fully functional GUI application—one that displays "Hello World!" when its button is clicked. If you examine the project's source, you will find that VS.NET inserted a significant amount of boilerplate code into the project behind the scenes. We will examine this code in depth in Chapter 3, but we can make a number of initial observations:

- To display a message box we used the `Show()` method of the BCL `MessageBox` class (note that `Show()` is a `static` method of the class). If you are familiar with VB, the `MessageBox.Show()` method replaces the old `MsgBox` function.
- As with our console applications, the GUI application contains a `Main()` statement where program execution begins.
- The `Main()` statement is contained within a class named `Form1`, which *inherits* from a BCL class named `System.Windows.Forms.Form`.
- The project contains a number of `using` statements at the top of the source file; these reference namespaces such as `System.Drawing` and `System.Windows.Forms`.
- The project contains additional boilerplate code to initialize the Form's components.

We will investigate the underpinnings of VS.NET's automation in Chapter 3, but for now simply appreciate that the development environment performs a lot of work on your behalf to simplify desktop development. The net result of VS.NET's efforts is that you can design GUI applications using the same rapid approach that is employed in Visual Basic.

Sorting Example Using the BCL

To round out this chapter let us consider a more functional example than Hello World: sorting an array of numbers. Remember that in C#, operations such as sorting are carried out by means of the BCL (of course, you could always write your own sorting algorithm from scratch). The C# program in Listing 1.9 utilizes two BCL classes—ArrayList and Random—to sort a list of random numbers and then print them out.

```
// C# Sorting Program
using System;
using System.Collections;

public class Sorting {

    static public void Main () {
        int index;
        //create the list and populate with random numbers
        ArrayList numbers = new ArrayList();
        Random rnd = new Random();

        for (index=0; index<=9; index++) {
           numbers.Add(rnd.Next() % 100);
        }

        // Sort the array
        numbers.Sort();   // That's it!

        // Print out the sorted numbers:
        for (index=0; index<=9; index++) {
          Console.Write(myArray[index]);
          Console.Write(",");
        }
    }
}
```

Listing 1.9   Sorting an array of numbers in C#

Save Listing 1.9 in a file called SortNumbers.cs and compile it from the command line by means of the C# compiler: `csc.exe Sort`

Numbers.cs. (Alternatively, you could create a console project in Visual Studio.NET.) The SortNumbers.exe application that is created produces output similar to the following: 10, 11, 61, 63, 74, 77, 80, 90, 94, 98.

The highlighted portions of Listing 1.9 illustrate areas where the Base Class Libraries are being used. Again, the first two using statements are based on the namespace concepts that we will examine in Chapter 3. The next two highlighted lines declare and instantiate two BCL classes that we are leveraging: ArrayList and Random. The ArrayList class is like a collection; elements can be added and removed, and it will automatically resize itself. The Random class generates the random numbers that we will sort.

The for loop in Listing 1.9 adds ten random numbers to the list and then sorts the array. Sorting the list is as simple as calling the Sort() method against the ArrayList class—the underlying operation is handled by the BCL. Keep in mind that we will examine C#'s loop structures (e.g., the for statement) and operators (such as the modulus operator (%)) in Chapter 4.

As you can see from Listing 1.9, using the BCL is simply a matter of understanding the conventions of the classes that you will be calling. In the example above, the functionality of the program (sorting and output) is provided by the BCL; C# simply acts as a forum to call it. Furthermore, the language neutrality of the CLR means that your knowledge of the Base Class Libraries is immediately transferable to other .NET languages such as VB.NET and J#.

In Chapter 3 we will examine the BCL more thoroughly and discover that console and desktop applications (.EXEs) are simply a subset of the possibilities with C#. By leveraging the Base Class Libraries you can write software components (.DLLs), web-based applications, web services, and many other programs that are difficult to construct using pre-.NET technology (such as Windows Services).

Chapter Summary

C# is the native language of the .NET Framework. To become a productive C# developer you must become familiar with two separate but equally important aspects of Microsoft's new programming language: the C# dialect, which is a simplified combination of Java and C++ (with a little Visual Basic thrown into the mix), and the .NET Framework, which fundamentally alters the manner in which applications run under the Windows Operating System.

Although C# is a derivative of C++ and Java, like a typical child it both amalgamates and evolves the characteristics of its parents. Absent from Microsoft's new language are C++ features such as multiple implementation inheritance and templates, whereas more complex constructs such as pointers are accessible only through special *unsafe* options. Carryovers from C++, such as preprocessing capabilities and operator overloading, will be new to Java developers, as will slight variations in C#'s facilities for in-line documentation, interfaces, and class inheritance.

Despite C#'s new features, such as first-class support for component-based development, it is the language's execution environment—the .NET Framework—that provides noteworthy innovation. In .NET, applications execute under the auspices of the Common Language Runtime (CLR), which can be thought of as a language-neutral Java VM. Like a Java VM, the CLR provides services such as automatic memory management, type-safety checking, and exception handling to applications. Unlike a Java VM, the CLR is not the sole privilege of programs written in Java. Any language that can be compiled to Microsoft Intermediate Language (IL) code can execute within the CLR. Code that executes inside the CLR is called "managed" code. Code running outside the CLR (such as code produced by VB6 and Visual C++) is said to be "unmanaged."

Functionality in C# is accessed through the Base Class Libraries (BCL), which serve as the building blocks for .NET applications. The BCL contains thousands of classes, for almost every conceivable operation your application might want to carry out, and also houses new versions of popular Microsoft technologies such as ADO and ASP.

In addition to a new execution environment for Windows applications, .NET brings about significant changes to many aspects of Windows architecture and language design. After the next chapter on installation we will delve into these details, which include a new self-describing software component and an enforced data–type system that allows C# to interoperate seamlessly with other languages.

Chapter 2

.NET INSTALLATION

To develop C# applications you must have the .NET Framework installed on your machine. This chapter outlines the installation procedure of the .NET Framework onto the Windows Operating System.

Requirements

OS REQUIREMENTS

.NET will run on every 32-bit version of the Windows OS with the exception of Windows 95. However, the following features of the framework will run only on Windows 2000, Windows XP, or the soon-to-be-released .NET Server OS:

- Web services
- ASP.NET
- Classes that leverage COM+ services

The restriction with respect to the first two technologies (web services and ASP.NET) is a by-product of an infrastructure requirement of both these frameworks; namely, that ASP.NET and .NET web services require Internet Information Server (IIS) version 5.0 or greater to execute. Therefore, operating systems that ship with earlier versions of the web server (such as NT4, which houses IIS 4.0, and Windows Millennium and 98, which use Personal web server) cannot be used to develop either web services or ASP.NET applications in .NET. Likewise, because COM+ is not available on operating systems prior to Windows 2000, .NET classes that leverage COM+ services are restricted to Windows 2000 or above.

SYSTEM REQUIREMENTS

In order to install the .NET Framework on your machine, Microsoft recommends the following system configuration:

- Processor: Minimum Pentium II-450Mhz (Pentium III-650Mhz recommended)
- Memory: Windows 2000 Professional: 96 MB (128 MB recommended); Windows 2000 Server: 192MB (256 MB recommended)
- Hard drive: 500MB available on the drive where the OS is installed (usually C:\), and 2.5 gigabytes available on the installation drive (where VS.NET will be installed)

.NET Distribution

VS.NET and the .NET Framework are distributed on four CDs. The first three contain the VS.NET development tools, and the fourth contains the *Windows Component Update*. The *Windows Component Update* will install the core framework files (the CLR and Runtime classes) and updated versions of system files that .NET requires in order to run on your machine. For information on obtaining the CDs either by mail or download, see ᶜᴺ⇨CS020001. Alternatively, you can install the framework by means of one large setup program roughly 2 gigabytes in size. Running this program will span the installation files to a hard drive, from where the installation program can also be executed. The installation procedure outlined here is identical for either approach.

Installing .NET

To install the .NET Framework, run SETUP.EXE found on the first CD or from the download. After a couple of minutes you will be greeted with the screen in Figure 2.1.

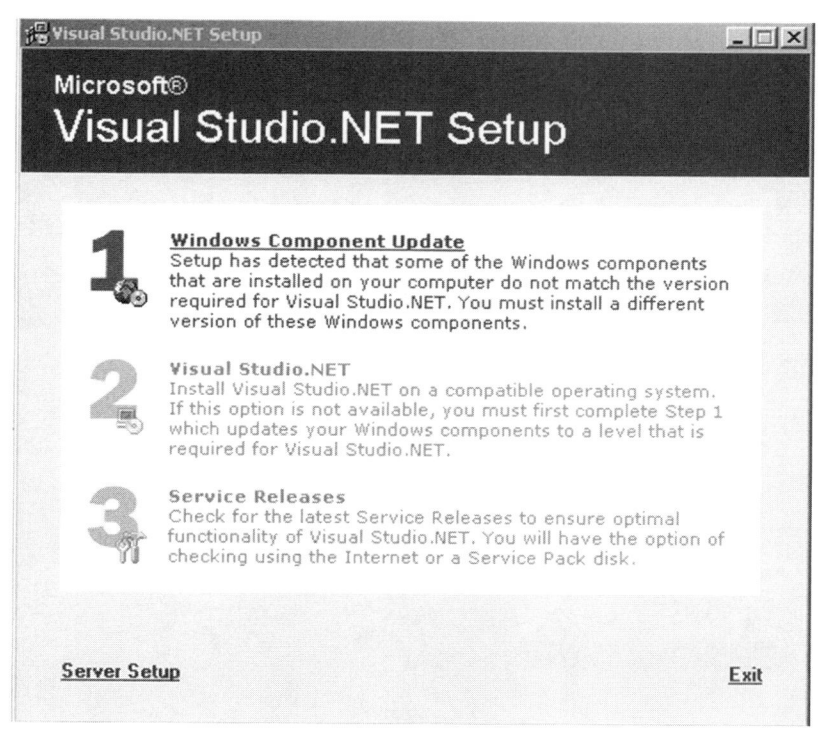

Figure 2.1 VS.NET setup

As Figure 2.1 indicates, you must run the *Windows Component Update* before installing VS.NET. After clicking *Windows Component Update,* the setup program will analyze your machine for a few minutes to determine which system files need to be updated. Depending on the operating system and the applications that you have already installed, the setup program may have to reboot the system several times during the installation process. Because of this requirement, it offers the *Automatic Log On* feature; by giving you a password to the installation program, the system can automatically log on and continue the installation every time it has to reboot the machine. Because the setup program may have to reboot the machine as many as seven times during the installation routine, this option can be a real time-saver. If you disable this option, you will have to log on the machine each time the computer reboots.

After you either enable or disable *Automatic Log On,* the setup program will begin the *Windows Component Update.* Depending on the files it must update, this procedure could take several minutes. During this time the setup program will detail its progress, as illustrated in Figure 2.2.

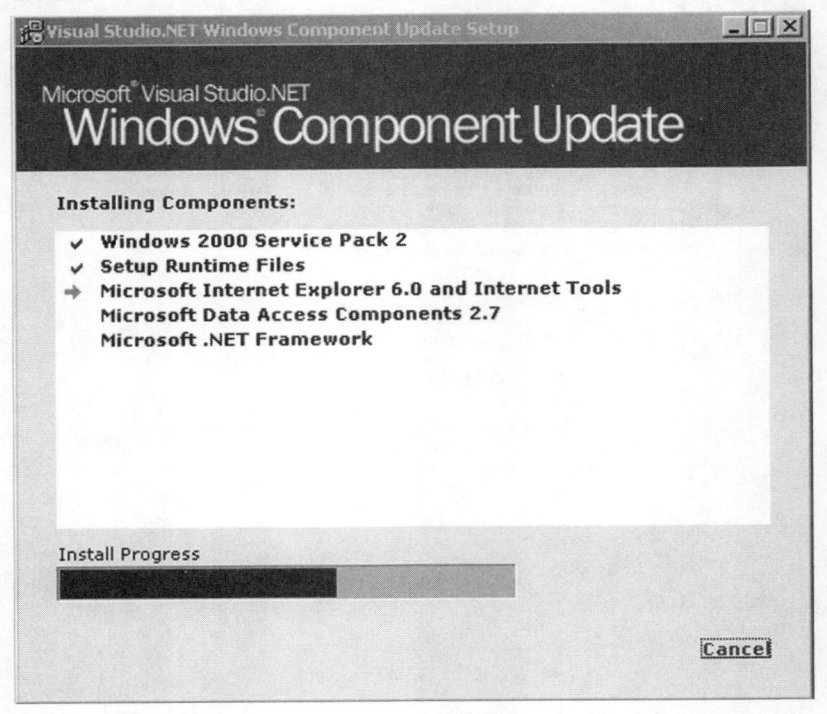

Figure 2.2   Windows Component Update in progress

After the Windows Component Update has finished, the setup program will prompt you for the first VS.NET CD. It will then ask you to choose the portions of VS.NET that you want to install (the IDE, MSDN documentation, etc.). The options screen is shown in Figure 2.3.

For the purposes of working with the examples in this book, we recommend that you accept the default install options. After selecting those aspects of VS.NET that you want included (C# is found under *Language Tools* in Figure 2.3), click *Install Now*. The setup program will begin. Depending on the options that you have selected, installation could take anywhere from twenty to sixty minutes. After the installation has finished, your computer will contain all the necessary tools to build and deploy .NET applications.

Program Locations
The .NET setup program will append two new items to your Start menu's Program folder. The first item is called *Microsoft .NET Frame-*

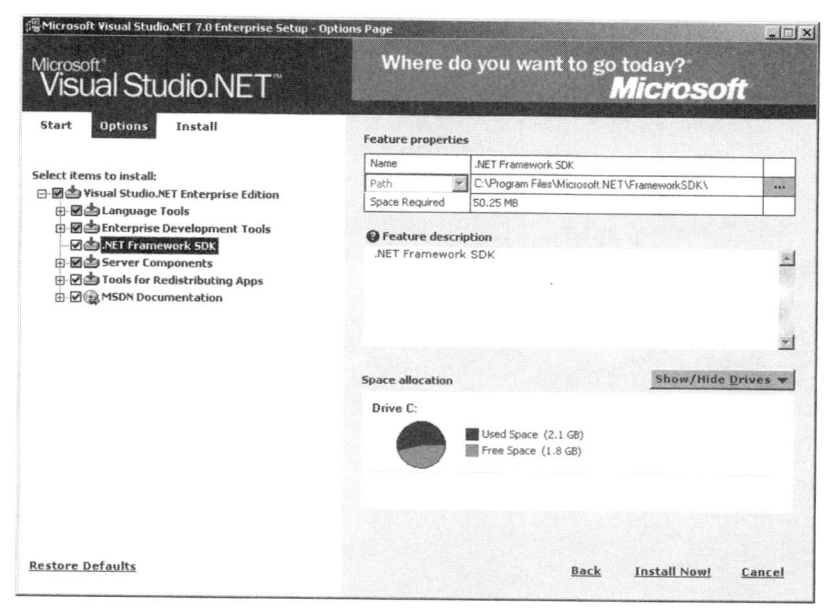

Figure 2.3 VS.NET installation screen

work SDK, and it contains MSDN documentation and code samples. The second item is called *Microsoft Visual Studio.NET 7.0,* and contains links to the VS.NET IDE and to another folder called *Visual Studio.NET Tools.* In this book we will often build programs from the VS.NET command line, which you can access by clicking the *Visual Studio.NET Command Prompt* icon shown in Figure 2.4.

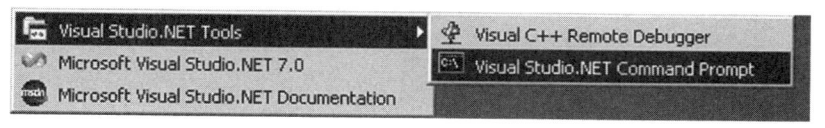

Figure 2.4 The Visual Studio.NET Command Prompt

Note that many utilities we use throughout this book (e.g., ILDASM.EXE in Chapter 3) are found in the `\%ProgramFiles% \Microsoft Visual Studio .NET\FrameworkSDK\Bin` directory. If you use the *VS.NET Command Prompt* in Figure 2.4, this directory will automatically be included in your PATH variable so that you can access the .NET Framework utilities from within any directory.

Chapter 3

THE .NET FRAMEWORK

The future of C# lies with the incarnation of the .NET Framework on Windows. Although it is true that efforts are under way to migrate the CLR (and, by extension, C#) to other platforms, as of this writing the C# language is undoubtedly tied to Microsoft's new software environment. In this chapter we investigate the following aspects of the framework:

- The *Common Language Runtime* (CLR), which executes all .NET applications
- The *Base Class Libraries* (*BCL*), which are a collection of classes that you can utilize from C#. The BCL is noteworthy because it is accessible to *all* .NET languages in a consistent manner
- *Assemblies,* which is the new name for software "components" in the .NET Framework

At the end of this chapter we will tie together these concepts and examine a fundamentally new paradigm in the realm of software development: cross-language inheritance.

Although the topics in this chapter are not specific to C#, they comprise the platform under which C# applications execute. Just as Visual Basic 6 developers had to understand the particularities of the Windows Operating System to develop in VB, you must appreciate the specifics of the .NET Framework to program in C#. In the next chapter we will get into the heart of the language when we survey the various elements that constitute the C# syntax. (Developers not at all familiar with C# syntax may want to skip ahead to Chapter 4 and then return to this chapter.)

CORE CONCEPTS

The Common Language Interface (CLI) and Non-Windows Platforms
Along with the C# language itself, Microsoft has submitted a specification called the Common Language Interface (CLI) to the ECMA standards body. This lengthy document describes the specifics of both the CLR and IL code, and essentially serves as a guideline for migrating the .NET Framework to other platforms.

What is notable about the CLI is that there is nothing OS-specific about it. Although the CLI describes the characteristics of .NET features such as garbage collection, metadata (described in this chapter), and common data types, it says nothing about their underlying implementations. Thus, a UNIX version of the CLR may utilize whatever OS-specific services are available to it. Such is the case with the open-source MONO effort, a version of the CLR ported to Linux. As of this writing, however, such ports are compromised efforts at best. As the on-line article at ᪽CS030001 describes, many aspects of .NET (e.g., ASP.NET and ADO.NET) are intrinsically dependent on Windows technologies such as IIS and COM, which greatly complicate the porting process. As of this writing, it is fair to say that complete C# development can only be carried out on the Windows platform.

Topic: The Common Language Runtime

At the heart of the .NET Framework is the Common Language Runtime (CLR). In addition to acting as a virtual machine, interpreting and executing IL code on the fly, the CLR provides many other services to applications, such as type-safety checking, memory management, garbage collection, and security enforcement. In this section we'll examine the primary services of the CLR.

CONCEPTS

Managed Code
Code that is executed by the CLR is said to be "managed." Code that runs outside the CLR is referred to as "unmanaged" or "native." How-

ever, there is more to managed code than this semantic classification. What does it mean to "run" within the CLR?

As we explained in Chapter 1, C# programs are converted from source code to Intermediate Language (IL) code by the C# compiler. The CLR then converts IL code into machine code, which can be executed by the Windows Operating System. By acting as a buffer between an application and the OS, the CLR can enforce security on the program and ensure that it has the proper resources to run. In other words, it can "manage" the application's execution. This is in contrast to applications authored before .NET, which are executed directly by the operating system and are thus "unmanaged."

Because managed code is executed by the CLR, the CLR can make decisions (at runtime) as to what an application can and cannot do. For example, the CLR can assign certain access rights to code depending on the origin of the code (the local drive, the Internet, etc.). This capability is referred to as Code Access Security (CAS) or Evidence Base Security; more information on this can be found at ⚓CS030002.

Another way to think of managed execution is to picture a .NET application running within a box that sits on top of the operating system. Within this box the application has access to a universal-type system referred to as the Common Type System (described below); numerous runtime services, such as garbage collection and exception handling (error checking); and thousands of classes that offer a variety of functionality. The application can also step outside the box if required (via COM Interop and Platform Invoke, both covered in Chapter 7).

Just-in-Time Compilation

Inevitably, developers mistakenly associate the managed execution of the CLR with slow performance. After all, if the CLR must convert IL code into machine code at runtime, it is reasonable to conclude that some overhead must exist. This line of reasoning derives from a common fallacy in the Java world: Because Java VMs interpret Java byte code line by line, Java programs are inherently slow.

In fact, both the CLR and modern Java VMs rapidly convert an application into native machine code the first time the application is run, a process referred to as Just-in-Time (JIT) compilation. Moreover, because the compilation process occurs at runtime as opposed to compile time, the CLR can optimize the compilation for the particular machine on which it is running. This capability is in contrast to C++ compilers, where optimization toward a particular processor is performed at compile time (Visual C++ 6.0, for example, exposes such compilation options as "Favor Pentium Pro").

Common Type System

The Common Type System (CTS) is a definition of permissible data types in the .NET Framework. To execute within the CLR, all languages, including C#, must derive their data types from the CTS.

There are two ways to use a variable in C#. You can use the language's built-in primitive types; alternatively, you can utilize the CTS types directly, which are usually more verbose. Listing 3.1 illustrates both approaches.

```
int a=4;              // C# primitive integer
System.Int32 b=5;     // CTS Integer
```

Listing 3.1   Built-in and CTS types in C#

C++ and Java users might prefer the first variation, since the type names are similar to those found in these languages (e.g., an Integer is declared as an `int`). Developers who are unfamiliar with such conventions may prefer the second technique, because it is more descriptive. Employing either option is really a matter of preference, since the primitive types translate into CTS types behind the scenes (i.e., their behavior and performance are identical). Table 3.1 lists common CTS types and their shorter C# equivalents.

C# Built-in Type	Underlying CTS Type
bool	System.Boolean
byte	System.Byte
decimal	System.Decimal
double	System.Double
float	System.Single
int	System.Int32
long	System.Int64
object	System.Object
short	System.Int16

Table 3.1   Primitive and CTS mappings in C#

The important principle to understand about the CTS is that it applies not only to C# but to *all* languages in the .NET Framework. This means that all .NET languages agree on the types they can use and the representation of those types. For example, both VB.NET and C# treat an integer as 32 bits. Prior to .NET, VB6 and Visual C++ had different standards for the representation of an integer (VB6 used 16 bits, C++ used 32). VB developers who have leveraged the Windows API will attest to the problems that arise because of such differing conventions. As we will see at the end of this chapter, the CTS greatly simplifies the interoperability among languages in the .NET Framework.

The Base Type: System.Object

All data types in the .NET Framework derive (inherit) from the System.Object type found in the CTS. We will cover the concept of type derivation in Chapter 6, but, basically, by deriving from an entity, a data type acquires the capabilities of that entity. Thus, every type in the .NET Framework automatically obtains the capabilities of System.Object. One of these inherited capabilities is a method called ToString(), which converts the contents of the variable to a string (similar to the Str$() function in VB). This allows any variable to be used easily in output operations, as illustrated in Listing 3.2.

```
int count=5;
double width=7.0;
MessageBox.Show(count.ToString());
MessageBox.Show(width.ToString());
```

Listing 3.2   The System.Object ToString() method

Furthermore, because all types in the .NET Framework derive from System.Object, it is useful in scenarios where a method may return one of several types. Consider Listing 3.3.

```
Class MyClass
{
  public System.Object Foo(int x)
  {
      // Return a range of types (int, string, etc)
  }
}
```

Listing 3.3   Returning an Object in a method

Because the Foo() method in Listing 3.3 returns a generic Object, the method can return anything that an Object encapsulates (such as a String, a Float, or an ArrayList class). We will investigate C# data types further in the next chapter.

VB Developers: Think Variant
From a functional point of view VB developers can think of the `Variant` and the `System.Object` type as equivalent. Each can store any of the permissible data types of its respective environment. So just as you used the `Variant` to store strings, integers, and classes in VB6, you can use `System.Object` to do the same in C#.

```
System.Object o;
o=4;
o=7.8;
o="Hello World";
```

Listing 3.4   The Object type in C#

As can be seen from Listing 3.4, an `Object` is very much like a `Variant`. VB developers can draw another parallel between the two: Just as Visual Basic 6 programs can use only the types that can be represented by a `Variant`, C# applications are confined to using those types within the CTS.

Garbage Collection

One of the most useful functions performed by the CLR is automatic memory management. Consider the code in Listing 3.5, which creates and uses an instance of a `Math` class.

```
class IllustrateGC
{
   public void DoSomething() {
      Math m = new Math();
      m.Add(1,2)
   }
}
```

Listing 3.5   Garbage collection in .NET

If Listing 3.5 had been written in C++, we would have had to release the `Math` class explicitly after using it (the functional equivalent of `Set m = Nothing` in Visual Basic). In C#, however, we can get away with this omission because the CLR will clean up after us. After the code executes, the CLR determines that the `Math` class is no longer being referenced and destroys it appropriately. In Chapter 5 we will examine the details of garbage collection along with C# cleanup mechanisms such as class destructors (the equivalent of `Class_Terminate` routines in VB).

Application Domain (AppDomain)

The Windows Operating System uses processes to protect concurrently running applications from one another. Internet Explorer (IE) and Microsoft Word, for example, each run in a different process. If Word executes an illegal instruction, Windows can shut down its individual process without adversely affecting IE.

Since processes predate .NET, they must provide robust protection against native code making them expensive to create and tear down. Because .NET applications operate within the CLR, they can be afforded the same protection without the costly construction of a process. The .NET Framework saves resources by allowing multiple Application Domains (AppDomains) to exist in one process. If the CLR must shut down an AppDomain, it can do so without disrupting other AppDomains within the same process. Therefore, it is proper to think of an AppDomain as a "lightweight" process made possible by the increased protection provided by the CLR. Just as a Windows process separates applications in the native realm, an AppDomain serves as the protective boundary for programs executing in the .NET Framework.

Where Does the CLR Live?

Our discussion of the CLR up to this point has been strictly theoretical; it sometimes helps to see things in a more tangible manner. Although the CLR provides services to applications that were previously responsibilities of the operating system, the CLR *itself* sits on top of the operating system. It must therefore exist as a tangible entity somewhere on your hard drive.

If you look inside the `\%winroot%\Microsoft.NET\Framework\versionNum\` directory (where `versionNum` is the particular version of the .NET Framework that you have installed), you will find two files: `mscorsvr.dll` and `mscorwks.dll`. These files, each roughly 2 megabytes in size, represent two versions of the CLR: one for single-processor machines and one for multiple-processor machines. .NET will load the appropriate version when an application runs, automatically taking advantage of additional processors if they exist. (In case you are wondering, the CLR itself was written in a few hundred thousand lines of mostly C code, a version of which has been publicly released. See ᴄɴCS030007 for more information on the Microsoft Shared Source CLI Implementation.)

EXAMPLE

The CLR is ubiquitous in the .NET Framework; virtually any C# example would demonstrate its usage. In this example we are going to further examine the Common Type System that the CLR imposes on C#. Save the following code in a file named CTSExample.cs.

```
// VB developers, note the array declaration
// and the 'for' loop.  We will revisit these in Chapter 4
using System;

class CTSExample
{
   static void Main(string[] args)
   {
     int a=0;
     double b=1.5;
     string c="Brent";

     // Declare an array of objects
     object []o=new object[3];

     // Populate array with our variables:
     o[0]=a; o[1]=b; o[2]=c;

     // Print out the types stored in the array:
     for (int i=0; i<=o.Length; i++)   {
      Console.WriteLine("element # {0} is a {1}"
                   ,i,o[i].GetType());
     }
   }
}
```

Listing 3.6 CTS C# example

Listing 3.6 illustrates some important aspects of the Common Type System. After declaring some primitive types (`int`, `double`, and `string`), we declare an array of `object`s. From Table 3.1 we can see that the `object` type maps to a `System.Object` in the CTS. Furthermore, the rules of the CTS prescribe that *all* data types in the .NET Framework derive from `System.Object` (which means that, in a sense, every .NET data type *is* an `Object`). Therefore, the object array can hold references to any .NET data type, including the primitive types we declared previously (a, b, and c).

After populating the array with the primitive data types, we iterate through the array and print out its contents. (Note that you can, as we have, place multiple statements on one line, provided that they are delimited with a semicolon.) To print out a variable's "type" we use a special method named `GetType()`. This method is implemented by `System.Object` and is thus automatically available to any .NET class.

The line that actually prints out the variable's type may require some explanation:

```
Console.WriteLine("element # {0} is a {1}",i, o[i].GetType());
```

Placing {0} and {1} in the `WriteLine()` output string instructs the `Console` class to replace these tokens with the arguments that follow. The first token, {0}, is replaced with the value of the `for` loop's counter variable (i). Similarly, {1} is replaced with the second argument, which is the element's type as reported by the `GetType()` method. Developers familiar with C or C+ will find this syntax similar to the % operator used with the `printf` function. (Similar to the `printf` function, the `WriteLine()` method allows one to control the spacing, width, and precision of the output string. For details see the reference card included with this book as well as ⌁CS030003).

Running the Example

Compile Listing 3.6 using the command-line compiler (csc.exe) and run the application file that is produced (CTSExample.exe). You will observe output similar to Listing 3.7.

```
element # 0 is a System.Int32
element # 1 is a System.Double
element # 2 is a System.String
```

Listing 3.7   Application output

As can be seen from the application's output, primitive types in C# map to types in the CTS according to the rules in Table 3.1. More important is the fact that an `object` can represent any type in the .NET Framework. Because of this all-encompassing capability, `objects` are useful:

1. for generic containers such as the object array in Listing 3.6.
2. when you are unsure of a variable's contents at design time (remember that an `object` is akin to a VB6 `Variant`).
3. when a method may return a variety of values (`double`, `int`, etc.). In such a situation the method can simply return an `object`, and the caller can infer its type by means of the `GetType()` method.

SUMMARY

All applications in the .NET Framework, including those written in C#, are executed by the Common Language Runtime. The CLR performs many valuable services for an application, such as garbage collection, application isolation, and security checking. The CLR also enforces a Common Type System (CTS) on all .NET languages, which greatly simplifies the interoperability among them.

Applications in the .NET Framework are translated into Intermediate Language (IL) code by a language compiler, which is Just-in-Time (JIT) compiled into machine code by the CLR the first time an application is run. .NET applications execute within Application Domains, the CLR's equivalent of Windows processes.

Topic: The Base Class Libraries

Whereas the CLR is the brains behind a .NET application, the Base Class Libraries are the building blocks. The BCL contains thousands of classes that can be used to construct applications in C#. Everything from data storage classes to XML parsers to .NET "subtechnologies" such as ASP.NET and web services are exposed through the BCL.

The Base Class Libraries are copied to your system automatically when you install the .NET Framework, and they exist as language-independent IL code. Thus, they are accessible to all .NET languages in a consistent manner. This is in contrast to pre-.NET technologies where there are different libraries for different languages (the MFC for C++, JCL for Java, etc.). Before we use the BCL, we must understand the essential concept of namespaces.

CONCEPTS

Namespaces

Because there are so many classes inside the BCL, there must be a system to organize them. In .NET, classes are grouped by means of namespaces.

Namespaces provide a scope (or container) in which classes and methods are defined. Several core BCL classes, for example, are found in the `System` namespace. If the BCL contained a class called `Foo`, you would have to *qualify* it by prefixing it with System: `System.Foo`.

Namespaces can also be nested. The `System.IO` namespace, for example, contains classes for I/O operations, whereas `System.Security` contains classes to access the CLR's security infrastructure. It is tedious to have to qualify BCL classes when you use them. For this reason C# allows you to reference namespaces implicitly by means of the `using` keyword. Consider the code in Listing 3.8.

```
using System;
using System.IO;
// Open a file and write to it:
StreamWriter sw = File.CreateText("MyFile.txt");
sw.WriteLine("This is my file");
sw.WriteLine("I can write ints {0} and floats {1}", 1, 4.2);
sw.Close();
```

Listing 3.8   Implicitly referencing a namespace

Because of the two `using` statements, we don't have to write the more verbose:

```
System.IO.StreamWriter sw =
    System.IO.File.CreateText("MyFile.txt");
sw.WriteLine("This is my file");
sw.WriteLine("I can write ints {0} and floats {1}", 1, 4.2);
sw.Close();
```

Listing 3.9   Explicitly identifying a class

As you can see, referencing namespaces implicitly can save you a lot of typing and make your code easier to read. We will use namespaces in C# to:

1. access the BCL classes.
2. access classes authored by other developers.
3. provide a namespace for your own classes that other .NET developers may use.

If you come from the Java world, you can think of a namespace as being equivalent to a package. Not only is the basic structure the same, but you also have to either fully qualify your C# classes with the namespace or import it with the `using` command.

BCL EXAMPLE: WINDOWS FORMS APPLICATIONS

Now that we understand the BCL, we are in a position to more thoroughly analyze the Windows Forms application that we wrote in Chapter 1. Reload this application in VS.NET, and you will see the following lines at the top of the project's source code:

```
using System;
using System.Drawing;
using System.Collections;
using System.ComponentModel;
using System.Windows.Forms;
using System.Data;
```

Listing 3.10 *Code from the Windows Forms application in Chapter 1*

VS.NET automatically inserted these lines into the project in order to reference certain BCL namespaces. Recall that several core classes (such as CTS types) reside in the System namespace. In addition, because we are constructing a desktop application, VS.NET references the System.Windows.Forms namespace so that we can easily access the Windows Forms classes.

Recall that the application we developed in Chapter 1 consisted of a simple form and button. If you peruse the source code, you will find a line similar to the following:

```
public class Form1 : System.Windows.Forms.Form
```

When we created this project in Chapter 1, VS.NET implicitly gave the project an empty form. Behind the scenes, the IDE generated a Form1 class that mapped to the empty form. Because Form1 inherits from the BCL Windows Forms class, it automatically garners some boilerplate capabilities, such as the ability to render itself when the application executes.

Similarly, when we added a button on the form, the environment gave the Form1 class a private member variable named Button1. This may not seem obvious when you look through the source code, but you can see it if you expand the Windows Form Designer *generated code* section as illustrated in Figure 3.1.

As Figure 3.1 illustrates, automatically generated code is enclosed within #Region and #End Region tags. Scan through this portion of the project's code (there is a lot of it), and you will find the following line:

```
    ▶Windows Form Designer generated code

    #region Windows Form Designer generated code
    /// <summary>
    /// Required method for Designer support - do not modify
    /// the contents of this method with the code editor.
    /// </summary>
    private void InitializeComponent()
```

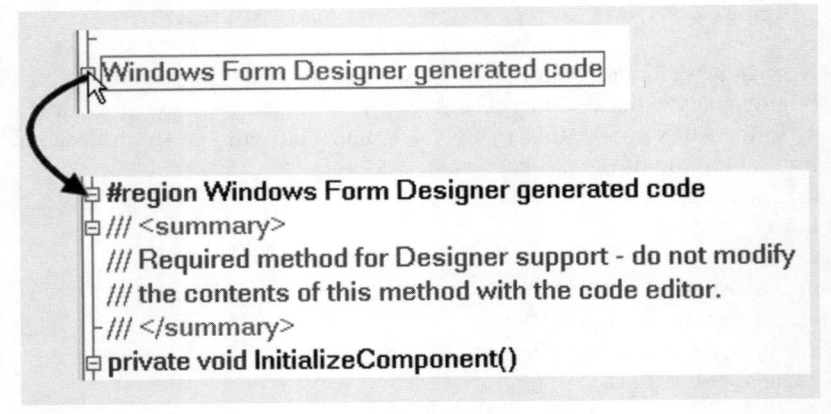

Figure 3.1   Expanding VS.NET generated code

```
private System.Windows.Forms.Button button1;
```

  This line declares the `Button` class as a private member variable of the `Form1` class. Note that `button1` is an instance of the BCL `Button` class found in the `System.Windows.Forms` namespace. Look closely at the project source again, and you will find private method named `InitializeComponent()`. This method is called from the form's constructor, which is similar to the `Form_Initialize` method in VB6 (it is called before the form loads).

  The `InitializeComponent()` method instantiates and configures the form's visual contents (buttons, labels, pictures, etc.). If you look within this method, you'll find lines similar to the following that determine the button's size and location.

```
this.button1.Location = new System.Drawing.Point(24, 16);
this.button1.Size = new System.Drawing.Size(240, 70);
```

Listing 3.11   Determining a button's size

  These lines were generated by VS.NET when you placed the button on the form. If you were to return to the form and resize the button, the IDE would change the second line of code to match your actions. Note that a control's location and size are specified by means of the `Location` and `Size` properties (although the Windows Forms classes still expose the `Left`, `Top`, `Height`, and `Width` properties for backward compatibility with VB6).

  You may be wondering if we can do the reverse; that is, can we change the underlying code and see a corresponding change in the button's size in the design environment? You can do this, but it is not advisable. Visual Studio doesn't expect you to modify the code it generates. If you make a change it doesn't understand, it could damage the entire project. For demonstration purposes, however, let's do something innocuous and change the first parameter in the button's size from 240 to 100. Return to the design environment, and the button's width will have decreased.

Look through (but don't touch!) the rest of the project's code, and you will begin to understand the intricacies of the Windows Forms classes. The entity in VS.NET that performs this magic is called the Windows Form Designer (WFD).

The Windows Form Designer
When you draw a button or textbox on a form, the WFD translates your actions into C# code that leverages the classes found in the `System.Windows.Forms` namespace. This code becomes an integral part of the project's source code, to which you can add your own logic.

Remember that the Base Class Libraries exist as neutral IL code. They are thus callable from any language that targets the .NET Framework. However, in order for the WFD to generate code automatically, as it did in this example, the language must support special Microsoft "Code Generation" extensions. As of this writing, only VB.NET, C#, and J# are so equipped. Therefore, although you can certainly call the Windows Forms classes from managed C++ or JScript.NET, you are not afforded the luxury of automatic code generation and must write such code manually.

The most difficult aspect of using the BCL is figuring out which classes you need to accomplish the task at hand. There are thousands of classes for many programmatic tasks including data access, Active Directory management, socket programming, and security. The most complete source for the BCL is the MSDN documentation, although descriptions of some of the more important classes can be found on-line at ᵔᴺ⁾CS030004.

Base Class Library Files
In the previous example VS.NET used the Windows Forms classes by referencing the `System.Windows.Forms` namespace that contained them. Where, however, do these classes actually reside (i.e., what file contains its implementation code)?

As of this writing, the BCL classes can be found in the following directory (where `versionNum` is the particular version of the .NET Framework you have installed):

```
\%winroot%\Microsoft.NET\Framework\versionNum\
```

If you look inside this directory, you will find several DLLs that contain the BCL classes for a given namespace (some DLLs actually contain numerous namespaces). The following table lists some of the more important files in the .NET Framework.

BCL FileName	Contents
Mscorlib.dll	Fundamental classes and data types
System.Data.dll	ADO.NET classes for database access
System.DirectoryServices.dll	Classes to manipulate Active Directory
System.Drawing.dll	GDI+ classes for drawing/manipulating images
System.EnterpriseServices.dll	Access to COM+ services
System.Runtime.Remoting.dll	.NET Remoting classes
System.Security.dll	CLR Code Access Security classes (policies, zones)
System.ServiceProcess.dll	Classes to write Windows Services
System.Web.dll	ASP.NET classes for HTTP-based applications
System.Web.Services.dll	Classes to author Web Services
System.Windows.Forms.dll	Desktop windows application classes
System.XML.dll	XML parsing, reading/writing classes

Table 3.1   DLLs containing important BCL classes

These files (and hence the .NET Framework) must be installed on a computer in order to execute .NET applications. When you (or VS.NET) use BCL classes such as `Form` and `ComboBox`, the CLR determines the file in which the method is located and loads it appropriately when the application executes. In the next topic we will see that these files are really *assemblies,* the new way that components are packaged in the .NET Framework.

Assemblies and Namespaces

The relationship between BCL files (assemblies) and namespaces can be confusing. An assembly houses executable code; a namespace simplifies the manner in which that code can be accessed. A single assembly can contain multiple namespaces. For example, an assembly that exposes mathematical functions might partition itself into standard and scientific services, and group them into two namespaces called `MyCalc.Standard` and `MyCalc.Scientific`. Even though the assembly would contain two namespaces, it would still be packaged in one file. (Note that it is also possible for an assembly to span multiple files [called modules] as well; see ⟲CS030005 for more information.)

In order to use a Base Class library you must reference the assembly explicitly in VS.NET (and optionally specify namespaces to make your code more concise). We have not referenced assemblies in VS.NET thus far, because the environment references a number of them for us by default. You can see this by opening up the *References* tree in the Solution Explorer as shown in Figure 3.2.

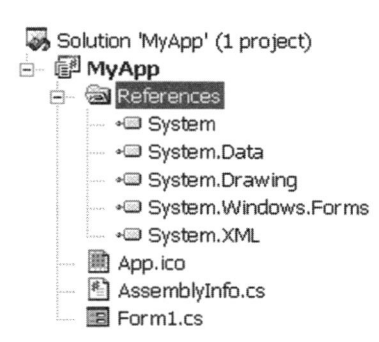

```
Solution 'MyApp' (1 project)
└─ MyApp
   └─ References
      ─ System
      ─ System.Data
      ─ System.Drawing
      ─ System.Windows.Forms
      ─ System.XML
   ─ App.ico
   ─ AssemblyInfo.cs
   ─ Form1.cs
```

Figure 3.2   BCL files automatically referenced by VS.NET

Compare Figure 3.2 with the file names given in Table 3.1, and you will see that, for Windows desktop applications, VS.NET automatically references Base Class Libraries for ADO.NET, GDI+, Windows Forms, and XML. If you want to use additional classes, you must reference the appropriate assembly manually, a process that we'll examine in the next topic.

SUMMARY

The Base Class Libraries is a collection of classes that form the building blocks of C# applications. The BCL contains thousands of classes for common operations such as database manipulation, file IO, and mathematical computations, as well as new Microsoft technologies such as Windows Forms, ASP.NET, and web services.

The BCL is organized by means of namespaces, which makes it easier to access and syntactically more concise. Core BCL classes are found in the System namespace or in nested namespaces within it (such as System.Collections and System.IO). Some of these namespaces are referenced automatically in VS.NET when you write C# applications.

To explicitly use a namespace in C#, you must leverage the `using` keyword.

Visual Studio.NET automatically generates code that leverages the BCL when you create certain projects within its environment. For example, desktop applications utilize `System.Windows.Forms` classes behind the scenes, whereas ASP.NET applications leverage the classes found in `System.Web`. As of this writing, automatic code generation in VS.NET is limited to VB.NET, J#, and, most important, C#.

Topic: Assemblies

A software component is an entity that exposes a number of services to other applications. For example, the ActiveX Data Object (ADO) library used for database access is a software component. On the Windows Operating System software components are usually packaged as Dynamic Link Library (DLL) files or, in some cases, executable (EXE) files.

Throughout the years a number of standards have emerged as to how components "offer" their services to clients, that is, the means by which clients can discover these services and invoke them if desired. The two prominent standards on the Windows platform are the following:

1. *Win32 DLLs:* These originate from the very early days of Windows and are usually written in C or C++. In addition to housing the Windows API, Win32 DLLs are often used to provide low-level system access to programs (device access, for example). In Chapter 7 we will see that Win32 DLLs can be called from C# by means of a technology called Platform Invoke (PInvoke).
2. *COM:* The Component Object Model (explained in Chapter 1) was the first evolution of the software component for Windows. The three noteworthy improvements of COM over traditional Win32 DLLs were language neutrality—any language could communicate with a COM component (theoretically); stricter versioning rules—COM tried to improve on how components evolved; and self-describing components—a client could "query" a COM object to determine whether it supported a particular service.

With .NET the software component has evolved yet again into the assembly. All assemblies in the .NET Framework contain two important entities: Intermediate Language (IL) code, which houses the assembly's executable logic, and metadata, which describes all the types (classes, methods, etc.) that the assembly exposes. Both of these features are illustrated in the upcoming example. There are two primary types of assemblies that you can create in C#:

1. *Executable files (EXEs) such as Console and Desktop applications.* Even though EXEs are not really components, they are still classified as assemblies because they contain IL code and metadata.
2. *Component Libraries (DLLs).* You will create component libraries in C# when you want to package a collection of services that are accessible to other applications. In this topic we will write and use such a component.

CONCEPTS

Type Library
COM components usually contain a type library that describes the methods they expose. A powerful feature in Visual Basic 6 is IntelliSense, in which a list of methods appears whenever you press a period following an object in the VB6 environment.

After selecting the particular method you wish to call, the VB6 environment also lists the parameters the method expects. Behind the scenes the VB environment queries the object's type library for information and displays it in an intuitive manner through IntelliSense. With the advent of assemblies, type libraries have evolved into metadata. Furthermore, assemblies *always* house type information (it is not optional, as in COM). This means that .NET components always support the IntelliSense feature.

The Registry
The registry is a database that stores configuration information for the Windows Operating System. One problem with COM is that version and type information is stored in two different places: the registry and the component's type library. For this reason COM components must be *registered* (using a utility called regsvr32.exe) before they can be used. Running this utility populates the registry with the component's type information.

.NET eliminates the need to keep component information in two locations; the metadata for an assembly is stored entirely within the component itself. .NET components are thus self-describing in that they contain both IL code and the necessary information needed to execute them.

Assemblies and DLL Hell

Assemblies are noteworthy because they end the "DLL Hell" problem that has plagued the Windows Operating System for many years. To understand how, you must appreciate that there are two types of assemblies in the .NET Framework: private and shared.

Private assemblies are not designed to be used by multiple applications. They are designed to be used by one application and *must reside in that application's directory or subdirectory*. This isolated methodology is reminiscent of the old DOS days when applications were fully contained within their own directories and did not disturb one another. By default, all assemblies (such as the one we will create in the upcoming example) are private.

For those components that must be distributed (if you want multiple applications to use a common component), Microsoft offers the shared assembly. The shared assembly concept is based on two principles. The first, called *side-by-side execution,* allows the CLR to house multiple versions of the same assembly on a single machine. The second, termed *binding,* ensures that clients obtain the version of the component they expect. Together, these two principles free developers from having to ensure that their components are compatible with their earlier versions. If a component evolves through versions 1.0, 1.1, and 2.0, the CLR will maintain separate copies of each version and deliver the appropriate version to each client.

Security and the Global Assembly Cache

What differentiates the shared assembly model from previous component models (such as COM and Win32) is that the versioning policy is not voluntary or based on considerate programming practices, but is enforced through public key cryptography. A full discussion of cryptography and its use by the CLR would quickly plunge us into the cryptic world of hashing, tokens, digital signatures, and other topics beyond the scope of this book. These subjects can quickly become overwhelming, but all you have to understand is that to enforce versioning, the CLR must ensure that:

1. shared assemblies can be updated only by authorized parties.
2. if a component is updated, clients expecting the older version receive it.

These requirements are facilitated by two entities. The first is a *private key*, which you obtain to "sign" an assembly, allowing you (and only you) to update it. The second is the Global Assembly Cache (GAC), which can house multiple copies of a shared assembly based on your "signature" and the version information used to build it. This information (signature and version) is stored in the metadata of all clients who wish to access the assembly, which allows the CLR to load the appropriate version at runtime. The process of creating a shared assembly is fairly straightforward and is illustrated on-line at ᴄɴCS030006.

EXAMPLE

A useful piece of information when debugging an application is the operating system account under which the application runs. For example, when you use a program such as Microsoft Word, the application attempts to access system resources (files, the registry, etc.) using the logged-in account (e.g., CODENOTES\bwilliams). In this example we will write a (private) Class Library (DLL) assembly that exposes a method to retrieve this information.

Writing a Class Library
To create an assembly, open VS.NET and create a new C# Class Library project named *myAssembly* (choose the Class Library template in the project dialog box). A Class Library is a DLL assembly that exposes a number of types that are callable from .NET applications.

After you click OK to create the project, VS.NET will create a project file where you can write the methods you wish to expose to the outside world. The file already contains some boilerplate code, as shown in Listing 3.12.

```
using System;

namespace myAssembly
{
   /// <summary>
   /// Summary description for Class1.
   /// </summary>
   public class Class1
   {
      public Class1()
      {
```

```
            //
            // TODO: Add constructor logic here
            //
        }
    }
}
```

Listing 3.12 Boilerplate code inserted by VS.NET

Recall from the namespace discussion in the previous topic that you access the Base Class Libraries by referencing the namespaces in which they are contained. Similarly, when you author a Class Library, you place it within a namespace that others must reference. By default, VS.NET places the project in a namespace equal to the project name (myAssembly, in this case). It also gives the project a default class (Class1) that will be exposed to client applications.

As it stands, our assembly is not very functional, the class it exposes doesn't do anything. At the beginning of this example we sought to write an assembly that would report the user account under which it was running. Start by changing the name Class1 to ProcessInfo, and delete the constructor from the source. (A constructor, covered in Chapter 6, is a method that gets called automatically when the class is instantiated.)

Next, we need a method in the class that determines the user account under which the class is running. But where can we find such functionality? As you may have guessed, there is a Base Class library that does exactly what we want.

Referencing a Base Class Library

Recall from the previous topic that in order to use a BCL class, you must first reference the assembly that contains it. The functionality we desire is exposed by the WindowsIndentity class located in System.Security.DLL. In the previous topic we also learned that certain BCL files are referenced automatically by VS.NET so that we don't have to reference them ourselves. Since Class Library projects do not automatically reference the DLL we require, we have to add a reference ourselves. Go to Project → Add Reference and explicitly select the System.Security component as shown in Figure 3.3.

Notice the addition of the two using commands at the top of the code. By inserting these lines we can work with the WindowsIdentity class rather than the more verbose System.Security.Principal.WindowsIdentity. Both names refer to the same class; however, the shorter version is much easier to type and read.

Figure 3.3 illustrates that you can also reference COM components,

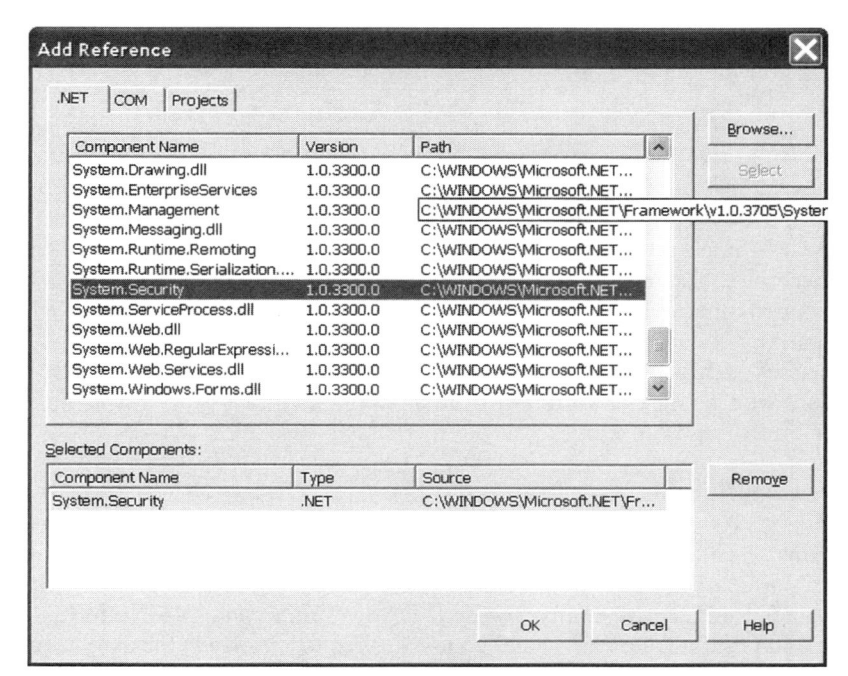

Figure 3.3 Adding a reference to a BCL class

an option that we will explore in Chapter 7. After selecting the
System.Security.DLL, click OK. Notice that the file is added to the References section of your Solution (Figure 3.2). Remember that referencing a BCL file is only part of the process; you must also reference the namespace of the particular class you want to use. With that in mind, replace the code in Listing 3.12 with the contents of Listing 3.13.

```
using System;
using System.Security.Principal;

namespace myAssembly
{
   public class ProcessInfo
   {
      public string UserID()
      {
         // Return the process user account:
         return WindowsIdentity.GetCurrent().Name;
      }
```

        }
}

Listing 3.13   myAssembly reports the userID of the host process

Build the library by going to Build → Build Solution, and you now have a Class Library that exposes a class named `ProcessInfo`, which in turn exposes a single method named `UserID()`.

It is important to realize that there is no particular relationship between the assembly name and the namespace(s) it contains. It just so happens that most system DLLs are named in a way that reflects the namespaces they contain (e.g., `System.Security.DLL` contains namespaces such as `System.Security` and `System.Security.Principal`). Before we use the Class Library from an application, let us take a look at the resulting DLL file.

The ILDASM Utility

The myAssembly.DLL file that you just built is an assembly that contains IL code and self-describing metadata. To look at this metadata we can use a tool provided by Microsoft called ILDASM.EXE, which stands for IL Disassembly. To use ILDASM bring up the VS.NET command prompt (Figure 2.4) and go to the directory in which the assembly file is located. By default, VS.NET stores the file in the project's bin\Debug directory. Next, execute the following command:
`ILDASM/adv myAssembly.DLL`

ILDASM will load the assembly and bring up a screen similar to the one depicted below.

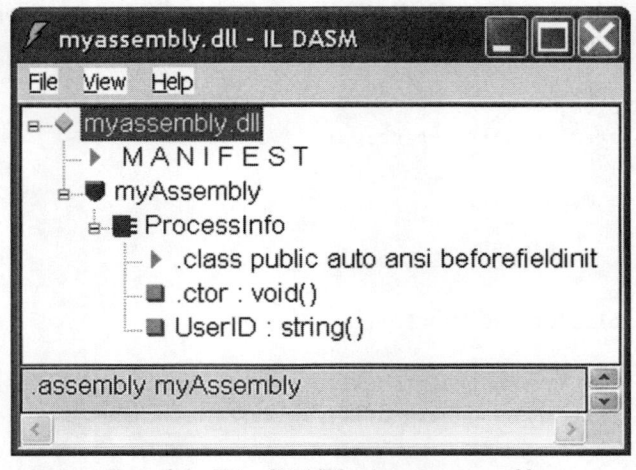

Figure 3.4   Using ILDASM to inspect an assembly

As illustrated in Figure 3.4, ILDASM lists the types exposed by an assembly, which in the case of our library consists of a single class named `ProcessInfo` that contains two methods: `ctor` and `UserID()`. Some of you may recognize the `ctor()` method as the class's constructor. (Even though we removed it from the source code, all C# classes are given constructors implicitly.) Also, note that the class is contained within the `myAssembly` namespace in accordance with Listing 3.13.

You can also use ILDASM to examine the assembly's metadata by going to its View menu and selecting Metadata → Show! The metadata listing is quite verbose, but looking through it you will find the following definition:

```
TypeDef #1
-----------------------------------------------------------
TypeDefName: myAssembly.ProcessInfo   (02000002)
Flags      : [Public] [AutoLayout] [Class] [AnsiClass]
Extends    : 01000001 [TypeRef] System.Object
Method #1
-----------------------------------------------------------
        MethodName: UserID  (06000001)
        Flags     : [Public] [HideBySig] [ReuseSlot]
        RVA       : 0x00002050
        ImplFlags : [IL] [Managed]   (00000000)
        CallCnvntn: [DEFAULT]
        hasThis
        ReturnType: String
        No arguments.

Method #2 ctor . . .
```

Listing 3.14   The assembly's metadata

The *TypeDef* section of the metadata lists the types exposed by the assembly, which includes our class, `ProcessInfo`. Recall from our discussion of the Common Type System at the beginning of this chapter that all types in the .NET Framework derive from the `Object` type. Therefore, it should come as no surprise that our class extends (inherits) from `System.Object`, as reported in Listing 3.14.

The metadata in Listing 3.14 also lists all the methods exposed by our class. This is important, because entities such as compilers and even the CLR itself can use this information to ensure that the class will be called in a correct fashion. This information also fuels IntelliSense inside Visual Studio.NET.

You can also examine the IL code for a particular method. For example, if you click on the `UserID()` method in Figure 3.4, you will see its underlying IL code. If you are familiar with assembly language, you will find IL code similar to high-level pseudo machine code.

To review, an assembly consists of the two main entities that we have examined using ILDASM: IL code, which is converted by the CLR into machine code when the assembly runs, and metadata, which describes all the types that the assembly exposes. Now that you understand the internals of assemblies, let us examine how you use them.

The Base Class Libraries

In writing our Class Library (`myAssembly`) we used the BCL `WindowsIdentity` class to determine the user account under which the application was running. To use this class we had to add a reference to the DLL file that contained it and also reference its namespace.

To use *our* Class Library, clients would repeat the exact same procedure. This similarity is reflective of an important aspect of the BCL: *The Base Class Libraries are themselves assemblies.* The only difference between our assembly and the BCL is that the BCL is authored by Microsoft and installed on your system as a part of the .NET Framework. Therefore, you can use ILDASM to examine the Base Class Libraries. (Remember, they can be found in the `\%winroot%\Microsoft.NET\Framework\versionNum\` directory). For example, if you use ILDASM to inspect `System.Windows.Forms.DLL`, you will find classes such as `Button`, `Label`, and `Form`.

Using the Assembly: The WhoAmI Application

To use the assembly we just developed, create a new C# Windows application in Visual Studio named `WhoAmI`. Drag a button and text box onto the form and then add a reference to our assembly by going to Project → Add References, clicking *Browse,* and selecting `myAssembly.DLL` from the directory in which it is contained. Again, note that the file is added to the Reference section of the project's solution.

Reference the assembly's namespace by adding the line `using myAssembly` at the top of the source file. Next, double-click the button and add the highlighted code in Listing 3.15 to its event handler.

```
private void button1_Click(...)
{
   myAssembly.ProcessInfo m = new myAssembly.ProcessInfo();
   MessageBox.Show(m.UserID());
}
```

Listing 3.15   Using our assembly in ASP.NET

Run the program by pressing F5, and after you click the button, the Class Library will report the user account under which the application is running: CODENOTES\sfernandez.

You will notice some interesting behavior as you type the second highlighted line into your source: The environment automatically lists the methods of the ProcessInfo class (thanks to IntelliSense). This behavior is made possible by the metadata in Listing 3.14. Behind the scenes, VS.NET consults this metadata to determine the methods that the class exposes, which it then converts into a user-friendly representation on the screen.

Assemblies—Not Just Class Libraries
Before we depart from the topic of assemblies, we must make an important clarification. Based on this example you may conclude that only Class Library files (DLLs) are classified as assemblies. In fact, *any* entity that contains IL code in the .NET Framework is an assembly. This includes .NET desktop applications (EXEs) and component libraries (DLLs). (However, you cannot add a reference to an EXE.)

HOW AND WHY?

How do I prevent a class in my assembly from being used by other programs?
Look at Listing 3.13, and you will see that the public keyword precedes the declaration of the ProcessInfo class. The public extension advises the C# compiler that the class should be accessible to all programs that reference the assembly. In C# you can specify the visibility of types to the outside world by means of visibility keywords that we will examine in the next chapter.

SUMMARY

Executable files in the .NET Framework consist of both IL code and metadata. Whereas IL is machine-neutral byte code that is executed by the CLR, metadata describes the types that the executable exposes. Both executable programs (EXEs) and software components (DLLs) under the .NET Framework are referred to as *assemblies*.

The presence of metadata in an assembly makes it self-describing in that the assembly fully describes its contents to the outside world. This metadata fuels VS.NET's IntelliSense feature and can be inspected by means of the ILDASM utility that is packaged with the .NET Framework.

Topic: C# Interoperability with Other Languages

The underlying theme in .NET Framework is uniformity. Because all .NET languages compile to IL code, they all derive their data types from the CTS, and they can all use the Base Class Libraries in a similar manner. Because the internal plumbing behind all languages is built into the CLR, .NET languages can interact very easily. This is most evident by a new feature made available in the .NET Framework called cross-language inheritance.

CONCEPTS

Cross-Language Inheritance

As we will see in Chapter 6, C# gives developers the ability to write classes that inherit from other classes. A fundamentally new feature in .NET is the ability to inherit from classes written in other languages. For example, imagine we start with a C# class named `Calculator`. We compile this class into a Class Library assembly. With .NET we can create a second class in VB.NET called `VBExtend`, which inherits from `Calculator`. If we want, we can create a third class in C# that inherits from `VBExtend`. This recursive process is illustrated in Figure 3.5.

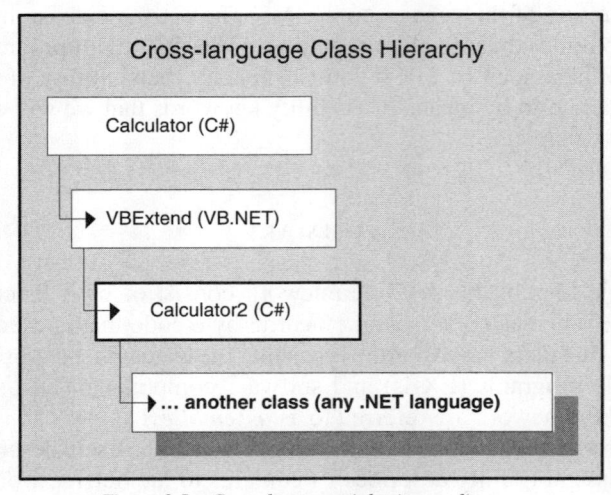

```
Cross-language Class Hierarchy

  Calculator (C#)
      │
      └─▶ VBExtend (VB.NET)
              │
              └─▶ Calculator2 (C#)
                      │
                      └─▶ ... another class (any .NET language)
```

Figure 3.5   Cross-language inheritance diagram

The virtues of cross-language inheritance are made possible by the standard platform of the CLR. A subtle yet important point is that when you inherit from a class in .NET, *you are really inheriting IL code.* In Figure 3.5, for example, VBExtend is not inheriting a C# class so much as it is inheriting an *IL class*. In other words, once a class is compiled into IL code, it loses its language affiliation. Because the VB.NET compiler understands IL, the Calculator class from which it derives could have been authored in *any* .NET language; the compiler has no idea that the class was originally written in C#.

Cross-language inheritance represents a significant innovation in the realm of software development. Although languages have been able to communicate with one another for some time (through communication protocols such as COM and CORBA), *never before has a language been able to treat a class authored in another language as if it were an intrinsic class of the target language itself.* For example, prior to .NET you could not write a class in Java and then inherit that class in C++.

The Caveat
Unfortunately, cross-language inheritance is not without its share of complexities. The unavoidable fact is that languages are intrinsically different from one another. For example, the concept of pointers, while central to C++ and also available in C#, is absent in Visual Basic and Java. OOP features such as inheritance and polymorphism play a pivotal role in VB.NET, C#, and C++, but may not have direct equivalents in COBOL or Pascal. In short, the features of two languages will never completely intersect, and so to communicate with one another there must be a common standard to which they adhere. In .NET this standard is called the Common Language Specification (CLS).

The Common Language Specification
The CLS is best understood in light of the following situation: Assume for a moment that you wished to write a new language for the .NET Framework called *Zebra*. Like C#, VB.NET, and managed C++, the Zebra compiler would translate Zebra syntax into IL code. As a language author you would have to make an important choice with respect to how Zebra would communicate with the outside world:

1. *No communication:* Zebra applications *cannot* communicate with other languages. Therefore, when you write a Zebra program, you cannot utilize the C# Calculator class we wrote in the previous topic. That is, you can't directly communicate with code in other languages as if it were native to your language. You could still use a system like CORBA or COM or web services. However, all of these systems require overhead and extra development.

2. *Communication:* Zebra applications *can* communicate with other languages. Thus, it should be possible for a Zebra program to inherit a C# class. Likewise, it should be possible for a C# program to inherit a Zebra class.

If you were to choose the second option, then your language would have to adhere to the CLS. In other words, for .NET languages to communicate with one another, they must all agree with the standard as outlined by the Common Language System. Because the standards of the CLS are employed only when languages communicate, they apply only to those types that are exposed to the outside world. (As we will see in Chapter 6, types marked with the `public` and `protected` keywords are accessible outside an assembly.) The CLS defines standards for:

1. Public classes
2. The public and protected members of public classes (such as public methods and public class variables)
3. The parameters and return types of public and protected methods

One of the parameters of the CLS, for example, is the manner in which arrays are passed. Consider the following method:

```
public ProcessEmployees(int [] employeeIds) {
    // process employees according to ID ...
}
```

Listing 3.16   Passing an array to a method

Another language using this method (such as VB.NET or JScript.NET) may be unsure as to the order in which array elements are to be delivered to `ProcessEmployees()`. For example, are array elements delivered first to last or last to first? When they are multidimensional arrays, are they passed in row order or column order? Because the CLS defines such a standard, ambiguities like these are no longer problematic.

To clarify: Whereas the Common Type System (CTS) defines the internal data types that a language may use, the Common Language System (CLS) prescribes the conventions that the language employs when it communicates with other .NET languages.

The CLS and C#

Matters become complicated because C# can go outside the boundaries of the CLS. For example, the CLS does not permit the use of *un-*

signed numeric types (data types incapable of representing negative numbers). However, several unsigned numeric types are built into the C# language. Thus, if you author a class with a method that accepts or returns a uint, it will not be usable by languages such as VB.NET. Consider the following class:

```
public class Math {
   public uint Add(uint a, uint b)
   {
     return a+b;
   }
}
```

Listing 3.17   Using non-CTS elements in C#

Because the Add() method in Listing 3.17 uses an unsigned integer, the Math class is not accessible from VB.NET. (The lack of unsigned integers in the latest version of Visual Basic is an unfortunate carryover from VB6.)

In a sense the CLS defines a subset of the functionality that is available in C#. If you are only working with C#, then you can ignore the CLS and its restrictions. However, if you are interoperating with other languages, then you must ensure that your C# code is CLS compliant. Thankfully, the C# compiler can monitor adherence to the CLS.

The CLSCompliant Attribute
The CLSCompliant attribute allows you to signify to the outside world whether the C# code you are writing is CLS compatible. Before we examine how this attribute works, we must understand what an attribute is in the first place.

Tangent Attributes
An attribute is a declarative statement in your code that embeds metadata into an assembly. This metadata can then be extracted at runtime in order to characterize aspects of an application or to influence its behavior. As Listing 3.18 illustrates, attributes are enclosed within the square bracket characters ([]) in C#. By convention, attribute names end with the word *Attribute*. Thus, if you look in the MSDN, you will not find an attribute called CLSCompliant but, rather, CLSCompliantAttribute. We can use the former, more succinct version in our code, however, because C# is smart enough to convert it to its longer equivalent.

Back to Our Example

Consider a modified version of the Math class source code:

```
[assembly: CLSCompliant(true)]
public class Math
{
   public uint Add(uint a, uint b)
   {
     return a+b;
   }
}
```

Listing 3.18   The CLSCompliant attribute

The CLSCompliant attribute in Listing 3.18 informs the C# compiler that the contents of the assembly (including our class) must be CLS compatible. (We will examine attribute notation in depth in Chapter 5.) Despite our declaration, however, the class is *not* compliant because it still exposes and consumes unsigned integers. It should come as no surprise, therefore, that if you attempt to compile the program, VS.NET will generate the following errors:

```
Argument type 'uint' is not CLS-compliant
Argument type 'uint' is not CLS-compliant
Return type of 'Math.Add(uint, uint)' is not CLS-compliant
```

From a practical perspective the CLSCompliant attribute instructs the compiler to warn you that you have stepped outside the boundaries of the CLS. To remove these errors we simply rewrite the class without unsigned integers:

```
[assembly: CLSCompliant(true)]
public class Math
{
   public int Add(int a, int b)
   {
     // You can still use non-CLS types internally:
     uint x,y,z;
     return a+b;
   }
}
```

Listing 3.19   A CLS-compliant Math class

As a result of the modification, the class is now accessible to languages such as VB.NET. Remember that the CLS applies only to data types that are externally visible to other applications. It is possible, therefore, to use `uints` *within* the `Add()` method and still keep our code CLS compliant.

HOW AND WHY

What aspects of the C# are not CLS compliant?
The following aspects of C# fall outside the boundaries of the CLS:

- Pointers (accessible through the unsafe options we will examine in Chapter 7)
- Operator overloading (covered in Chapter 6)
- The following primitive data types: `sbyte`, `ushort`, `uint`, and `ulong`

Otherwise, C# is fully compliant with the CLS.

SUMMARY

Cross-language communication has traditionally been a thorny issue involving numerous trade-offs, intricate plumbing, and complex technologies such as COM and CORBA. The architectural standards of the .NET Framework allow languages to Interoperate with unseen power and ease. Because all languages compile to IL code, it is possible to treat a class authored in another .NET language as it if were a native class in the target language itself. Thus, classes written in C# are inheritable in VB.NET, J#, JScript.NET, and managed C++. Conversely, classes written in other .NET languages can be used and extended in C# by means of the inheritance features that we will discuss in Chapter 6.

In order to communicate with other .NET languages, C# programs must adhere to the framework's Common Language System (CLS). This can be problematic because certain C# features (such as pointers and unsigned data types) fall outside the CLS specification. You can instruct the C# compiler to warn you if a program is using CTS-incompatible features by marking it with the `CLSCompliant` attribute.

Chapter Summary

C# applications execute within the .NET Framework, which consists of an execution engine (the CLR), a class framework to construct applications (the Base Class Libraries), and a standard manner in which applications are packaged (assemblies). Assemblies contain both IL code and metadata, which describes all the types that an assembly exposes.

The C# language employs these aspects of the framework on varying levels. By leveraging the BCL for functionality, developers can create a wide variety of C# applications that target the web, the desktop, or the enterprise. The BCL classes are organized by means of namespaces, which makes them easier to access and syntactically more concise. Namespaces are also used whenever you author your own components in the .NET Framework.

Much of the programmatic plumbing that complicated C and C++ development is now provided by the CLR. In addition to garbage collection, the CLR provides important services such as program isolation through Application Domains (AppDomains) and a uniform type system for all .NET languages (the CTS). The CLR makes it easy for languages to communicate with one another since all languages compile down to standard IL instructions and agree on the representation of data types.

Chapter 4

SYNTAX AND CONCEPTS

In this chapter we examine the major elements of the C# syntax. Developers familiar with Java and C++ will find many parallels between the two languages because C# derives from the C language on which Java and C++ are based. Visual Basic developers will also notice that C# borrows some language elements from VB, but to a lesser degree. A few concepts in this chapter will be new to all developers because they are specific to the .NET Framework.

Whereas the previous chapter illustrated the building blocks of .NET applications (the Base Class Libraries), this chapter illustrates the tools required to string them together. In the first topic we examine the data types that store information in C# as well as the operators that manipulate them. The second topic illustrates ways to control program flow, and the final topic takes an in-depth look at how strings and arrays are handled by C# and the CLR.

CORE CONCEPTS

Comments

A comment can be inserted into a C# source file in one of three ways. Listing 4.1 illustrates each technique.

```
Single-line comments:
int nSum;      // Keeps a running sum of numbers
```

```
Multi-line comments:
/* The following method accepts three parameters:
   Age (integer) : your age in years.
   Height (float): your height in feet
   Sex (Boolean) : true for male, false for female

   Given this information it returns your ideal weight
   as a float variable */

public float IdealWeight(int Age, float Height, bool Sex)

XML-based comments:
/// <summary>
/// Generate monthly sales reports.
/// </summary>
class Monthly { ... }
```

Listing 4.1   Comments in C#

A single-line comment is inserted in source code by prefixing the comment with two slashes. This technique is appropriate for short comments such as describing the purpose of a variable. Multi-line comments should be enclosed within the /* and */ delimiters, and are appropriate for more elaborate comments such as documenting what a method does. Finally, XML comments can be embedded in a source file by prefixing each XML line with three slashes. XML comments can be very useful because they can be extracted by the C# compiler into a single XML file that documents the source file. For a close look at XML comments in C#, see ᴄɴ➔CS040001.

Topic: Data Types and Operators

In this topic we survey the data types in the C# language and the operations you can perform on those types. Whereas a data type (such as an integer) is simply a *container* for information, an *operator* (such as addition) provides the ability to modify the contents of that container. Like many of the programming languages with which you have worked previously, C# offers powerful constructs to manipulate and scrutinize its containers.

CONCEPTS

The C# Type System

The permissible data types in C# must fall within the confines of the Common Type System of the CLR. This requirement leads to a rich assortment of types that you can use for a variety of purposes. The C# type system is illustrated in Figure 4.1.

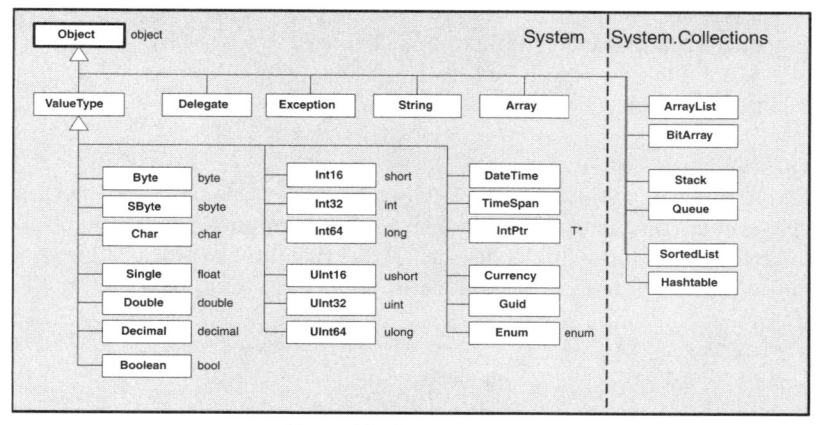

Figure 4.1 Data types in C#

As explained in the previous chapter, all C# data types inherit from the base `System.Object` type at the top of Figure 4.1. Note that some types do not derive from `Object` directly, but instead inherit from the `ValueType` object that we will explain later in this topic. Many of the types in Figure 4.1 (such as integers and strings) are easily recognizable, while others (such as the `DateTime` and `BitArray`) require further investigation.

The types in Figure 4.1 can be broken into the following groups:

- *Integral data types,* which are capable of representing whole numbers. These types can be either *signed* or *unsigned*. A signed type can store both negative and positive numbers, whereas an unsigned type can store only positive numbers. Therefore, unsigned types can store higher positive values than their signed counterparts (because an extra bit is not needed to store whether the value is positive or negative). For example, a `short` variable can store values between -32768 and 32767, whereas a `ushort` variable prescribes a limit between 0 and 65535. Unsigned types will be new to VB developers.
- *Floating point types,* which can store decimal numbers such as

1.4, 19.0, and -202.1. Types in this family include `single`, `double`, and `decimal`, each of which can store values with varying ranges and degrees of precision as highlighted in Table 4.1.
- *Character data types,* such as `char` and `string`, which store character data. Strings are examined in the final topic in this chapter.
- *Containers,* which can store a collection of values in numerous ways (e.g., queues, stacks, hashtables, etc.). Most of these data types are found in the `System.Collection` namespace and are discussed in the last topic of this chapter.
- *Miscellaneous types,* such as Booleans, enumerations, and date types, which we will examine shortly.

Variable Declaration

Recall that when you declare a variable in C#, the type precedes the variable name. You can also initialize a variable during its declaration, as illustrated in the following code block. Note that unlike C++, C# does not allow you to reference a variable until it has been initialized.

```
uint a = 4;
long b = 0x82AF;        // hexadecimal
short c = -1282;
float d = 8.324F;       // note the F suffix for float
float e = 3.21E3F;      // scientific notation
double f = -1.0128;
double g = 8.2e-127;    // a really small number
string h = "c:\\windows\\system32";
string i = @"c:\windows\system32";
bool j = false;

int x,y,z=4.0;          // only z = 4
```

Listing 4.2 Variable declaration in C#

Listing 4.2 illustrates some common data types and the manner in which they can be declared. Many of these declaration techniques are similar to those in Java and C++. For example, to utilize hexadecimal in-line constants, simply prefix the number with `0x`. Along these lines, when you declare a float constant, you must suffix the number with the `F` character. There are numerous other declaration formats that permit the use of scientific numbers, implicit conversions, etc. We detail these techniques at ᶜᴺCS040002, but some of the more important constructs are discussed below. (C++ and Java developers: Note that octal in-line constants have been dropped in C#.)

String Declaration

String declaration in C# is based on the concept of escape characters. Escape characters (sometimes called escape sequences) are used to embed special characters such as \ (slash) and " (double quote) into a string. For example, to initialize a string to "This is a backslash:\", you would write the following:

```
string s = "\" This is a backslash:\\\"";
```

Observe that in C# we must prefix special characters with backslashes. For example, to embed a backslash into a string we write \\, and to embed a single quote we use \'. This requirement, which is a carryover from C++ and Java, can make in-line strings cryptic to read and is especially annoying when you are dealing with directory paths. To this end, C# offers an improvement over its predecessors. You can tell the compiler to ignore escape sequences by prefixing the declaration of a string with the @ character:

```
string s = @"C:\windows\system32\kernel32.dll";
```

This new form of declaration is sometimes referred to as a *verbatim string literal*. Note that verbatim literals can also span multiple lines:

```
string sappyPoem = @"Tis a wandering dove with flight unbound,
          A heart attached to a love once found,
          But a heart so colored is blind to see,
          That to truly love is to set one free";
```

A verbatim string literal will also maintain the indentation and white spaces of the string. For more information on this string declaration format, see ⸙CS040003. We will revisit the important topic of strings later in this chapter.

Variable Ranges

Numerous data types in C# store numbers (int, double, long, and float, to name a few). Each type offers a compromise between the amount of memory it occupies (measured in bits) and the range of numbers it can store. Table 4.1 lists the size and range for these types.

Type Name	Size (bits)	Range
sbyte	8	-128 to 127
byte	8	0 to 255

Type Name	Size (bits)	Range
char	16	Any Unicode character
short	16	-32768 to 32767
ushort	16	0 to 65535
int	32	-2147483648 to 2147483647
uint	32	0 to 4294967295
long	64	-9223372036854775808 to 9223372036854775807
ulong	64	0 to 18446744073709551615
float	32	1.54×10^{-45} to 3.4×10^{38} for positive numbers -3.4×10^{38} to -1.54×10^{-45} for negative numbers (7 digits of precision)
double	64	5.0×10^{-324} to 1.7×10^{308} for positive numbers -1.7×10^{308} to -5.0×10^{-324} for negative numbers (15-16 digits precision)
decimal	128	1.0×10^{-28} to 7.9×10^{28} for positive numbers -7.9×10^{28} to -1.0×10^{-28} for negative numbers (28–29 digits precision)

Table 4.1 Data type ranges

Table 4.1 can serve as a guideline for numerical type usage in C#. For example, to store a person's age it would make the most sense to use the `byte` type because a person's age cannot be negative and will almost certainly not exceed 255. Using a `byte` instead of a `uint` or a `ulong` would save you 24 and 56 bits of memory, respectively. The `decimal` type is the most suitable for applications where numerical precision is important because it can store numbers that are accurate to 28 or 29 decimal places.

Narrowing Conversions and Casting
The variety of numerical data types in C# comes at a cost. Specifically, when transferring data from one type to another, you must make special provisions for *narrowing conversions*. A narrowing conversion is an assignment that results in the possible loss of data. Consider the following code.

```
int i = 50;
long z = 100;
i = z;
```

Listing 4.3   An unsafe assignment

Listing 4.3 assigns the contents of a `long` variable to an `int`. This assignment is dangerous because a `long` variable can store values outside the allowable range of an `int` (see Listing 4.2). In other words, a narrowing conversion occurs when the target data type is less capable than the type to which it is being assigned.

Because of the dangers associated with such conversions, the previous listing does not compile. To rectify this error you must perform an *explicit cast*, as illustrated in Listing 4.4.

```
int i = 50;
long l = 100;
i = (int)l;
```

Listing 4.4   Explicit casting in C#

As illustrated above, to cast a variable to a particular type in C#, you precede the assignment with the type name enclosed within brackets. Casting is permissible not only on numerical types but also on class hierarchies, as will be discussed in Chapter 6.

Note that the reverse assignment (i.e., the assignment of an `int` to a `long`) does not require an explicit cast to compile. Because a `long` type has the wider range of the two (and can thus store anything an `int` can), C# performs the cast *implicitly*.

Casting Rules and Boolean Casting

Casting is the conversion of one type to another type. As you might expect, there are limits to the capabilities of casting operations. For example, it would hardly make sense to cast an `ArrayList` class to a decimal (how would C# carry out the process?). Because of problematic conversions such as this, explicit and implicit casting in C# must adhere to a set of rules as outlined by the .NET Framework.

For example, a `float` variable can be implicitly converted only to a `double` type. Likewise, if you extend a class in C#, it can be cast to any parent class in the hierarchy. The casting rules for C# (the list of what types can be converted to other types) are described on-line at CS040004. In Chapter 6 we will see that you can prescribe custom casting characteristics for classes that you author. For example, you can determine what occurs when a certain class is cast into an integer or Boolean (similar to C++ cast overloading).

Casting Boolean
One caveat to keep in mind with respect to casting is the lack of flexibility of the Boolean (`bool`) data type. As with most programming languages, a Boolean data type in C# can take on values of `true` or `false`. Unlike many languages (but similar to Java), Boolean variables cannot be converted into numerical values (or vice versa). For example, the following code, which is permissible in C++, will not compile in C#.

```
bool a=true;
int b=(int)a;  // ERROR!
```

Listing 4.5 *C++ code—implicit conversion of a Boolean*

Although languages such as VB and C++ have numerical representations for `true` and `false` values (usually 1 and 0, respectively), C# does not. Therefore, in C# you must use more explicit means in order to extract the contents of a Boolean, as the following `Boolean2Int()` method demonstrates.

```
public class Convert {

    static int Boolean2Int(bool b)
    {
        if (b==true)
            return 1;
        else
            return 0;
    }

    static void Main(string[] args) {
        bool a=true;
        int b=Boolean2Int(a);
    }
}
```

Listing 4.6 *Converting a Boolean into a numerical type*

Value Types and Reference Types

A variable in C# is stored in one of two locations: (1) the stack, which is a fixed amount of memory that the CLR gives each .NET application to store frequently accessed data items such as method parameters and return values, and (2) the heap, which is a block of memory that can change its size dynamically depending on an application's requirements.

Types that are housed on the stack are referred to as *value* types; types that are located on the heap are called *reference* types. Primitive types in C# such as integers, floats, and bytes are value types, whereas class constructs such as ArrayList, Console, and System.Object are reference types. Because value and reference types are stored in separate locations, there are some notable differences between them from a C# perspective.

Type Declaration

The first difference between value and reference types is the manner in which an instance of a type is created. As Listing 4.7 illustrates, reference types are instantiated by means of the new keyword, whereas value types are not.

```
int a;                       // declaring a value type
ArrayList l=new ArrayList(); // declaring a reference type
```

Listing 4.7 Declaration of value types versus reference types

In order to understand the different conventions in Listing 4.7, we must understand what is transpiring behind the scenes. When you declare a value type variable such as an integer, C# implicitly reserves memory for it on the stack. Thereafter, when you use the value type (when you change its contents, etc.), you are directly manipulating the area of the stack that houses the variable. A reference type, on the other hand, is simply a handle (or a pointer) to an area of memory on the heap. When a reference type is manipulated, its underlying contents are modified *indirectly* by the CLR (the heap is almost never altered directly by the developer, the exception being the unsafe constructs explained in Chapter 7). It helps if you think of a value type as a placeholder that resides *directly* on the stack, in contrast to a reference type that simply points to a location on the heap. This important distinction is illustrated in Figure 4.2.

As shown in Figure 4.2, a reference variable simply points to a location on the heap where the actual type resides. It should become apparent why the new keyword is a crucial part of the declaration. Consider the following line of code:

```
ArrayList myList;
```

Although this line declares an ArrayList variable named myList, as it stands a does not point to anything (or, more formally, it points to null).

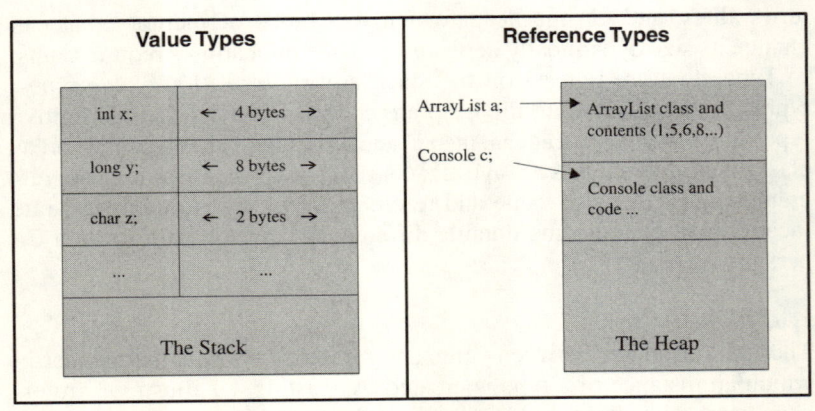

Value Types	Reference Types
int x; ← 4 bytes →	ArrayList a; → ArrayList class and contents (1,5,6,8,...)
long y; ← 8 bytes →	Console c;
char z; ← 2 bytes →	→ Console class and code ...
...	
The Stack	The Heap

Figure 4.2   Value types versus reference types

That is, space on the heap has not been reserved for this variable. By adding the new keyword to the declaration

```
ArrayList myList = new ArrayList();
```

C# reserves a section of memory on the heap, populates the reserved memory with an instance of the `ArrayList` class, and then sets the `myList` variable so that it points to that memory. There is no stipulation that the new keyword be used during declaration. The following code is also permissible in C#:

```
ArrayList a;    //Initially, a points to nothing
// do some operations…
a = new ArrayList();
```

Listing 4.8   Using new outside type declaration

To review, the primary differences between a value type and a reference type are:

1. Value types reside on the stack, and the memory for them is reserved implicitly by C# during declaration.
2. Reference types reside on the heap, and you must explicitly allocate memory for them by using the new keyword.

As we will see in the following topics, the internal differences between value and reference types have practical implications as they are used by C#.

Copying Types

An important area where value and reference types differ is the manner in which they are copied (when a variable is assigned to another variable). Consider the following block of code, which illustrates the copying characteristics of both a value type (an integer) and a reference type (a class named Foo).

```
using System;

class Foo {
   public int x=0;
   public int y=0;
}

class Class1 {

static void Main(string[] args) {
   Foo a,b;    // Reference types
   int c,d;    // Value types

   // Value copying
   c=4;
   d=c;
   c=5;       // Change c after assignment

   // Reference Copying:
   a = new Foo();
   b = a;
   a.x = 1;   // Change a after assignment
   a.y = 2;

   // Print out contents of b and d:
   Console.WriteLine("b.x={0}, d={1}",b.x,d);
}
}
```

Listing 4.9 Value copying versus reference copying

Let's consider the simpler case first: the copying of a value type. Because both integers in Listing 4.9 (c and d) are value types, they are each given 4 bytes on the stack when they are declared. When the line d=c executes (when the value type is copied), the contents of c are *physically copied* into d's placeholder. Thereafter, if the contents of c change, the contents of d remain unaffected. In other words, after the copy operation has been performed, d no longer has any relationship with c. When the value of d is printed at the end of Listing 4.9, it reports the value it received during the copy operation, which is "4" rather than the modified value of variable c, which is "5."

The behavior of reference type copying is more complex. Once again let us consider the operation of Listing 4.9. First, we declare both a and b variables as type Foo. Because we have not used the new keyword, however, memory on the heap has not been reserved for either variable (they initially point to nothing or null). Next, we reserve memory on the heap for the a variable by means of new. Finally, the line b=a copies the reference types.

The important point is that *when a reference type is copied in C#, both variables simply point to the same location on the heap*. In other words, nothing is physically copied during a reference assignment other than a memory address. After the copy operation, both a and b point to the same location on the heap (technically, this is known as *aliasing*).

The subtle yet crucial by-product of this behavior is that changes to a still affect b. Because both variables point to the same location on the heap, modifications to a (a.x = 1) will propagate to b. Therefore, when we print out b.x in Listing 4.9, we get the value of a.x, which is "1," as opposed to its original value of "0."

Shallow Copying and Deep Copying

This behavior—the fact that reference copying results in two variables that point to the same location—is called *shallow copying*. Conversely, value type copying, whereby each variable refers to a separate memory location and the contents of one variable are physically copied to another, is referred to as *deep copying*.

As you can see from Listing 4.9, shallow copying can have unintended results if you are not careful. For this reason it is sometimes desirable to perform deep copying on reference types. That is, in Listing 4.9 we may want to replicate the contents of a such that both a and b point to separate memory locations with the same contents. The difference between deep and shallow copying of reference types is illustrated in Figure 4.3.

The deep copying of reference types (the diagram on the right in Figure 4.3) can be accomplished by using the IClonable interface that is exposed by the .NET Framework. Details on this interface as well as examples that illustrate its usage can be found at ᥤCS040005.

Type Destruction

Another notable difference between value and reference types is the manner in which they are removed from memory. Value types are immediately

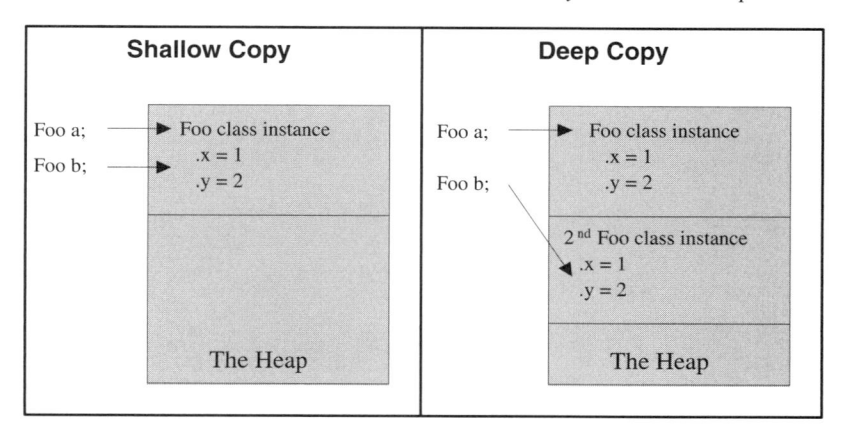

Figure 4.3 Shallow copying versus deep copying

removed from the stack once they go out of scope; reference types are garbage collected by the CLR at ongoing intervals. Consider Listing 4.10:

```
void SomeMethod()
{
  Foo a = new Foo();   // Reference type
  int b;               // Value type

  // use a and b.
  // b destroyed here (before exiting scope)
}
// a destroyed at some later point…
```

Listing 4.10 Type destruction in C#

After `SomeMethod()` has finished executing, both the reference variable a and the value variable b are removed from memory. The difference is that whereas b's memory is reclaimed immediately, the memory occupied by a is not deallocated until the CLR's garbage collector runs. In other words, entities on the stack are destroyed immediately when they go out of scope, whereas entities on the heap are subject to the unpredictable timings of garbage collection. Therefore, with respect to memory utilization, value types are more efficient than reference types because of their timely destruction. We will revisit reference type garbage collection in Chapter 5.

Tangent: Visibility and Scope
You may wonder what exactly it means to "go out of scope." In C#, code is compartmentalized into blocks (or scopes). A block of code is en-

closed within the { and } curly bracket characters. Thus, in Listing 4.10 the code within SomeMethod() constitutes a block of code or a scope. Similarly, the code within the following if statement is a code block.

```
if (b==5) {
  // anything here is within a code block
    int x;
}
```

Listing 4.11   Code blocks in C#

The lifetime and visibility rules governing code blocks are straightforward:

1. A variable is only accessible (visible) within the code block where it is declared and in nested blocks within that block.
2. The value types that are declared within a code block are destroyed (removed from the stack) after the block finishes executing. (Reference types involve the more complex procedure of garbage collection, which is explained in Chapter 5.)

Therefore, in the preceding code the x variable is not accessible outside the if statement block.

Code blocks can also be nested. For example, the if code block in Listing 4.11 must reside within a method code block. When you utilize nested code blocks in C# (as you most certainly will), you must ensure that an inner code block doesn't "hide" the variables in an outer code block. Consider Listing 4.12.

```
void SomeMethod() {
  int foo, b=0;
  if (b==0) {
     int foo=5;  // error, foo exists in the outer block.
  }
}
```

Listing 4.12   Nested code blocks

Because the inner block declares a variable (foo) that exists in the outer block, the C# compiler generates an error. For a closer look at scope and visibility in C#, see ᶜᴺ⇨CS040006.

Comparing Types

A final point to keep in mind with respect to value and reference types is the manner in which types are tested for equality. Value types can be compared via the straightforward equality operator (==). However, the same does not hold true for reference types. The following code, which uses the Foo class from Listing 4.9 , illustrates the dangers with reference type comparison.

```
static void Main() {

  Foo a = new Foo();
  Foo b = new Foo();
  int c,d;

  // Initialize reference types:
  a.x = 1; a.y = 2;
  b.x = 1; b.y = 2;
  // Initialize value types:
  c=3; d=3;

  if (c==d) {
     // Will always get here
  }

  if (a==b) {
     // Will never get here!
  }
}
```

Listing 4.13 Comparing value versus reference types

Even though both instances of Foo contain identically constructed classes (with member variables x and y set to 1 and 2, respectively), the second if statement in Listing 4.13 does not consider a and b equal.

Remember that a reference type is simply a pointer to the heap. When testing for reference equality, C# simply compares the address of each object. If each variable is pointing to the same location (i.e., if they represent the same instance on the heap), then the equality operator returns true. If the variables are pointing to different heap locations (as is the case in Listing 4.13), then the equality operator returns false. To determine whether two reference types are equal in terms of *content*, you must use the special Equals() method that we will examine in Chapter 6.

Exception to the Rule: Strings
The rules we have given for value and reference types would be simple and succinct were it not for one exception: strings. Although strings are

reference types (they are allocated on the heap and garbage collected), they adhere to value type semantics. This means that strings can be declared without the `new` keyword and can be tested for equality via the `==` operator.

You may wonder why the CLR stores strings on the heap and not the stack. Recall that the heap is an area of memory whose size can change dynamically (whereas the stack's cannot). Because the size of a string can change, it makes sense to store it on the heap. (Actually, as we will see in the final topic in this chapter, a string's contents do not change. Instead, the CLR creates a new string object for every corresponding change in content.)

Converting Between Value and Reference Types (Boxing)

Given the differences between value and reference types, it may seem confusing that value types ultimately derive from the `System.Object` base class, which is itself a reference type. In fact, if you examine Figure 4.1, you will discover that all value types actually inherit from a class named `System.ValueType`. How can a value type inherit from a reference type? Furthermore, what exactly is .NET trying to accomplish through this counterintuitive setup?

As you delve into the .NET Framework, you may frequently have to convert between value and reference types. Consider the following code:

```
int a=5;
object b=a;
```

Listing 4.14   Converting between value and reference types

The second line in Listing 4.14 takes the contents of the integer (a value type) and places it within an `object` (a reference type). Because of the different storage locations of each variable, the CLR must copy the value of a, which is located on the stack, into the memory of b, which is located on the heap. This process—the physical conversion of a value type into a reference type—is called *boxing*. The reverse process—the extraction of a reference type into a value type—is called *unboxing*.

As you develop .NET applications, you will often use boxing without realizing it. Consider the following code:

```
int a=3500;
Console.WriteLine("a = {0}",a.ToString());
```

Listing 4.15   Implicit boxing in C#

Recall from our discussion in Chapter 3 that methods such as `ToString()` are exposed by `System.Object` and are thus callable on any

.NET type. In Listing 4.15, however, we are referencing an integer as if it were a `System.Object`. Behind the scenes, C# *boxes* the integer into an `object` type so that the `ToString()` method can be invoked against it. This process is illustrated in Figure 4.4.

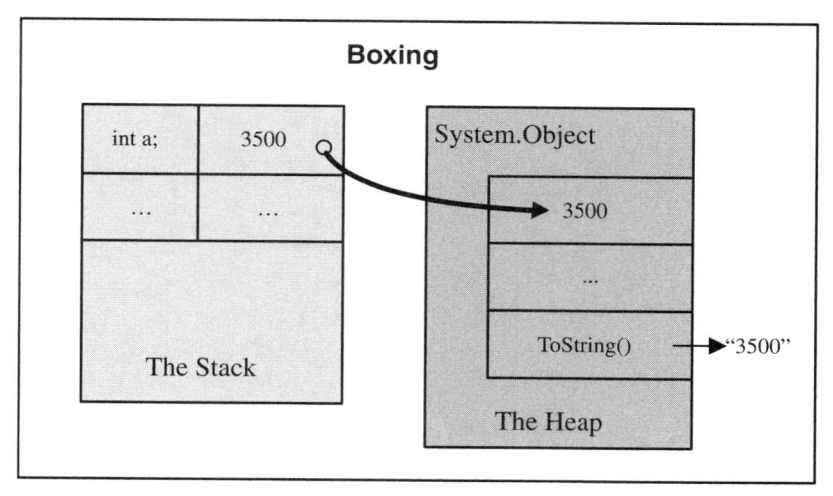

Figure 4.4 The boxing process

Although the process of boxing is certainly useful, it may seem like nothing more than an internal implementation detail of the framework. After all, if the procedure is performed implicitly by the CLR as needed, of what concern is boxing to developers other than a runtime service to be employed as necessary? As is frequently the case, convenience comes at a cost.

Boxing: Performance Implications
From a functional point of view, boxing is invisible to developers because it is performed behind the scenes. From a performance perspective, however, there is more to boxing than meets the eye. Every time the process of boxing is carried out, the CLR must copy the contents of the value type variable to the garbage-collected heap. If the procedure is performed repetitively, performance can be adversely affected. The following code illustrates the slowdown that results from unnecessary boxing.

```
using System;

class BoxingTest
{
```

```
static void Main()
{
   long TimeStamp;
   double seconds,seconds2;

   // no boxing:
   TimeStamp = DateTime.Now.Ticks;
   for (int k=0; k<=10000000;k++)
   {
      int a=k+1;
      a++;
   }
   TimeStamp = DateTime.Now.Ticks - TimeStamp;
   seconds = (double)TimeStamp /
      (double)TimeSpan.TicksPerSecond;

   // boxing:
   TimeStamp = DateTime.Now.Ticks;
   for (int j=0; j<=10000000;j++)
   {
      System.Object a=j;
      a=(int)a+1;
   }
   TimeStamp = DateTime.Now.Ticks - TimeStamp;
   seconds2 = (double)TimeStamp /
      (double)TimeSpan.TicksPerSecond;

   Console.WriteLine("no boxing: {0}",seconds);
   Console.WriteLine("boxing: {0}",seconds2);
}
}
```

Listing 4.16   Performance problems associated with boxing

Listing 4.16 contrasts a boxing-free operation with one that employs boxing. In the first loop, the program times how long it takes to assign an integer variable to ten million numbers. Because both the loop counter variable (k) and the target variable (a) are integers, value type copying is performed, and the process does not involve boxing. (We will examine the for loop construct in the next topic.) In the second loop, however, the target variable is a System.Object, and so the CLR must employ boxing. (Look closely and you'll see that unboxing is also performed because the a variable is cast into an int). The time spent in both loops is computed by means of the TimeSpan class in the BCL, which we explain later in this topic.

Save Listing 4.16 in a file named Boxing.cs and compile it using the C# compiler. Run the application, and the program will report how long each loop takes to execute. Results will vary, but the first loop will be significantly faster than its boxed counterpart. On our machines it was *twenty to thirty times faster*. Clearly, the convenience of boxing comes at a cost, which is something to keep in mind as you move information between value and reference types. For some metrics on boxing performance, see oCNpCS040007.

System.ValueType

The role of the System.ValueType object in the .NET Framework is, at first glance, confusing. How can a primitive type such as an integer inherit from this object, given that an integer is not a class construct (it is simply 4 bytes of memory on the stack)?

System.ValueType is simply an abstraction; its inclusion in Figure 4.1 is somewhat misleading because value types don't inherit from this class in an object-oriented sense (we discuss object inheritance in Chapter 6). Instead, System.ValueType is simply a representation for any type that is stored on the stack. For example, you can employ this class when you want a method to accept any value type parameter:

```
void AcceptOnlyValueTypes(System.ValueType v) {
  // do something with the value-type
}
```

Listing 4.17   Using System.ValueType

In C# you rarely interact with this class directly. Its inclusion within the framework provides the CLR with necessary boilerplate functionality (such as boxing capabilities). For a closer look at System.ValueType, see oCNpCS040008.

User-Defined Value Types

In addition to primitive value types such as integers and bytes, C# allows you to create custom value types (also referred to as user-defined value types). Specifically, the framework allows you to create *enumerations* and *structures*. Like all value types, both of these entities reside on the stack when they are instantiated.

Enumerations

An enumeration (enum) is simply a list of constant values. Consider a method that accepts a parameter specifying the day of the week. One strategy would be to have the method accept an integer:

```
bool IsWeekend(int day) {
   if (day==1)
      // Sunday
   if (day==2)
      // Monday
   //remaining code omitted for brevity
}
```

Listing 4.18   The ComputeSomething method

Although this is an acceptable approach, it requires the caller of the method to be familiar with the convention being employed (i.e., Sunday=1, Monday=2, etc.). An enumeration allows you to establish such a relationship more explicitly:

```
enum DayOfTheWeek {
   Sunday,
   Monday,
   Tuesday,
   Wednesday,
   Thursday,
   Friday,
   Saturday
}

bool IsWeekend(DayOfTheWeek day)
{
   if (day==DayOftheWeek.Sunday)
     // Sunday - return true;
   if (day==DayOftheWeek.Monday)
     // Monday - return false;
   //remaining code omitted for brevity
}
```

Listing 4.19   An enumeration in C#

As illustrated in Listing 4.19, enumerations can make code easier to read and methods easier to call. Internally, enumerations are stored as numeric values by the C# compiler. By default the first element in an enumeration is given a value of zero, and subsequent elements are incremented by one. Thus, in Listing 4.19, C# assigns the following values implicitly: Sunday=0, Monday=1, etc. You can override this default behavior, however, as illustrated in Listing 4.20.

```
enum DayOfTheWeek
{
    Sunday=2,      // Set new first value
    Monday,        // Monday = 3
    Tuesday,       // Tuesday = 4
    Wednesday,     // Wed = 5
    Thursday=8,    // Change sequence!
    Friday,        // Friday = 9
    Saturday       // Saturday = 10
}
```

Listing 4.20   Initializing the values in an enumeration

Enumerations are an inherited feature of C and C++ (and may therefore be new to Java and VB developers). C# enumerations are more versatile than their C++ counterparts. They can be used very easily in string output operations such as `Console.WriteLine` because it is possible to ascertain the string equivalent of an enumerated element given its numeric value (i.e., to obtain "Sunday" in Listing 4.20 given a value of 2). Finally, with C# you can also easily prescribe the data type that is used to represent the elements of the enumeration internally (a byte, an integer, etc.), a specification that is frequently obscured in C++. See CS040009 for details.

Enumerations can also be used with a construct called `FlagsAttribute`, which allows their members to be used as *bit fields*. This construct is frequently employed when an enumeration's members might be used in combination, for example: `File.Open | File.Append (File.Open OR File.Append)`, for VB developers. The `FlagsAttribute` is discussed at CS040010.

Enumerations are also exposed extensively by the Base Class Libraries. For example, when you use the BCL `FileStream` class to manipulate a file, the `FileMode` enumeration is used to specify the manner in which the file is opened (`FileMode.Create`, `FileMode.CreateNew`, etc.). We will leverage this enumeration in the next chapter when we write to a stream (Listing 5.7). For a closer look at enumerations and their use in the BCL, see CS040011.

Structures (Structs)
The second kind of user-defined value type that you can create is a *structure*. A structure is similar to a class in that it exposes method and mem-

ber variables. Unlike a class, however, a structure is allocated on the stack and is therefore more efficient than a class from a memory standpoint. In Chapter 6 we will examine the important topic of user-defined structures.

DateTime and TimeSpan Types

To illustrate the deficiencies associated with boxing, Listing 4.16 timed a boxing operation versus a nonboxing one. In order to do this, the program marked two separate points in time (before and after the `for` loops) and then computed the interval between them.

Time and dates in .NET are exposed through the `DateTime` and `TimeSpan` structures. Note that because both of these entities are structures, they are allocated on the stack for fast access and derive from `System.ValueType`.

Prior to .NET, different languages had different conventions for representing times and dates. VB, for example, used the internal `Date` data type, whereas C++ used the various functions in the C-Runtime library. Because both the `DateTime` and `TimeSpan` structures are a part of the Common Type System, you can easily pass dates between C# and other .NET languages. (Both of these structures occupy 8 bytes of memory.)

The `DateTime` structure can represent any moment in time between 12:00:00 midnight, January 1, 0001 C.E. (Common Era), to 11:59:59 P.M., December 31, 9999 C.E. Moreover, it can represent time with very fine granularity—100 nanosecond intervals (a nanosecond is one billionth of a second).

Whereas `DateTime` is used to represent a moment in time, the `TimeSpan` structure is used to represent an interval between two points in time. Together these structures can be used to carry out date and time calculations. For example, you can subtract an instance of a `DateTime` structure from another to obtain the time interval between them, or you can add a `TimeSpan` to the current `DateTime` to calculate a future date. The second operation is illustrated in Listing 4.21.

```
// Get the current date
DateTime t = DateTime.Now;

// Initialize a TimeSpan of 250 days:
TimeSpan ahead = new TimeSpan(250,0,0,0);

Console.WriteLine("The date today is: {0}",t);
Console.WriteLine("The date in 250 days will be:
   {0}",t.Add(ahead));
```

Listing 4.21   Calculating a future date using TimeSpan and DateTime

More information on the `TimeSpan` and `DateTime` structures can be found at ⚡CS040012.

OPERATORS

An operator allows you to modify or scrutinize a data type. As the previous section illustrated, C# exposes a rich set of types that can represent numerous forms of information: strings, numbers, dates, etc. In this section we examine the built-in operators in C#. In Chapter 6 we will examine the concept of *operator overloading,* which allows developers to define new operator functionality for classes that they write.

There are four types of operators in C#. The first three are classified according to the number of variables (or constants) on which they "operate." A unary operator is used with one type, a binary with two, and a ternary with three. The last class of operators falls into a miscellaneous category that we will examine shortly.

Unary Operators
The most widespread unary operators in C# are the so-called shortcut operators, which make common arithmetic operations syntactically more concise. These shortcut operators, which should be familiar to Java and C++ developers, are listed in Table 4.2.

Shortcut operator	More Verbose Equivalent
A++;	A=A+1;
A--;	A=A-1;
A+=2;	A=A+2;
A-=3;	A=A-3;
A*=4;	A=A*4;
A/=5;	A=A/5;

Table 4.2 C# shortcut operators

The first two operators in Table 4.2 are also referred to as the increment and decrement operators, respectively. Increment and decrement operators can be written in two ways: a++ or ++a. Although both techniques produce the same result (the value of a is incremented by one), they have subtle yet differing conventions as to when the addition is actually carried out. For details see ⚡CS040013.

Bitwise and Binary Complementors

Two other unary operators in C# are the Boolean complement (!), which negates Boolean values, and the bitwise complement (~), which inverts bitwise values. These operators are illustrated in Listing 4.22.

```
bool Ok=true;
byte a = 7;      // = 00000111 binary

Ok = !Ok;        // Ok = false
a = (byte)~a;    // a = 11111000b = 248
```

Listing 4.22   The Boolean and binary complementors

Note that the bitwise complement returns an `integer` by default, which is why we have to explicitly cast it to a `byte` in the listing.

Binary Operators

Whereas a unary operator works with one variable, a binary operator operates against two. There are three types of binary operators in C#: arithmetic, relational, and logical. Each class of operator is explained in the code snippets below.

Arithmetic Operators

C#'s arithmetic operators are best illustrated by example. In addition to standard operations such as multiplication and division, C# offers modulus and bit-shifting operators as illustrated in Listing 4.23.

```
int a = 1*1;
int b = 2/2;
int c = 3+3;
int d = 4-4;
int e = 5 % 2 ;     // remainder operator (modulus)
int f = 1 << 1;     // left bitshift
int g = 255 >> 5;   // right bitshift
```

Listing 4.23   Arithmetic operators in C#

The modulus operator (sometimes called the remainder operator) returns the remainder of a division operation. Thus, in Listing 4.23 e is set to one, since the remainder of 5 divided by 2 is one. The listing also demonstrates the left and right bitshift operators, which are used to shift the binary representation of the first variable by a prescribed number of bits. Thus, after Listing 4.23 has finished executing:

```
    f = 00000011 (3) shifted by 2 places to the left =
                    00001100 = 12
    g = 11111111 (255) shifted by 5 places to the right =
                    00000111 = 7
```

Relational Operators
Relational operators are used to compare two data types. These operators include equals (==), not equals (!=), less than (<), greater than (>), less-than-or-equal (<=), and greater-than-or-equal (>=). Note that these operators return Boolean values, which indicate the result of the comparison. Most often, relational operators are used with the control and flow constructs that we examine later in this chapter.

VB developers should note that C# does not have either the NOT or <> operators; instead, you must use ! and !=, respectively. Also note that equality in C# is tested via *two* equals signs (==). C++ developers should bear in mind that the following code, which compiles in C++, is flagged as an error in C# (a restriction borrowed from Java).

```
int x=0;
if (x=4) {
   // In C++ the if statement is always true and x is
   // given a value of 4. This confusing behavior is a
   // common source of bugs in C++, hence removed in C#
}
```
Listing 4.24   *C++ syntax not allowed in C#*

Logical Operators
Logical operators perform Boolean logic on either bitwise or Boolean expressions. That is, you can use a logical operator to perform a bitwise AND (&), OR (|), or XOR (^) on two variables, or you can combine a number of operators to create complex Boolean expressions. The following examples clarify the use of these operators.

```
// Logical bitwise operators

byte a = 3;       //00000011
byte b = 201;     //11001001
byte c,d,e;

c = (byte)(a&b); // Logical AND c = 00000001 = 1
```

```
d = (byte)(a^b); // Logical XOR  c = 11001010 = 202
e = (byte)(a|b); // Logical OR   c = 11001011 = 203
```

Listing 4.25 Logical bitwise operators

As illustrated in Listing 4.25, bitwise operators can be used to amalgamate two variables on the bit level. Conditional logical operators work in a similar fashion, but they are instead used to combine the value of two Boolean expressions, as the following example demonstrates.

```
double price = 20.08;
bool isSale = false;

if (isSale && (price > 20))
{
   // A sale AND price > 20
}

if (isSale || (price > 20))
{
   // A sale OR price > 20
}
```

Listing 4.26 Conditional operators

VB developers should note that the && and || operators should be used in place of VB6's AND and OR constructs, respectively.

The one shortcoming with Listing 4.26 is that the first `if` statement can fall prey to a phenomenon called *short circuit evaluation*. Short circuit evaluation occurs when the compiler determines the result of a combined expression without evaluating *both* of the individual expressions. Consider the first `if` statement, which prescribes that the `isSale` variable must be `true` and that the `price` variable must be greater than 20. Because the first condition is `false` (i.e., `isSale` is `false`), C# knows the result of the combined expression before it evaluates the second expression (whether the price is greater than 20). The compiler saves time by simply skipping the evaluation of the second expression.

Although short circuit evaluation can increase performance, it can have some unforeseen side effects. For example, if the second expression contains a method such as

```
if (isSale && SomeFunctionThatReturnsAboolean())
```

then you cannot be sure whether or not the method will be called. Because of this precarious behavior, C# offers Boolean logical operators, which are functionally identical to conditional operators except that both expressions are always evaluated (i.e., short circuiting is never performed). Boolean logical operators are illustrated in Listing 4.27.

```
double price = 20.08;
bool isSale = false;

if (isSale & (price > 20))
{
   // A sale AND price > 20
}

if (isSale | (price > 20))
{
   // A sale OR price > 20
}
```

Listing 4.27 Boolean conditional operators

As you can see, the only syntactical difference between conditional and Boolean operators is the presence of one character (&& versus & and || versus |, etc.).

Note that Boolean operators (|, &, and ^) are identical to the bitwise operators in Listing 4.25, except that they operate against Boolean expressions. In other words, when you use the |, &, and ^ operators in C#, the compiler determines whether a bitwise or a Boolean operation is performed depending on the expressions involved.

Keep in mind that you cannot mix expressions. That is, you cannot use these operators against both Boolean and bitwise expressions as shown in Listing 4.28.

```
byte b=255;
bool isSale = false;

if (isSale & b) // Problem here!
{
}
```

Listing 4.28 Mixing Boolean and bitwise expressions

Ambiguous code such as this generates the following compile-time error:

```
Operator '&' cannot be applied to operands of type 'bool'
                    and 'byte'
```

Ternary Operators

A ternary operator works against three expressions. C# has one such operator, which is a carryover feature from C and C++. Again, this operator is best illustrated in code.

```
double price=25;
string discount;

// C#'s Ternary operator:
discount = (price >20) ? "10% off" : "5% off";

// The previous line is functionally IDENTICAL to:
if (price >20)
   discount = "10% off";
else
   discount = "20% off";
```

Listing 4.29   C#'s ternary operator

The ternary operator is a condensed version of an `if` assignment statement. If the Boolean expression evaluates to `true`, then the target variable (`discount`) takes on the value of the *first* expression (the one after the ? character). If the Boolean expression evaluates to `false`, then the variable is set equal to the second expression (the one after the : character). VB developers can think of this operator as the equivalent of the `IIf()` function.

Other Operators

C# also exposes some other operators for miscellaneous functionality, which we will revisit throughout this book. A quick synopsis of some of the more important ones is given in Table 4.3.

Operator	Purpose	Covered in...
is()	Determines if a variable is of a specific type	Chapter 6
as()	Converts a variable to a specific type (similar to casting)	Chapter 6
sizeof()	Determines the amount of memory a variable occupies	CSO40014
typeof();	Obtains the variable's type information; used with reflection	Chapter 5

Operator	Purpose	Covered in...
checked();	Used in overflow arithmetic operations	CS040015
unchecked()	Used in overflow arithmetic operations	CS040015

Table 4.3   Other C# operators

SUMMARY

Data types in C# are divided into two categories: value types, which reside on the stack, and reference types, which are housed on the heap. Because value and reference types are stored in different memory locations, the manner in which each type is instantiated, destroyed, and copied also differs. Specifically, value types are instantiated automatically during declaration, whereas reference types must be instantiated by means of the new keyword. Value types are *deep copied* (meaning that a variable's contents are physically replicated to another variable), whereas reference types are shallow copied (which means that both variables simply point to the same location on the heap). Lastly, value types are efficiently removed from the stack when they go out of scope, in contrast to reference types that must undergo garbage collection by the CLR.

C# allows developers to translate value types into reference types through a process called boxing. Boxing takes a value type located on the stack and converts it into a reference type that resides on the heap. Through this process, methods that are callable on reference types such as ToString() can be invoked against value types such as integers. Boxing introduces a performance overhead, however, because replicating data from the stack to the heap is an expensive operation.

C# offers a rich array of operators that can be used to manipulate its types. In addition to requisite features such as arithmetic and comparison operators, C# exposes operators to manipulate bits, combine Boolean expressions, and convert types to other types (i.e., casting). In later chapters we will examine the powerful type() operator, which is used to inspect the structure of a given data type, as well as the is and as operators, which are used with class hierarchies.

Topic: Controlling Program Flow

On the most basic level a computer application consists of two features: the storage of data and the logical skeleton of the program, which dictates how the manipulation of that data is carried out. In the previous topic we saw that C# exposes a rich collection of data types and operators that allow one to store and modify data, respectively. In this topic we examine the constructs that allow one to determine the flow of a program (that is, the execution path that an application takes at runtime). Many of the constructs depicted in this topic are recognizable from other languages (especially C++ and Java).

CONCEPTS

Looping

Looping constructs allow a sequence of instructions to be performed repetitively. C# supports four kinds of loops: the `for` construct, which is a counted loop (i.e., it repeats a certain number of times); `while` and `do while`, which repeat until a certain condition is satisfied; and `foreach`, which iterates through a collection of objects. Let's consider each construct in turn.

For Loop

Similar to the `for` constructs in VB, C++, and Java (and many other languages), a C# `for` loop executes a block of statements repeatedly. As illustrated in Listing 4.30, the syntax for a `for` loop is somewhat different from the equivalent in Visual Basic.

```
// Loop from 1 to 10:
for (int k=1; k<=10; k++)
{
    Console.WriteLine("k={0}",k);
}

// Loop from 10 to 1:
for (int j=10; j>=1; j-)
{
  //do something
}

// Loop from 1 to 10 in steps of 2:
int m;
for (m=1; m<=10; m+=2)
{
```

```
        //do something
}
```

Listing 4.30   For loops in C#

As the preceding highlighted lines illustrate, a for loop is divided into three parts that are separated by semicolons: the initializer, the condition, and the modifier. The first part, the initializer, initializes the variable that performs the counting. As illustrated in the first two loops, the initializer can also declare the variable or, as in the third loop, initialize a variable that has been declared previously. Note that the variable (the counter) must be an integral type (e.g., integer, long, etc.). Also note that if the initializer declares the counter variable (as in the first two loops), then the variable cannot be referenced outside the loop (recall the scoping rules outlined in the previous topic). For example, the k variable in the first loop cannot be used outside that loop's code block.

The second part of the for loop is a condition expression. The rule is straightforward: The for loop repeats as long as this condition is true. Thus, the first loop executes as long as k is less than 11 (k<=10). Conversely, the second loop executes provided that k is greater than 1. The condition expression can, in fact, be any expression that evaluates to a Boolean value. You can, for instance, loop until the end of a file is encountered, as illustrated at ᶜᴺ→CS040016.

The third and final part of the loop is called the modifier. The modifier increments or decrements the counter variable upon each iteration of the loop. Because we are counting up in the first loop, the counter variable is successively incremented by 1 (note from Table 4.2 that k++ is equivalent to k=k+1). In the second loop, however, we are counting down and thus decrement the counter variable accordingly. Finally, in the last loop we are counting up in increments of two, and hence we increase the counter variable by that amount (m+=2). (The third loop is equivalent to For m = 1 To 10 Step 2 in VB.) Note that in many cases the condition section may be decoupled from the modifier. You may not even need the modifier at all (see the I/O example at ᶜᴺ→CS040016). If you do not need the modifier, you can omit it from the for loop declaration; however, you do need to put in the second semicolon as a placeholder.

While and Do While

The while and do while constructs continually execute a sequence of instructions provided that a given condition is true. The following code, for example, executes repeatedly until the user enters "FooBar" as the password.

104 · CodeNotes® for C#

```
string password;
do
{
   Console.Write("Enter your password: ");
   password = Console.ReadLine();
} while (password!="FooBar");
```

Listing 4.31   A do while loop

The `do while` construct can be made even simpler by turning it upside down into a `while` loop.

```
string password="";
while (password!="FooBar")
{
   Console.Write("Enter your password: ");
   password = Console.ReadLine();
}
```

Listing 4.32   A while loop

Note the subtle difference between these two constructs. In a `do while` loop, the code block executes *before* the expression is evaluated, whereas in a `while` loop, the code block executes *afterward*. Thus, the code within a `do while` block is guaranteed to execute *at least once*. Because this is not the case with the `while` block in Listing 4.32, we must initialize the `password` variable before the loop executes, in accordance with the following very important rule in C#: *Variables must be initialized before they can be used in comparison statements. An attempt to access an uninitialized variable generates a compile-time error.*

Foreach

The `foreach` construct is one of a handful of C# features that was borrowed from Visual Basic. This construct allows you to iterate through a collection of items. Listing 4.33 illustrates the use of `foreach` in conjunction with an array.

```
// Array of integers. We'll explore the way they are
// declared in the last topic in this chapter.
int []numberList={1,2,3,4,5};

foreach (int number in numberList)
{
```

```
    Console.WriteLine("{0}",number);
}
```

Listing 4.33 A foreach loop

The foreach loop requires that you declare the type of variable for the collection that you are iterating through. Because we are traversing through an integer array, Listing 4.33 declares an integer variable called number. Upon each iteration of the loop, number takes on the next value in the array (1,2,3, etc.).

As you can see, foreach can be cleaner than an equivalent for loop, which would require you to keep track of a counter variable and to set up the appropriate loop condition. As we will see in Chapter 6, foreach works not only with arrays but with any .NET object that supports a special interface called IEnumerable.

Jumping Out of a Loop: Break
As with C++ and Java, you can jump out of a loop prematurely by using the break statement, which simply transfers execution to the line after the loop's code block.

```
for (int k=0; k<=100; k++)
{
   if (k==7)
      break; // Exit loop
}
// Control is transferred here after the break
```

Listing 4.34 The break statement

Even though the loop in Listing 4.34 should execute one hundred times, the break statement causes it to exit after only eight (counting from zero to seven) iterations. You can use the break command to jump out of any type of loop. Java developers should note that C# does *not* support labeled break and if statements, though it does support the more general-purpose goto statement, covered in the following section.

Continue
Closely related to the break statement is continue, which transfers program flow to the beginning of a loop (the next iteration in the loop).

```
for (int k=0; k<=10; k++)
{
   if (k<=7)
```

```
        continue; // Skip to next iteration
    Console.WriteLine("{0}",k);
}
```

Listing 4.35   The continue statement

Because the `continue` statement precedes the `WriteLine()` method, the numbers 0 to 7 will not be printed because control is transferred to the beginning of the loop with the counter variable incremented. For the numbers 8 to 10, however, the `continue` statement is not executed, and they are printed. As with `break`, you can use `continue` on any type of loop.

Condition Statements

Condition statements allow you to prescribe the execution path that a program takes. C# supports three such statements: `if/else`, `switch`, and `goto`.

If/else

It is arguably unnecessary to illustrate a construct as simple as the `if` statement, but for the sake of completeness, the following code does just that. Note that unlike VB, the condition expression of an `if` statement must be enclosed within brackets.

```
double discount,price=100.45;

if (price > 100)
{
    // 20% off on items $100 or more
    discount = 20;
}
else if (price > 50)
{
    // 10% off on items between 100 and 50
    discount = 10;
}
else
{
    // 5% off all others
    discount = 5;
}
```

Listing 4.36   If/else statements

When Listing 4.36 executes, the CLR scans through the `if` and `else if` statements. When one of the conditions is true, control is passed to that code block. If none of the `if` or `else if` conditions is met, the code within the `else` block executes. Note that `else if` and `else` are optional portions of an `if` statement. Thus the following code is also valid:

```
if (x>20) {
   a = 4;
}
b=5;

// Another variation (with a twist)
if (x>20)
   a = 4;
   b = 5;
```

Listing 4.37 An if statement with no else

The second `if` statement in Listing 4.37 illustrates a common oversight in C#. Although `if` statements can be used without enclosing characters ({}), *only the first subsequent statement is processed conditionally*. This means that in the second `if` statement, b=5 will *always* execute (the behavior is functionally identical to the first `if` construct). For this reason it is a good idea to always use enclosing characters with an `if`, especially when you want to execute multiple statements under that condition.

Switch

Similar to the `if` construct, the `switch` statement is used to partition a program into multiple execution paths. Unlike an `if` statement, `switch` can only be used for direct comparisons (not >= or <= operations, as in the previous listing). In addition, the syntax behind a `switch` statement is somewhat unorthodox. Consider Listing 4.38.

```
string user="Greg";

switch(user)
{
   case "Greg":
      Console.WriteLine("Funny Guy");
      break;
   case "Brent":
      Console.WriteLine("Not so Funny");
      break;
```

```
    case "Sheldon":
    case "Alim":
       Console.WriteLine("Canadian Boys");
       break;
    default:
       Console.WriteLine("Nice to meet you!");
       break;
}
```

Listing 4.38   The switch statement

In the preceding code we branch to various execution paths, depending on the contents of the `user` variable. For example, if the `user` is Greg, then we appropriately report that Greg is a funny guy. The important point is that unlike the `if` construct, the `switch` statement does not have multiple code blocks (notice there are not numerous block separators (`{}`) in Listing 4.38). Thus, after each `case` statement we must `break` out of the `switch` block.

In the absence of a `break` statement, control simply propagates to the next line in the `switch` block. Thus, if the user is *either* Sheldon or Alim, Listing 4.38 informs us that they are Canadian. This portion of the code would be equivalent to:

```
if (user="Sheldon" || user="Alim" {
   Console.WriteLine("Canadian");
}
```

Listing 4.39   Obtaining "switch" logic using if statements

As you can see, the careful placement of `break` statements within a `switch` block allows you to perform the equivalent of Boolean ORs. Note that the `switch` statement in C# is considerably more versatile than C++, which allows one to switch on only single character values.

The Goto Statement

The final flow construct in C# is the controversial `goto` statement. The `goto` statement is controversial because throughout the years there has been considerable debate about its merit as a program flow statement. Instead of taking a position on the controversy, we'll simply illustrate how to use the `goto` statement.

```
goto SaveUs;
BlowUpMachine();
//Note, BlowUpMachine() will never execute!
```

```
SaveUs:
   Console.WriteLine("We are alive!");
```

Listing 4.40   The goto statement

As illustrated in Listing 4.40, the goto statement is simply an unconditional jump to another area in the program. (VB users: Note that you cannot use line numbers such as goto 10.) However, the use of goto in C# is more restrictive than in VB or C++. Specifically, you cannot jump to a more deeply nested block of code.

```
// This code will NOT WORK!
  {
    OverHere:
    Console.Write("I'm Here");
  }
  goto OverHere;
```

Listing 4.41   Illegal use of the goto statement

Listing 4.41 generates a compile-time error because the OverHere label is not defined in the outer code block where the goto statement resides. Note that this restriction precludes one from jumping *into* a loop construct such as a for or while loop.

Structured Exception Handling

Like C++ and Java, C# exposes structured exception-handling constructs by means of three keywords: try, catch, and finally. Structured error handling allows you to trap any errors that might arise in a given code block. Consider the implementation of the Divide() method in Listing 4.42.

```
double Divide(int num, int den)
{
   double result;
   try
   {
      // Perform the division.  Note the
      // explicit casts to doubles.
      result = (double)num/(double)den;
   }
   catch
   {
      // Error! Set the denominator to 1 and
```

```
    // reperform the division
    den = 1;
    result = (double)num/(double)den;
}
finally
{
    // This block of code always executes
}
return result;
}
```

Listing 4.42   Structured error handling in C#

Any code that might raise an error is placed within the try block. If this code executes without fail, then the code in the finally block is executed. If the code generates an error, however, control is transferred to the catch block where the error can be remedied. (Notice that the catch block in Listing 4.42 rectifies the situation where a divisor may be zero.)

Note that a finally block will *always* execute after the code in a try block. Thus, even if the code in a try block does something abrupt (performs a goto or return), the code in finally will execute before the jump is performed. The finally block normally houses clean-up code, such as the closing of file handles and database connections. Also note that finally is an optional keyword in the try/catch structure—use it only if you have code that must execute upon the termination of an exception block.

Nested Exceptions
You may wonder what occurs when the code within a catch or finally block raises an error. The answer to this question is based on the concept of a *stack walk*. If an error is raised in the Divide() method for which there is no catch block (as is the case of code located within the catch block itself), the error propagates to whoever called Divide(). If the calling routine doesn't have an error handler, the error propagates to its caller, and so on. If subsequent callers cannot handle the error, the error will eventually propagate to the CLR, which will shut down the application.

Although the propagation behavior just described is an adequate defense against problematic error handlers, structured exception handling offers a more elegant solution. You can enclose one try block within another, a technique referred to as *nested exception handling*.

```
try
{
```

```
   // a second try block
   try
   {
      // some code
   }
   catch
   {
      // rectification code
      int a=0;
      int b=1/a;   // divide by zero!
   }
}
catch
{
   // The error is caught here
}
```

Listing 4.43 Nested exceptions

Now if the inner `catch` or `finally` blocks do something illegal, the outer `catch` block will trap the error.

Listing 4.43 may seem like a contrived example. After all, what are the chances that our own error-handling code will result in an error? (Nonetheless, a good developer always plans for the boundary cases.) Not surprisingly, nested exceptions have other uses. We can prescribe, for example, that an inner `try` block will handle only certain types of errors, while the outer `try` block handles the rest. In order to use nested exceptions in this fashion, we must understand how errors are represented in the .NET Framework via exception classes.

Exception Classes

Errors in the .NET Framework are communicated through exception classes that are defined in the BCL and derive from `System.Exception`. A divide-by-zero error, for example, is represented through the `DivideByZeroException` class. Similarly, a file-not-found error is signified through the `FileNotFoundException` class. Like all BCL classes, exception classes are located in an appropriate namespace. `FileNotFoundException`, for example, is found in `System.IO`, while `HttpException` is found in `System.Web`.

Catching an Exception

Exception classes are used in the following manner:

```
using System.IO; // needed for FileNotFoundException class

try
{
   // Execute some code here
}
catch (DivideByZeroException divError)
{
   // A divide by zero occurred
   Console.WriteLine(divError.Message);
}
catch (FileNotFoundException fileError)
{
   // A filenote found error occurred
   Console.WriteLine(fileError.FileName);
}
catch
{
   // All other errors are caught here
}
```

Listing 4.44   Exception classes

As Listing 4.44 illustrates, you can have multiple catch statements within one try block, each of which handles a different type of error. If the code in Listing 4.44 generates a division-by-zero error, control is transferred to the first catch block. Once inside this block we can scrutinize the divError object for information. In this case, we simply print out error information by using the class's Message property.

Notice that in Listing 4.44 each catch block deals with a different exception class (excluding the last catch block, which we will get to momentarily). So whereas divError is a DivideByZeroException class, fileError is a FileNotFoundException class. Not surprisingly, fileError has methods that divError does not. For example, in Listing 4.44 we print out the name of the problematic file by means of fileError's FileName() method. A file name does not make sense in the context of a division error, so DivideByZeroException does not expose a FileName() method.

Another important point is that the exception object names (divError and fileError) that are used within a given catch block are arbitrary; you determine what they are called. You will commonly see try/catch blocks where the exception objects are more succinctly and consistently named.

```
catch (DivideByZeroException e)
{
   //Handle exception
}
catch (FileNotFoundException e)
{
   //Handle exception
}
```

Listing 4.45   Exception class convention

Catching All Exceptions

The last `catch` block in Listing 4.44 catches any errors that are not handled in the first two blocks. The downside of a block declared in such a manner (a `catch` construct by itself) is that there is no exception object that you can query for error information. The way around this shortcoming is to replace the last `catch` line with the following line: `catch (Exception e)`.

This line catches any type of error and stores associated information in a generic `Exception` class. As we will explain in the inheritance topic in Chapter 6, all exception classes in .NET derive from the base `Exception` class. Thus, the line above will catch *all* exceptions, assuming that the exception has not been caught by a previous `catch` block. Realizing this, you should be able to spot the problem with the following code:

```
try
{
   // Execute some code here
}
catch (Exception e)
{
   // A general error occurred
}
catch (DivideByZeroException e)
{
   // A divide by zero occurred
}
// other catch blocks...
```

Listing 4.46   Problematic try/catch code

As you may have guessed, the order of your `catch` blocks matters! In Listing 4.46, all exceptions would be caught by the first `catch` instead of traveling down to a more specific and appropriate exception class (such as `DivideByZeroException` if the exception was a division by zero). Thankfully, in this situation the C# compiler will generate an error informing you of the problem:

```
A previous catch clause already catches all exceptions of
         this or a super type ('System.Exception')
```

Note that you can also define your own types of exceptions by writing custom exception classes. For details see ⊶CS040017.

Back to Nested Exceptions
Our understanding of exception classes allows us to use nested exceptions very powerfully. You can write an inner `try` block that handles only certain errors, and handle the remaining ones in the outer `try` block. The advantage of this approach over the single block technique in Listing 4.44 is that the outer block will also catch any errors generated by the inner block's error-handling code.

```
try
{
   try
   {
      // Execute some code here
   }
   catch (FileNotFoundException e)
   {
      // error handling code
   }
}
catch
{
  // Catch non-file errors or errors in the preceding catch
}
```

Listing 4.47   Nested catches and exception classes

Throwing Exceptions
Just as you can catch errors in C#, you can also raise them. To generate an exception you first instantiate the appropriate exception class and then use the `throw` keyword.

```
// Throw a division by zero exception
DivideByZeroException d = new DivideByZeroException();
throw d;
```

Listing 4.48   Throwing an exception

This exception class will then propagate to the caller of the code, who can `catch` it appropriately. You can also perform a `throw` inside a `catch` block, in which case the exception will propagate to the caller of the code, where it can be caught via an outer `catch` block (assuming there is one).

```
try
{
   // Execute some code here
}
catch (Exception e)
{
   // Throw the exception to an outer catch block
   throw;
}
```

Listing 4.49   Throwing inside a catch block

The C# Preprocessor and Directives

A preprocessor manipulates source files before they are compiled. (The C# preprocessor is really a part of the C# compiler, but this technology is still referred to as preprocessing for consistency with C terminology.) The C# preprocessor is based on the following *directives,* which should be recognizable to C++ developers: `#define`, `#if`, `#else`, and `#endif`. (Note that directives are prefixed with the `#` character.) Most often these directives are used to toggle the printing of debug statements, as illustrated in Listing 4.50.

```
#define Debug

using System;
using System.IO;

class Preprocess
{
  static void Main() {
    #if Debug
      Console.WriteLine("Program is in Debug Mode");
```

```
    #else
      // Program is in release mode so don't print anything.
    #endif
  }
}
```

Listing 4.50   The C# preprocessor

The first line of the listing defines an *identifier* called Debug. Thereafter, we can use the #if, #else, and #endif directives to toggle whether or not certain portions of the program are compiled based on this identifier. If the Debug identifier in Listing 4.50 is defined, then we print out a message informing the user we are in debug mode. If Debug is not defined (as would be the case if we removed the first line of the listing), then we know we are in release mode and nothing is printed.

At this point, those unfamiliar with the techniques of preprocessing might question its value. After all, can we not accomplish the same functionality with the following, more intuitive code?

```
static void Main() {
  bool Debug=true;
  if (Debug) {
     Console.WriteLine("Program is in Debug Mode");
  }
  else {
     // Release Mode, so don't print anything
  }
}
```

Listing 4.51   Alternative to preprocessing

Although Listing 4.51 is an acceptable alternative to using the #define directive, the preprocessing technique is preferable for two primary reasons. Remember that preprocessing occurs *before* the C# compiler translates the source file. Therefore, what the C# compiler really sees in the previous example (Listing 4.51) is the following:

```
using System;
using System.IO;

class Preprocess
{
  static void Main() {
     Console.WriteLine("Program is in Debug Mode");
```

```
    }
}
```

Listing 4.52 Code after preprocessing

Notice that the directives in Listing 4.52 have been removed from the source file. Compare this stripped-down version of the source file with the non-preprocessor version in Listing 4.51, and you will find that preprocessing eliminates both a `bool` variable and the `if` logic associated with it. The C# preprocessor can also work with a combination of identifiers. For example, you can compile code conditionally based on the presence of two identifiers.

```
#if Debug && Verbose
   // Verbose debugging on
#endif
```

Listing 4.53 Boolean preprocessor expressions

For a more involved discussion of C# preprocessing as well as some helpful caveats, see ⌁CS040018.

Note that the C# preprocessor is not as flexible as its C++ counterpart. First, `#define` statements must always be placed at the top of the source file, as illustrated in Listing 4.50. Second, C# does not permit the use of macros or defined constants. Thus, the following code, while permissible in C++, does not compile in C#.

```
#define PI 3.14159   // defined constant
#define write(a) System.Console.WriteLine(a)  // macro
```

Listing 4.54 Prohibited C# preprocessing code

SUMMARY

Like all programming languages, C# offers numerous constructs to control program flow. Many of these features (such as `switch` and `while`) are carryovers from C++ and Java, while some constructs are borrowed from Visual Basic (`foreach`). In addition, some C# syntax elements might function or behave differently from those in your present language. The `switch` statement, for example, is more versatile than the version in C++. Likewise, the structure of C#'s `for` loop is somewhat different from the one found in VB. Java developers will also be happy (or possibly unhappy) to discover that they can now "`goto`" in C#.

C# exposes structured exception-handling constructs similar to those found in C++ and Java. Structured exception handling is implemented by means of the try, catch, and finally keywords. Program code is placed in a try block, and resulting errors are caught in the catch blocks that follow. Errors in the .NET Framework are differentiated by means of exception classes, which are special BCL classes that communicate error information.

Finally, C# houses a less capable version of the C++ preprocessor, which allows you to compile code conditionally based on identifiers that are signified with the #define directive. Preprocessing is frequently used in testing scenarios to toggle the display of debug statements.

Topic: Strings, Arrays, and Collections

In this topic we investigate the manner in which strings and arrays are handled by CLR and C#. As this topic illustrates, some special architectural considerations must be made for both strings and arrays as they exist in the .NET Framework. This topic also surveys the special collection classes inside the BCL, which, like arrays, can be used to store groups of information.

CONCEPTS

Strings

The handling of strings among various programming languages ranges from tedious to transparent. Some languages, such as C, require developers to manipulate character data manually by means of pointers on a byte-by-byte basis. Others, such as Visual Basic, abstract the complexities of strings through straightforward built-in data types. A VB string, for example, is really implemented as a COM BSTR type that hides the complexities of dealing with textual information.

With C#, developers can manage strings through either the "low-level" char and byte data types or by means of the more intuitive and powerful string data type. The string type offers capabilities akin to those exposed by VB and Java. In this section we will focus exclusively on the string type and relegate a discussion of the less capable char and byte to ᶜᴺ⇥CS040019.

As explained in this chapter's first topic, built-in C# types really map to types found in the Common Type System (CTS). It should come as no surprise, therefore, that the `string` data type maps to a `System.String` class. Thus, the following two variable declarations are equivalent:

```
string cSharpString;
System.String CLRString;
```

Listing 4.55   Declaring a string

Because the `string` data type is really a class, it exposes methods to manipulate the character data it is storing. Listing 4.56 illustrates two such methods.

```
string s = "Hello World";
s = s.Substring(0,5);        // extract "Hello"
s = s.ToLower();             // convert to lowercase
Console.WriteLine("{0}",s);  // print out "hello"
```

Listing 4.56   The string class

Whereas the first method extracts a sub string from the string (similar to VB's `Mid()` operator), the second converts the string to lowercase. As this example illustrates, utilizing the `string` type is fairly straightforward. The `string` data type also exposes methods to remove white spaces, determine the string's length, and search the string for a given sequence of characters. For a closer look at such methods, see CS040020.

Strings: Value Type Semantics

Recall from the first topic in this chapter that although strings are reference types that are stored on the heap (an important occurrence that we will explore momentarily), they are used in a value type manner. This means that strings are not declared by means of the `new` keyword, and they can be compared for equality using the == operator.

```
string s = "Hello World";
string a = "\tHello World\n".Trim();
if (a==s)
{
    Console.WriteLine("The strings are equal");
}
```

Listing 4.57   Comparing strings

In addition to the equality operator, the `string` class also exposes a method named `Compare()`, which can compare strings more powerfully.

For example, if two strings differ, this method will tell you where they differ. Examples that illustrate this method can be found at ⸰⇨CS040021.

Strings: The Immutable Problem
On the surface, utilizing strings in C# is fairly straightforward. Underneath the hood, however, matters become more complex. As we stated in the first topic in this chapter, strings are stored on the application's heap. The revealing (and sometimes confusing) point is that they are *immutable*. This is a formal way of saying that a string, once created, can never change. But how is this possible, given that we modified the string in Listing 4.56 by means of the ToLower() method? The unfortunate answer is that *every time you modify a string in C#, the CLR creates a new modified representation of the string on the heap*. Consider Listing 4.56, which extracts a portion of the string and then converts it to lowercase. Behind the scenes, the CLR performs the operations illustrated in Figure 4.5.

String Manipulation

Initial string → "Hello World"
Substring(0,5) → "Hello"
ToLower() → "hello"

Physical replication of the string on the heap

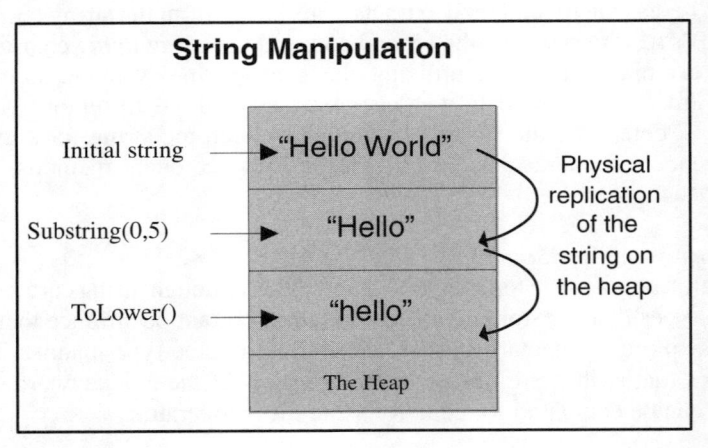

The Heap

Figure 4.5   Immutable strings in C#

As you can imagine, the behavior depicted in Figure 4.5 can severely degrade performance. For example, if you add one character to a string that is 10,000 characters in size, the CLR must first replicate the string before the character is added. Thus, to add simply one character to a string, the CLR must copy 20,000 bytes onto the heap (internally, strings are stored as full UNICODE characters that consume 2 bytes of memory each) before adding the character. Furthermore, the original string must be discarded and eventually garbage collected. Clearly, the manipulation of strings in C# is inefficient.

The StringBuilder Class

Because of the manipulation problems of the built-in `string` type, the .NET Framework exposes an efficient alternative by way of the `StringBuilder` class found in the `System.Text` namespace. Unlike a `string`, the `StringBuilder` class can modify character data without creating a new string object for every modification.

Imagine, for example, that we wanted to construct a string that contained a list of numbers from 1 to 10,000 ("1,2,3,..., 9999,10000"). One option would be to concatenate the `string` type repetitively by means of a `for` loop. A second option would be to utilize the `StringBuilder.Append()` method. Although both techniques produce the same result, they take dramatically different paths to get there. Figure 4.6 illustrates the difference.

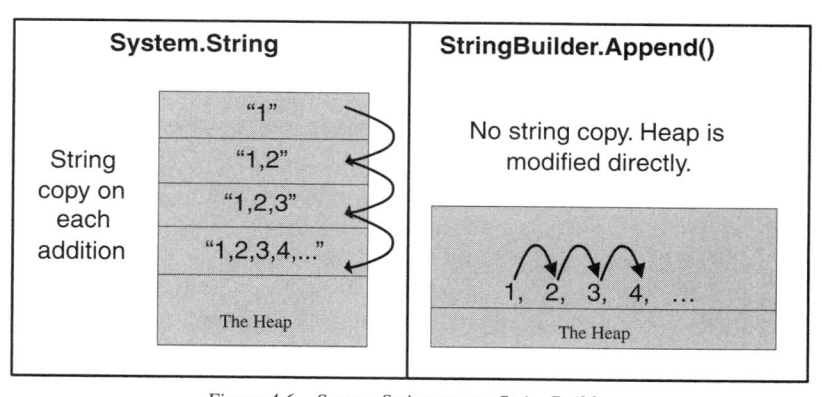

System.String	StringBuilder.Append()
String copy on each addition "1" "1,2" "1,2,3" "1,2,3,4,..." The Heap	No string copy. Heap is modified directly. 1, 2, 3, 4, ... The Heap

Figure 4.6   System.String versus StringBuilder

As shown in Figure 4.6, adding a character to the `string` type requires a new `string` object for each insertion. By contrast, the `StringBuilder.Append()` method performs each addition directly on the string itself, the net result of which is a remarkable difference in execution time. Listing 4.58 completes our comparison by timing how long each technique takes to construct a list of ten thousand numbers.

```
string s ="";
StringBuilder  b =  new StringBuilder("");
long TimeStamp;
double seconds1,seconds2;

// Time construction using a regular string:
TimeStamp = DateTime.Now.Ticks;
for (int j=0; j<=10000;j++) {
   s=s+j.ToString();
```

```
}
TimeStamp = DateTime.Now.Ticks - TimeStamp;
seconds1 = (double)TimeStamp /
   (double)TimeSpan.TicksPerSecond;

// Time construction using the StringBuilder:
TimeStamp = DateTime.Now.Ticks;
for (int j=0; j<=10000;j++) {
   b.Append(j.ToString());
}
TimeStamp = DateTime.Now.Ticks - TimeStamp;
seconds2 = (double)TimeStamp /
   (double)TimeSpan.TicksPerSecond;

Console.WriteLine("System.String time = {0}",seconds1);
Console.WriteLine("StringBuilder      = {0}",seconds2);
```

Listing 4.58 System.String manipulation versus StringBuilder

Compile and run the application (the complete code can be found at CS040022), and you will discover that constructing the list by means of the `StringBuilder` class is significantly faster than using the built-in `string` type. Results will vary from machine to machine, but on our systems the `StringBuilder` technique was roughly a hundred times faster. As you can see, understanding the internal operations of C# and the CLR is an imperative part of increasing performance under the .NET Framework.

The `StringBuilder` class exposes many other methods to manipulate strings efficiently. For a closer look at these methods, see CS040023.

Arrays

An array is a collection of elements, each of which can be accessed and modified individually. Like strings, arrays are stored on the heap and are garbage collected when they are no longer referenced. To instantiate an array in C# you must use the `new` keyword.

```
// Declaring arrays in C#:
int a[10];              // WRONG!
int[] b = new int[10];  // CORRECT
int []c;
c = new int[20];        // ALSO CORRECT
c[10] = 4;
```

Listing 4.59 Declaring arrays in C#

As illustrated in Listing 4.59, the number of elements in an array is determined by way of an argument to the new keyword. As with Java and C++, arrays are zero-based (the first element always begins at zero). Unlike C++ and VB, the size of an array in C# is not specified directly within the array declaration (see the first line of code in the listing). Note that arrays can never be resized; for dynamic sizing we'll soon examine the ArrayList class. Also note that when you declare an array in C#, the array subscript characters ([]) precede the type name, which is in contrast to VB and C++, where the subscript characters are placed *after* the variable name.

When you access an array in C#, the CLR checks that a valid element is being referenced. In other words, you cannot access an array element that does not exist.

```
int[] b = new int[10];
b[901] = 3;   // Error
b[10]  = 7;   // Error - but why?
b[2]   = 1;   // Ok
```

Listing 4.60   Array boundaries in C#

You might wonder why the second line in Listing 4.60 generates a runtime error. Remember that arrays are zero-based. By dimensioning an array of size 10, you are reserving space for elements 0 to 9. Accordingly, an attempt to reference the array's tenth element elicits an exception. This point is especially relevant for Visual Basic developers because VB forgoes such errors by reserving 11 elements for an array of size 10 (0 to 10).

Array Initialization
All the elements of a newly created array are given initial default values (0 for numeric types, null for reference types). In C# it is also possible to supply initial values during declaration.

```
int []a = new int[5] {1,2,3,4,5};
double []b = {0, 6.6, 102.2, 10.1};
string []c;
c = new string[3] {"Pear","Orange","Apple"};
```

Listing 4.61   Initializing arrays

As the first and third examples in Listing 4.61 illustrate, the number of initial values that are provided must match the size of the array. However, it is also possible to supply initial values without declaring an array size, at which point C# reserves memory for the array implicitly. Thus, in the second example, the compiler sees that b has been given four initial values, and it reserves four integer elements on the heap to store them.

Multidimensional Arrays
The arrays we have illustrated thus far have been one-dimensional. To create multidimensional arrays in C# you must use the conventions outlined in Listing 4.62.

```
int [,]b = new int[10,10];        // two dimensional array
int [,,]c = new int[10,10,10];    // three dimensional array
b[1,2] = 3;
c[0,0,2]=2;
```

Listing 4.62   Multidimensional arrays in C#

Initializing multidimensional arrays is as straightforward as doing the same with their one-dimensional counterparts, albeit a little more verbose.

```
// Initializing a multidimensional array:
int [,]b = new int[3,3] { {1,2,3},{4,5,6},{7,8,9}};
```

Listing 4.63   Initializing multidimensional arrays in C#

As with the procedure for one-dimensional arrays, the number of initial values supplied for a multidimensional array must match its size.

Arrays Are Reference Types
Because arrays are reference types, you cannot copy an array by means of the equals operator. That is, the following operation may not function as you would expect.

```
int []b = new int[10];
int []c = b;
c[1]=5; // b is affected!
```

Listing 4.64   Shallow copying arrays in C#

In Listing 4.64 both c and b point to the same location on the heap. Therefore, the modification to the first element of c also modifies the first element of b.

Recall from this chapter's first topic that this behavior is referred to as a *shallow copy*. In order to perform a *deep copy*, whereby b's elements are physically copied into a separate section of the heap reserved for c, you must leverage the array's CopyTo() method.

```
int []b = new int[10];
int []c = new int[10];
b.CopyTo(c,0);
c[1] = 1; // does not affect b
```

Listing 4.65 Deep copying arrays in C#

The CopyTo() method accepts two parameters: the array on which to perform the copying and the element where the copying should begin. (This method works only with one-dimensional arrays.) Note that the target array, c in this case, must be big enough to handle the elements that are being copied. Listing 4.65 thus replicates the contents of b to c. At the end of the operation we have two arrays that point to different locations on the heap, each with ten elements, all set to zero (recall that C# sets the elements of a numeric array to zero by default). Thereafter, changes to c do not affect b.

System.Array
It may seem odd that an array exposes a method named CopyTo(). As you might expect, C# is performing some trickery for us behind the scenes. All arrays inherit from the base System.Array class in the BCL, which exposes properties and methods suitable for array usage. In addition to CopyTo(), this base class contains methods that can be used to query the array for information (e.g., the number of elements, the number of dimensions, etc.) and to manipulate the array (sort, reverse, etc.). We discuss these methods on-line at ᴄɴCS040024. Another useful by-product of inheriting from this base class is that the foreach construct we examined in the previous topic can be used to iterate through arrays.

```
int []b = new int[10];

// Initialize the array using a for loop
for (int k=0;k<=9;k++)
   b[k] = k;

// Print out elements using foreach:
foreach (int i in b)
   Console.Write("{0},",i);
```

Listing 4.66 Iterating through an array using foreach

Jagged Arrays
Multidimensional (MD) arrays have one primary limitation, namely, that the number of elements in each dimension of the array must be

fixed. In other words, multidimensional arrays are "rectangular" in structure. Consider the array in Listing 4.67.

```
int [,]b = new int[4,3]
          {{1,2,3},
           {3,4,5},
           {4,5,6},
           {7,8,9}};
```

Listing 4.67 A 4x3 multidimensional array

Because b is a 4x3 dimensional array, each element in the first dimension of b must refer to another array with three numbers each (this symmetrical constraint is what we mean by "rectangular"). Another way to think of an MD array is to imagine it as an array of arrays. Thus, a 4x3 array is really a one-dimensional array with four elements. Each element, in turn, refers to another one-dimensional integer array with three elements. This simplified relationship is shown in Listing 4.67. Although multidimensional arrays have a variety of uses, they are unsuitable for some data representations.

Consider how we would represent a calendar, for example. Presumably, the first element of the array would refer to the month (and would therefore contain twelve elements). Different months, however, have different numbers of days. In this case, the squared nature of an MD array is problematic. A more efficient alternative would be to use a *jagged array*.

Like an MD array, a jagged array is an array of arrays. Unlike MD arrays, however, jagged arrays can point to secondary arrays of varied sizes. In other words, jagged arrays remove the symmetric constraints of their MD counterparts. Figure 4.7 contrasts their in-memory representations.

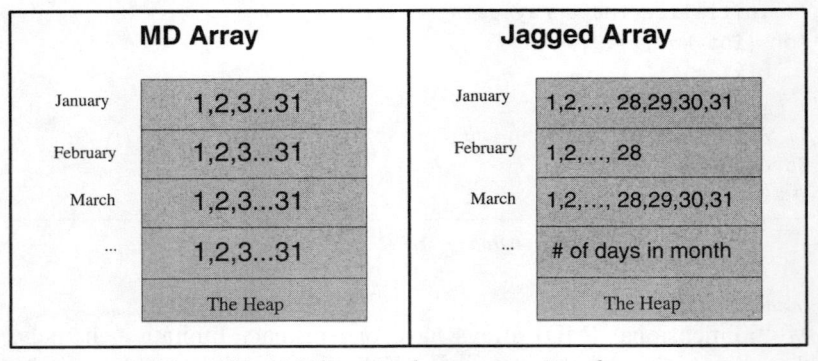

MD Array		Jagged Array	
January	1,2,3...31	January	1,2,..., 28,29,30,31
February	1,2,3...31	February	1,2,..., 28
March	1,2,3...31	March	1,2,..., 28,29,30,31
...	1,2,3...31	...	# of days in month
	The Heap		The Heap

Figure 4.7 Multidimensional arrays versus jagged arrays

It should be apparent why the jagged array in Figure 4.7 is more appropriate to represent a calendar than the MD array to its left. Because each of the "individual" jagged arrays can be a different size, storing a different number of days for each month is not problematic. In contrast, if we were to employ an MD array, we would have to reserve thirty-one elements for each month, as illustrated in Figure 4.7—clearly a waste of memory. The following listing completes our example by using a jagged array to represent a calendar.

```
// Declare Jagged array (notice the double subscripts)
int [][]Calendar = new int[12][];

// The array now points to twelve individual arrays
// which we can dimension individually:
Calendar[0] = new int[31]; // 31 days in Jan
Calendar[1] = new int[28]; // 28 (or 29) days in Feb
Calendar[2] = new int[31]; // 31 days in March
Calendar[3] = new int[30]; // 30 days in April
//Remaining code omitted for brevity
```

Listing 4.68   *Using a jagged array to represent a calendar*

At first glance you might find the declaration of a jagged array counterintuitive. Recall that a jagged array is really an array of arrays. It is therefore always declared with *two* empty array subscripts, as illustrated by the highlighted line in Listing 4.68. The new construct then stipulates that our jagged array will point to twelve one-dimensional arrays. By contrast, if we wanted a two-dimensional jagged array—that is, an array of two-dimensional arrays—our code would look like Listing 4.69.

```
// Declare a two-dimensional Jagged array
int [][,]jagged= new int[10][,];

jagged[0] = new int[4,4]; // first array is 4x4
jagged[1] = new int[2,7]; // second array is 2x7
jagged[2] = new int[6,1]; // third array is 6x1
```

Listing 4.69   *A multidimensional jagged array*

More information on jagged arrays can be found at CS040025.

Collections
Despite their usefulness, arrays have two primary limitations. First, unlike the ArrayList class, they cannot dynamically resize themselves as required. For example, if you instantiate a one-dimensional array with

ten elements, you cannot increase its size should you decide to add an eleventh item. Second, an element of an array can only be accessed by its index (its position in the array); there are no built-in provisions for accessing an element by its contents (i.e., there are no look-up facilities). To overcome these shortcomings, developers frequently write utility functions or turn to alternative storage mechanisms such as linked lists.

The .NET Framework exposes an extensive number of classes that also address the limitations of traditional arrays. These classes, which are found in the System.Collections namespace, offer numerous ways to store and retrieve groups of data. We will concentrate on two of these classes in this section, and relegate a further exploration of this namespace (which contains classes for stacks, queues, etc.) to ₒ^{CN}↦CS040026.

ArrayList

We used the ArrayList class in Chapter 1 (Listing 1.9) to sort a list of numbers. From a functional perspective the ArrayList class is similar to a regular C# array with two important differences: (1) you do not have to dimension it, and (2) it will automatically resize itself as you add elements to it. Furthermore, the ArrayList class exposes methods that a regular array does not (such as a BinarySearch() method, which can be used to locate the elements within the list quickly). The ArrayList is also more versatile than an array in that it can store different data types. (By contrast, arrays are homogenous: An integer array can store only integers, an array of strings can store only strings, and so on.)

```
using System.Collections;
...
ArrayList a = new ArrayList();
a.Add(4);
a.Add("Hello World");
a.Add(5.5);

foreach (object o in a)
    Console.WriteLine("{0}",o);
```

Listing 4.70 The ArrayList class

As Listing 4.70 demonstrates, an ArrayList can store numerous types (an integer, string, and double, in our case). However, there are some side effects to using an ArrayList in such a fashion. Most notably, functions that assume single-type storage—such as the Sort() method—will no longer work. (However, you can manually make

Sort() work with heterogeneous types; see ⌕CS040027 for an explanation and example.)

ArrayList: The Downside
Although the ArrayList class is a powerful storage mechanism, it does have some drawbacks. Because an ArrayList can house numerous types (it is most accurate to think of it as a list of objects), adding value type elements to the list involves the expensive operation of boxing, which we examined earlier in this chapter. Performance is further degraded because the ArrayList class must resize itself as required.

Although there are techniques to increase performance (such as reserving memory for the ArrayList ahead of time), this class will never be as fast a native array when it comes to adding elements. Nevertheless, the functionality offered by this class makes it a viable option to store dynamic lists in the .NET Framework.

Hashtable
An important concern when it comes to storing lists of information is how to find a particular element in the list. With an array the answer is straightforward and inefficient: Simply traverse the array until you find what you are looking for. The System.Array and ArrayList classes offer a more sophisticated alternative by means of the BinarySearch() method, which searches the array efficiently by first sorting it. Another technique is to determine an element's location in the list according to a key value. In this way the key can be used at a later point to rapidly retrieve the element without having to search the list whatsoever. This setup—the storage and retrieval of elements based on a key value—is known as a *hashtable*.

The theory behind hashing is extensive. For example, how exactly do we use the key to compute an element's location in the list (called a hashing function)? What do we do if the hashing function returns the same element location for different key values (called a collision)? Thankfully, such questions have been buried by Microsoft's implementation of the System.Collections.Hashtable class, which allows you to store and retrieve list elements by supplying a key for the item you are adding. Listing 4.71 illustrates the process.

```
Hashtable h = new Hashtable();

// Add people according to their S.I.N. number:
h.Add("136-01-28011","Carol Polacco");
h.Add("136-01-18701","Paras Dharamshi");
```

```
h.Add("131-17-17913","Aisha Habib");

// Print out whoever has an S.I.N. of 131-17-17913:
Console.WriteLine("{0}",h["131-17-17913"]);
```

Listing 4.71 Using the hashtable class

To add an item to the `Hashtable` class you must provide both a key and a value. The key can be used later to look up the value in question and should therefore be unique within the `Hashtable` (which is why we use Canadian S.I.N. values in Listing 4.71). Adding different values with the same key generates an exception. Once items have been added to the `Hashtable`, they can be extracted by referencing the class in an array-like fashion. Instead of referencing an element number, however, you supply the key associated with the specific item. For a closer look at the `Hashtable` class, see ⟿CS040026.

SUMMARY

There are many ways to store a group of elements in C#. Like C++ and Java, the language exposes native arrays that are accessed by index (a[4] = 4). Native arrays are dimensioned by means of the `new` keyword and reside on the heap. Unlike C++, the C# compiler constantly performs bounds checking on arrays, in order to ensure that you are referencing valid elements.

Like the arrays of most languages, C# arrays can be multidimensional, although the convention for creating them is different from C++ and VB. C# also introduces the jagged array, which is an array of arrays. Unlike multidimensional arrays, jagged arrays can refer to arrays of different sizes. Whereas a multidimensional array takes on a symmetrical structure (e.g., 3×2, 5×5, etc.), a jagged array can embody an uneven arrangement. For example, the first element of a jagged array can reference an array with ten elements, the second element can reference an array of five elements, and so on. Jagged arrays are useful in representing incongruous data.

Storage mechanisms that are more versatile than simple arrays can be found in the `System.Collections` namespace. The `ArrayList` class exposes array-like properties but can automatically resize itself, while the `Hashtable` class allows array elements to be retrieved easily via associated key values. The classes in `System.Collections` offer an additional advantage over native arrays because they are not bound to a particular type. For example, a single `ArrayList` class can hold (among others) `string`, `float`, and `byte` values, whereas a `double`-specific array is limited to `double` types. This added benefit comes at the cost of performance since the values that are added to these classes must be boxed into `System.Objects`.

Chapter Summary

The C# syntax is a combination of the features of C++, Java, and Visual Basic, with some improvements to boot. As with C++ and Java, C# code is partitioned into blocks that are denoted with "curly braces" ({ }). Variables defined inside a code block are visible only within that code block.

Like all programming languages, C# exposes ways to store and manipulate information. The language derives its data types from the Common Type System of the CLR, which allows C# to interact easily with other languages in the framework. The C# language also offers an extensive set of operators, such as arithmetic and bitwise elements, which can modify variables.

Controlling program flow in C# is made easy by the `if`, `switch`, and `goto` constructs, as well as the many looping constructs exposed by the language. Many of the constructs are similar to those found in C++ and Java, with some slight twists. C# also exposes a rich assortment of tools for storing and manipulating lists. Native arrays are a simple means of storing groups of elements, while more sophisticated entities found in the `System.Collections` namespace can be utilized for advanced list storage, manipulation, and lookup.

In the next chapter we will utilize many of the constructs discussed in this chapter to investigate the particularities of the .NET Framework, such as delegates, reflection, and garbage collection.

Chapter 5
—
.NET LANGUAGE FEATURES

In this chapter we examine some of the language features of the .NET Framework. These features are not specific to C# but are, rather, services provided by the language-neutral CLR and new paradigms exposed by the framework. As such, the topics discussed in this chapter are afforded to any .NET language, but we will obviously consider them from the perspective of C#. The last two topics in this chapter discuss delegates and garbage collection, which provide type safety for callback functions and automatic memory management, respectively.

CORE CONCEPTS

Metadata, Reflection, and Attributes
As you will recall from Chapter 3, metadata makes an assembly self-describing, and assists the CLR in ensuring that clients call methods in a type-safe manner. Reflection extends the benefits of metadata by allowing developers to inspect and use it at runtime. Using reflection, for example, one can dynamically determine all the classes contained in a given assembly and invoke their methods if desired.

As we saw at the end of Chapter 3, attributes are declarative tags in code that insert metadata into an assembly where it can be retrieved by the CLR, or possibly yourself, to influence some aspect of your application (how it behaves, how it is deployed, etc.).

Delegates
C++ programmers can think of delegates as glorified callback functions, whereas Visual Basic developers can draw analogies with VB's `AddressOf()` operator. Delegates facilitate "multicasting," which is equivalent to a single source calling several function pointers or raising multiple events.

Garbage Collection
Garbage collection is a service afforded to any application running within the CLR, and it destroys objects when they are no longer being referenced. Although garbage collection may seem like an innocuous operation, as we shall see it has important implications for the manner in which objects must release their resources.

Threading
Another new .NET feature also found in Java is support for threading classes. Threads allow an application to have multiple streams of execution, and they can decrease program response time while increasing the number of tasks an application can perform in parallel. Utilizing threads in C# can be an involved procedure that raises concerns such as thread safety and synchronization. .NET threads, which are exposed via classes in the `System.Threading` namespace, are discussed on-line at CS050001.

Topic: Attributes

Attributes are nonprogrammatic statements that embed additional metadata into an assembly. This metadata can then be extracted at runtime to characterize aspects of an application or to influence its behavior. In the section on shared assemblies in Chapter 3, we saw how the `AssemblyVersion` attribute was used to specify an assembly's version number:

```
[assembly:AssemblyVersionAttribute("1.0.0.0")]
```

This attribute (which is enclosed within square brackets, like all attributes in C#) embeds the following metadata into the resulting assembly:

```
.assembly Mathlib as "Mathlib"
{
  // other metadata
```

```
.ver 1:0:0:0
}
```

Listing 5.1   Metadata created by the Version attribute

When an application uses the assembly, the CLR extracts this section of the metadata to determine whether the versioning requirements of the application have been met.

Attributes are used throughout the .NET Framework. The CLR uses them to determine how objects are serialized (as we will see), whether or not a class will be utilizing COM+ services, etc. The CLR is not the only consumer of attribute-generated metadata, either. As we will see in Chapter 7, the `DLLImport` attribute allows one to utilize Win32 DLLs directly from C#.

The .NET Framework contains two types of attributes: predefined attributes, such as `AssemblyVersion`, which already exist in the BCL, and custom attributes, which you write yourself by inheriting from the `System.Attribute` class. We will discuss custom attributes in the next section on reflection once we have a better understanding of how attributes work. To this end we will now explore two predefined attributes: `Conditional`, which is used to write conditional compilation statements in C#, and `Serializable`, which prescribes how a class serializes (persists) itself to disk so that it can be re-created at a later point.

CONCEPTS

Conditional Attribute: Example

For years developers have relied on conditional compilation techniques to reduce the size of their applications and to debug their programs. In the previous chapter we saw that C# exposes this functionality by means of the `#define` directive:

```
#define DBG
...
#ifdef DBG
        Console::WriteLine("[TRACE]: In Function . . . ");
#endif
```

Listing 5.2   The #define directive

In the .NET Framework you can also use the `Conditional` attribute found in the `System.Diagnostic` namespace to facilitate conditional compilation. This may not seem terribly exciting, until you realize that this attribute allows an assembly to determine *how its client will com-*

pile, depending on the directives defined in the client. The following C# class library example clarifies the attribute's usage.

```
using System;
using System.Diagnostics;

namespace ToPrintOrNot
{
   public class CondPrint
   {
      [ConditionalAttribute("DBG")]
      static public void MyFunction()
      {
         Console.WriteLine("DBG directive is defined...");
      }
   }
}
```

Listing 5.3   condClass.cs—the Conditional attribute

Note that nothing in Listing 5.3 is conditionally compiled. Rather, the Conditional attribute poses the following question to all compilers that are compiling applications which reference this assembly: *Does the application you are compiling have DBG defined?*

YES: I'll allow your client to call MyFunction(). Compile your application as if it called it.

NO: Your client cannot call MyFunction(). Compile your application as if it never called it.

In other words, the Conditional attribute allows a class library component to enforce conditional compilation properties on its client. This information is communicated via the assembly's metadata, which, if examined via the ILDASM tool, resembles the following text (don't forget to create the assembly by using the C# compiler csc.exe /t:library condClass.cs):

```
MethodName: MyFunction (06000001)
  //other metadata
    System.Diagnostics.ConditionalAttribute . . .
  //other metadata
    ctor args: ("DBG")
```

Listing 5.4   Resulting metadata from the Conditional attribute

Keeping this metadata in mind for a moment, consider the following C# client that uses the assembly.

```
using System;
using ToPrintOrNot;

public class MyClass
{
   public static void Main()
   {
      CondPrint.MyFunction();
      Console.ReadLine();
   }
}
```

Listing 5.5   condClassClient.cs

When we compile this application as follows:

```
csc.exe /r:condClass.dll condClassClient.cs
```

the C# compiler asks itself the question implied by the Conditional attribute to determine whether or not MyFunction() is called. In this case there is no DBG defined in the client application, and so MyFunction() is not called. (It would be as if the line were never in the source code in the first place.) However, if you were to add the following line:

```
#define DBG
```

to the top of the listing, MyFunction() would be called, resulting in the following program output:

```
DBG directive is defined . . .
```

You can confirm that the presence of the #define DBG statement toggles whether or not the method is being called by using ILDASM to examine the application's IL code under both scenarios.

An even more powerful aspect of this attribute is that it can span across .NET languages. For example, a VB.NET client that used the class library in Listing 5.3 could toggle debug statements by means of the #Const directive (VB.NET's equivalent of #define). Because the Conditional attribute manifests itself as metadata in the language-neutral assembly, conditional compilation across languages is possible (an unseen capability prior to the introduction of .NET).

This is just one example of using attributes, but it highlights the underlying premises behind them:

1. An attribute embeds additional metadata into the assembly.
2. Metadata is used in some fashion to influence application behavior.

The Serializable Attribute

The Serializable attribute informs the CLR that a class can be persisted to a stream. This stream could be a file, a communication channel such as TCP/IP, or even a message queue (MSMQ). An object marked with this attribute is said to be *persistable,* and a persistable object also knows how to reconstruct itself from the stream to which it was saved.

The following code illustrates the application of this attribute on a class named NumberList, which maintains a list of integers in memory.

```
[Serializable]
public class NumberList
{
   private int []s;
   public NumberList ()
   {
     // populate a list of 5000 numbers upon instantiation:
     s = new int[5000];
     for (int k=0; k<5000;k++)
        s[k]=k;
   }
   public long Sum()
   {
      long total=0;
      for (int k=0; k<5000;k++)
         total+=s[k];
      return total;
   }
}
```

Listing 5.6 The Serializable attribute

As Listing 5.6 illustrates, using the Serializable attribute is remarkably easy; you simply apply it on the desired class. Because of NumberList's serializable designation, we can save instances of the class to disk and re-create them at later times. The serialization of classes in the .NET Framework is based on two concepts: a stream and a formatter.

Streams and Formatters

A stream is an abstraction for a sequence of bytes. The destination of these bytes is ultimately determined by the properties of the stream. Some stream classes, such as `FileStream` and `MemoryStream`, store the bytes in a persistable area (a file and memory, respectively). Other streams, such as a `NetworkStream`, simply send the bytes over a communication channel to a client.

Whereas a stream ultimately represents the destination of a sequence of bytes, a formatter determines how a `Serializable` class is converted into those bytes in the first place. The .NET Framework provides two formatters: the `BinaryFormatter` class, which converts a class into a binary byte representation, and the `SoapFormatter` class, which translates a class into user-friendly XML.

Serializing: An Example

The following code uses the `Stream` and `BinaryFormatter` classes to save an instance of our `NumberList` class to a file named `List.bin`. Thereafter, it reconstructs a new instance of the class from this file and calls the `Sum()` against the newly created instance. Note the use of the `FileMode.Create` enumeration member, which specifies the manner in which the destination file is opened (in this case the file is created if it doesn't exist).

```
using System;
using System.IO;
using System.Runtime.Serialization.Formatters.Binary;

class Class1
{
  static void Main()
  {
    NumberList list = new NumberList();
    // Save the class to disk:
    Stream s = File.Open("List.bin", FileMode.Create);
    BinaryFormatter b = new BinaryFormatter();
    b.Serialize(s,list);
    s.Close();

    // Populate a new instance of the class from
    // the saved file:
    NumberList list2;
    s = File.Open("List.bin", FileMode.Open);
    list2 = (NumberList)b.Deserialize(s);
```

```
    s.Close();
    Console.WriteLine("{0}",list2.Sum());
  }
}
```

Listing 5.7   Saving a Serializable class to disk

Note that we had to import the appropriate namespaces in Listing 5.7 in order to use both the `Stream` and `BinaryFormatter` classes. After creating an instance of our class, the `Serialize()` method of the formatter saves it to disk. It is important to understand that this process saves all the information required to instantiate the class at a later point, which for our class is the list of 5,000 numbers. In other words, the process of serialization saves a class's "state," which consists of its member variables.

After saving the class to disk, we use the `Deserialize()` method of the formatter to populate a new instance of the `NumberList` class with the previously saved state. Although the `Serialize()` and `Deserialize()` operations are performed sequentially in this example, there is no requirement that this be the case. We could have serialized the class to disk and then reconstructed it a couple of days later. Thus, another way to think of serialization is the decoupling of a class's lifetime from the application that creates it.

The process of serialization is often used with the .NET Remoting technology that we discussed in Chapter 1 to "send" an object to a remote machine where it can be reinstantiated and used. For an example of the two models working together, see ᴄᴺCS050002.

Serialization: A Little Too Simple?
The simplicity of .NET serialization—the fact that a class can be made persistable by simply applying an attribute on it—may trouble developers who have worked with serialization in other frameworks (such as COM). In many other frameworks you have to describe *how* the class serializes to a stream; you simply don't wave a magic wand and make it so as we did in Listing 5.6.

The simplicity behind Listing 5.6 is a by-product of the common framework of the CLR. Remember that a class must be built from the entities exposed by the Common Type System. Because these are all built-in types in the framework, the CLR knows how to serialize them. In other words, it is the CTS that allows for intrinsic serialization support in .NET.

However, for some operations you may wish to override the CLR's default serialization behavior. This can be accomplished by means of the `ISerializable` interface, which allows a class to determine its own serialization procedure. For details on implementing this interface, as well as some other serialization tips, see ⟿CS050003.

Attribute Naming

By convention, the names of all of the predefined attributes found in the BCL end with "Attribute" (e.g., `AssemblyVersionAttribute`, `ConditionalAttribute`, etc.). To make your code less verbose, C# allows you to use attributes without specifying this redundant ending. Thanks to this property we can reference `ConditionalAttribute` simply as `Conditional`, a convention we will follow throughout the remainder of this book.

HOW AND WHY

Why do I get the following compile-time error?

```
error CS0578: Conditional not valid on 'MyFunction()'
    because its return type is not void.
```

The `Conditional` attribute can only be used on methods without return values. If you think about what this attribute does, it should become apparent why this is the case. Consider what would happen if a client had the following line of code:

```
result = someConditionalFunction();
```

Remember that the `Conditional` attribute stipulates that if the client doesn't have a certain directive defined, the client will be compiled as if the call to the method had never proceeded. If this occurs, what value will `result` receive? Other portions of the client that depend on `result` containing a valid value will be thwarted. Because of the problems associated with this scenario, the `Conditional` attribute can be used only on methods without return values.

SUMMARY

There are two types of attributes in the .NET Framework, both of which embed additional metadata into an assembly. *Predefined* attributes exist in the BCL, and the metadata they produce is used by some Microsoft entity (such as the CLR or the Windows Form Designer) for descriptive purposes or to influence application behavior. Custom attributes allow developers to place their own metadata into assemblies, which can be retrieved by using the reflection technique examined in the next section.

Topic: Reflection

Metadata is the information that glues the .NET Framework together. In Chapter 3 we saw that assemblies use metadata to describe the types they contain so that applications can communicate with them effectively. In the previous section we learned that predefined attributes embed additional metadata into an assembly that is used by some entity in the .NET Framework (such as the CLR) for informational purposes or to affect application behavior.

The virtue of self-describing metadata becomes most apparent when we consider the process of reflection, which allows developers to probe and use an assembly's metadata directly. For example, you can determine all the classes that an assembly contains, the members each class exposes, and the parameters that the members expect without prior knowledge of the assembly. Using this information you can call a class's method dynamically by constructing its parameters at runtime.

From an external point of view, an assembly is nothing more than a collection of exposed types. These types could be the basic types found in the Common Type System (CTS), such as integers and strings, or more complex constructions of them, such as your own classes, structures, and enumerations. Recalling that .NET applications execute within `AppDomains`, we can list the following hierarchy of elements within the .NET Framework:

```
AppDomains:
   Assemblies:
      Types:
            Fields
            Properties
            Events
            Methods
            Other Types
```

Listing 5.8 AppDomain hierarchy

The classes found in the `System.Reflection` namespace allow you to probe through an assembly's metadata in a similar hierarchical fashion. You can, for example, ascertain all the types contained within an assembly (its classes, structures, etc.). Similarly, given a class, you can determine the types it contains (the class's methods and member variables) as well as their constituent types (method parameters and return values).

CONCEPTS

Simple Reflection

In the following example we will consider how reflection can be used to probe and call a mathematical library called `MathLib`. In the spirit of our previous examples, `MathLib` exposes two methods, `Add()` and `Factorial()`, in addition to a public member variable named `SomeVar`.

```
using System;

namespace MathLib
{
  public class MathClass
  {
    public string SomeVar;
    public long Factorial(long a)
    {
      long nDigit, nAnswer;
      nAnswer = 1;
      for (nDigit=1; nDigit<=a; nDigit++)
        nAnswer = nAnswer*nDigit;
      return nAnswer;
    }
    private int Add(int a, int b)
    {
      return a+b;
    }
  }
}
```

Listing 5.8   MathLib.cs—the MathLib class

As usual, we create a MathLib.DLL assembly by means of the C# compiler:

```
csc.exe /t:library MathLib.cs
```

From our discussion in Chapter 3 we know that the resulting assembly contains the metadata that describes the members of `MathClass`: the public member variable SomeVar, and the public and private methods Factorial() and Add(). A client program can probe this metadata by using the System.Reflection classes, as the following program demonstrates.

```
using System;
using System.Reflection;
using MathLib;   // remember to reference MathLib.DLL

public class Reflect
{
  public static void Main()
  {
    MathClass MyClass;
    MyClass = new MathClass();

    // Print out the member information of MathClass:
    Type T = MyClass.GetType();

    MemberInfo[] Members = T.GetMembers(
      BindingFlags.Public|
      BindingFlags.NonPublic|
      BindingFlags.Instance);

    foreach (MemberInfo mi in Members)
      Console.WriteLine(" {0} = {1}", mi.MemberType,mi);
  }
}
```

Listing 5.10   Reflect.cs—simple reflection in C#

Compile and run this program (don't forget to reference the class library we created from Listing 5.9), and it will print out all the members of MathClass as given in Listing 5.11. Note that some methods, such as GetHashCode(), were inherited from the System.Object base class.

```
Field  = System.String SomeVar
Method = Void Finalize()
Method = Int32 GetHashCode()
Method = Boolean Equals(System.Object)
Method = System.String ToString()
Method = Int64 Factorial(Int64)
Method = Int32 Add(Int32, Int32)
```

```
Method = System.Type GetType()
Method = System.Object MemberwiseClone()
Constructor = Void .ctor()
```

Listing 5.11   Reflection output

The key to understanding the process of reflection is to familiarize yourself with the underlying classes in the BCL. An object's metadata is accessed through its `Type` class, which is retrieved by means of the `Object.GetType()` method. The `GetType()` method is implemented by the `System.Object` class from which all classes derive; thus, it can be called on any object (the bold line in Listing 5.10).

The metadata for `MyClass` can now be accessed through the `Type` class, `T`. The `Type` class exposes a method called `GetMembers()`, which returns the members of the underlying object as an array of `MemberInfo` objects.

```
MemberInfo[] Members = T.GetMembers(
        BindingFlags.Public |
        BindingFlags.NonPublic |
        BindingFlags.Instance);
```

Listing 5.12   Extracting MemberInfo

Recall from our array discussion in Chapter 4 that the `Members` array will automatically dimension itself with the number of elements returned by `GetMembers()`. This method also accepts an optional parameter that specifies which members it will return. In this case we have requested that it return public and private members on the instance of our class (`MyClass`). We specify these requirements by using OR (|) to combine the various members in the `BindingFlags` enumeration found in the `System.Reflection` namespace.

Having executed this method, we are now left with an array of `MemberInfo` objects, each of which represents a member of the `MathClass` class. By iterating through each element in the array by means of a `foreach` loop, we print out the class's members given in Listing 5.11.

You are encouraged to investigate the `System.Reflection` classes and explore the world of reflection. If there is information embedded in an assembly's metadata, you can most certainly retrieve it by using one of these classes; it is just a matter of finding the appropriate class (or classes). For some additional reflection examples, see ◦⇾CS050004.

Advanced Reflection

The above program may not seem particularly impressive, as it doesn't yield any information that we probably don't already know. After all, if we have access to MathLib.DLL, then we can determine MathClass's methods using the ILDASM tool instead of using reflection to interpret the metadata ourselves. The true versatility of reflection becomes apparent when you consider the following program, which calls the MathLib assembly without prior knowledge of its makeup.

```
using System;
using System.Reflection;

public class Reflect
{
  public static void Main()
  {
    // Dynamically load the assembly:
    Assembly asm = Assembly.LoadFrom("MathLib.dll");

    // Iterate through the Assembly, and search all its classes
    // for a method named "Add" that takes two Int32s as
    // parameters:

    foreach (Type t in asm.GetTypes())
    {
      MethodInfo[] miarr = t.GetMethods(
        BindingFlags.Instance| BindingFlags.NonPublic|
        BindingFlags.Public);

      foreach (MethodInfo mi in miarr)
      {
        if (mi.Name == "Add")
        {
          ParameterInfo[] pInfo = mi.GetParameters();
          // Does this Add() take two Int32 parameters?
          if (pInfo.Length == 2)
          {
            if (pInfo[0].ParameterType.Equals(typeof(Int32)) &&
              pInfo[1].ParameterType.Equals(typeof(Int32)))
            {
              Console.WriteLine("Add() method found.");
              // Create an instance of the class:
              object o = Activator.CreateInstance(t);

              // Construct the parameters required
              // the call the Add method using Invoke():
```

```
                    Object returnValue;
                    Object [] arguments = new Object[2];
                    arguments[0] = 1;
                    arguments[1] = 2;

                    // Dynamically Invoke Add():
                    returnValue = mi.Invoke(o,arguments);
                    Console.WriteLine("Dynamically Invoked Add()");
                    Console.WriteLine("1+2={0}",returnValue);
                  } //If int32 add
                } //If two arguments
              } //If add method
            } /foreach MethodInfo
          } //foreach Type in assembly
      } /Main method
} //class
```

Listing 5.13   ReflectCall.cs: Dynamically calling MathClass.Add()

This program works in a manner similar to the previous one, by using the classes found in System.Reflection to probe the various types in the assembly. The difference is that the assembly is loaded dynamically at runtime by using the Assembly class's LoadFrom() method. Every class in the assembly is then searched for an Add() method that accepts two integer parameters. When such a method is found, it is called using the Invoke() method of the MethodInfo class.

```
Object returnValue;
Object [] arguments = new Object[2];
arguments[0] = 1; arguments[1] = 2;
returnValue = mi.Invoke(o,arguments);
```

Listing 5.14   Invoking a method dynamically

As Listing 5.14 illustrates, parameters are passed to the Invoke() method as an array of objects, with the first element corresponding to the first parameter, and so on. As the developer it is your responsibility to deliver an object array whose size and contents match the parameters and types that the method is expecting. If you fail to do this, the CLR will throw a TargetParameter or Argument exception. In other words, at some point you must know what the add method actually does and what arguments it expects.

Note that unlike the previous program, this one does not require referencing the class library assembly (i.e., compilation with the

/r:MathLib.DLL switch). Everything from loading the assembly to calling its `Add()` method is done dynamically at runtime. In fact, we could have passed the DLL name into the program as a command-line argument (instead of in-lining it as a string), thereby eliminating all references to the specific assembly.

Keep in mind that when loading the assembly by means of the `LoadFrom()` method, you should appropriately specify the directory within which the assembly is contained (i.e., use `Assembly.Load From(@"\SomeDir\MathLib.dll"` or use the proper escape characters for the file path).

Running the Example
Compile and run the program, and it will produce the following output:

```
Add() method found.
Dynamically Invoked Add().
1+2 = 3
```

Listing 5.15 Advanced reflection output

Look carefully and you'll realize that we have done something we shouldn't have been able to do. `Add()` is a `private` method in `MathClass`. In addition to dynamic invocation services, reflection has the added benefit of allowing you to invoke `private` methods on classes. This can be useful for diagnostic utilities that need to interact with classes beyond their `public` interfaces, but it raises security concerns for class authors who thought that `private` methods would be, well, `private`. Whether or not code can invoke `private` methods by means of reflection depends on the security policy of the code's origins (locally, the Internet, etc.). By default, code that originates from the local hard drive can detect and invoke the private methods of a class. You can alter this behavior by using the .NET Configuration tool. Details on the utility can be found at ᴄᴺ/CS050005.

Custom Attributes and Reflection
Reflection can also be used to retrieve the metadata that has been embedded as a result of an attribute. This is especially important for custom attributes whose metadata you will want to retrieve and use in some meaningful way. Together, custom attributes and reflection allow you to extend the metadata infrastructure of the .NET Framework. For example, you can write a custom attribute, as illustrated in Listing 5.16.

```
[HasBeenTested(50)]
Class SomeClass { ...
```

Listing 5.16   The HasBeenTested custom attribute

Clients can use this attribute to specify the extent to which a class or method has been tested. A value of 0 would indicate that the entity has not been tested, whereas 100 would indicate complete and rigorous testing, and values in between would indicate partial testing. Because this information would be embedded in the assembly itself, an install utility could extract it at runtime by means of reflection to determine whether the assembly was ready for deployment (i.e., if any type in an assembly is rated less than 70, it could be rejected for installation).

To write a custom attribute such as HasBeenTested you must write a class that inherits from the System.Attribute class in the BCL. The source code for such an attribute, along with a reflection utility that uses it, can be found at ⟶CS050006.

Reflection.Emit and Code Generators

Just as the process of reflection can be used to retrieve and interpret metadata, it can be used to construct and emit it. The classes found in the System.Reflection.Emit namespace allow metadata for new types to be generated in memory and used at runtime. In fact, you can dynamically create an entire assembly, its classes and methods, and the IL code behind them. The "in memory" assembly can then be used by other applications.

Although this namespace contains a number of powerful classes, their primary limitation is that you must learn to code in IL in order to build classes dynamically. Furthermore, even if you took the time to learn IL, writing an object of any complexity in this assembly-like language is a daunting task.

It would be ideal if we could put C# source code into a string variable and then simply compile that string into a proper assembly. Fortunately, the C# compiler itself is exposed through classes located in the Microsoft.CSharp and System.CodeDom.Compiler namespaces. Using these classes you can produce in-memory assemblies dynamically by compiling string variables. This procedure is illustrated on-line at ⟶CS050007.

SUMMARY

Reflection allows you to access an assembly's metadata by using classes found in the `System.Reflection` namespace. This can be the standard metadata that is produced by the IL compiler and describes the types contained within an assembly, or the metadata that is embedded by a predefined or custom attribute.

Using reflection, one can traverse through the .NET entity hierarchy (AppDomain → Assembly → Module → Class, etc.), ascertaining information about the types one is interested in and invoking them if desired. The reverse process is facilitated by the classes found in the `System.Reflection.Emit` namespace, whereby .NET entities can be constructed dynamically in memory and invoked.

Topic: Delegates

Asynchronous notification schemes are incredibly efficient. If you call a friend and he is not home, you don't wait on the line for hours to speak with him. Most often you leave your phone number with the person on the line so that when your friend does get home, he can notify you of his arrival by calling you back. By not waiting idly on the line for an extended period of time, you are free to do other things.

Callback functions facilitate exactly this type of asynchronous behavior. When calling a class's method (your friend's telephone number), you provide it with a callback function (your telephone number) so that you can be alerted when a particular event occurs (your friend returns home). As a result of this exchange, your program (you) is free to do other things in the interim.

Callback functions are equivalent to function pointers in C and C++, and the `AddressOf()` operator in Visual Basic. Both of these constructs serve the same purpose: to provide the address of a method (phone number) that should be called back when an event occurs. The problem with callback functions is that they do not communicate parameter/return value information or make guarantees about where they point. In other words, the person taking down your phone number cannot verify that it is in the proper format or that it even exists.

With the .NET Framework, callback functions have evolved into delegates. Delegates differ from callback functions in three respects:

1. They are type-safe, which means that they make guarantees about the parameters they expect (the phone number is in the correct format).
2. The CLR will always ensure that they point to a valid class method (the phone number exists).
3. They allow for multicasting, which means that you can specify a chain of methods in one or many different objects and locations that should be called back. This would be equivalent to leaving numerous phone numbers at your friend's place and having him call all of them back when he got home.

A delegate is a class that inherits from the `System.MulticastDelegate` class and wraps the callback functions you specify. By acting as a buffer between the real callback function and its caller, it can provide the guarantees and services listed above.

Delegates also remove one notable limitation of C++ function pointers and `AddressOf()`: They can point to a class's method, whereas traditional callback schemes only allow a global function to be used. You may be wondering how delegates handle a scenario in which a callback class has been deallocated. Remember that because both the class and the delegate are running within the CLR, such a situation will never occur. The class will never be garbage collected if a delegate is wrapping one of its methods.

CONCEPTS

Example: The AlarmClock Class

We illustrate delegates through a class called `AlarmClock`, which "wakes up" a client application after a given period of time. To wake up client applications (to call them back when it is time), `AlarmClock` must first define a delegate that clients will use to request wakeup calls:

```
public delegate void WakeMeUp(DateTime mTime);
```

As we will see, this definition prescribes that clients must provide the `AlarmClock` class with a method that accepts a `DateTime` structure (`AlarmClock` will populate this structure with the time when the client was woken up).

Once `AlarmClock` wakes up the application by invoking the delegate, the client can do whatever it wants with the `DateTime` structure (print it on the screen, write it to a file, etc.). To request a wake-up call, `AlarmClock` exposes a method called `RequestWakeup`:

```
public void RequestWakeup(WakeMeUp wakeupFunc, int
                SecondsTillWake)
```

The first argument of this method is the delegate that we previously defined. The second parameter is the number of seconds that `AlarmClock` should wait before calling back the client application.

Building the AlarmClock class
The full `AlarmClock` source is given below.

```
using System;

namespace Alarms
{
  public class AlarmClock
  {
    public delegate void WakeMeUp(DateTime mTime);
    public void RequestWakeup(WakeMeUp wakeupFunc,
        int SecondsTillWake)
    {
      // Delay until it is time to wake the client up
      Thread.Sleep(SecondsTillWake*1000);
      // Time has expired, so wake the client up by
      // calling the delegate:
      wakeupFunc(DateTime.Now);
    }
  }
}
```

Listing 5.17 AlarmClock.cs—our alarm clock class

As shown in Listing 5.17, `RequestWakeup` delays for the specified period of time before waking up the client application by calling the provided delegate:

```
wakeupFunc(DateTime.Now);
```

Remember that delegates are really classes deriving from `System.MulticastDelegate`. This being the case, it doesn't seem as if the line above should compile; you can't invoke a class in such a manner. What you're seeing, however, is some trickery by the C# compiler. Behind the scenes, the compiler is calling the `Invoke()` method of `System.MulticastDelegate`, which calls whatever method(s) the delegate wraps. You can confirm this by using ILDASM to inspect the generated IL code.

The Client
Compile the `AlarmClock` class into a Class Library assembly and then consider the following code that uses it.

```
using System;
using Alarms;

public class MyClass
{
  static void Wakeup(DateTime mTime)
  {
    Console.WriteLine("I got my wakeup call at:");
    Console.WriteLine(mTime.ToString());
  }

  public static int Main()
  {
    AlarmClock mClock;
    mClock = new AlarmClock();
    AlarmClock.WakeMeUp WakeUpCall = null;
    WakeUpCall = new AlarmClock.WakeMeUp(Wakeup);
    Console.WriteLine("Requested Wakeup Call...");
    mClock.RequestWakeup(WakeUpCall,3);
    return 0;
  }
}
```

Listing 5.18   Alarmclient.cs—our alarm client application

As the highlighted code in Listing 5.18 illustrates, a delegate must be constructed before we can request a wakeup call from `AlarmClock`. Unlike `AlarmClock`, which *accepts* a delegate, the client application that *provides* one does not use the `delegate` keyword. Instead, it first declares a method whose signature matches that of the delegate:

```
void Wakeup(DateTime mTime).
```

Next, the client application creates a delegate that "wraps" the method. In C# you create a delegate as you would a class by using the new keyword (remember that behind the scenes a delegate is a class). When declaring a delegate, you pass it the method that it will wrap:

```
WakeUpCall = new AlarmClock.WakeMeUp(Wakeup);
```

By employing this roundabout process, C# can ensure that the method being wrapped by the delegate accepts the same parameters as the delegate itself. If you were to modify `WakeupFunction()` so that it accepted an integer instead of a `DateTime` structure, C# would inform you that:

```
error CS0123: Method 'MyClass.Wakeup1(int)' does not match
delegate 'void Alarms.AlarmClock.WakeMeUp(System.DateTime)'
```

Such compile-time checking is in contrast to the ambiguous function pointers in C++ or `AddressOf()` in VB, which cannot ensure that callback functions accept the proper number (and type) of parameters. As you can see, the type-safe nature of delegates leads to a more robust notification scheme.

Compile and run the client application in Listing 5.18, and you will see the following output:

```
Requested Wakeup Call...
I got my wakeup call at:
5/3/2002 1:58:05 PM
```

Listing 5.19   Application output

Three seconds after the first line of the output is printed, the client application will be awoken by the `AlarmClock` class and will display the second and third lines.

But Is It Asynchronous?

You could argue (correctly) that the `AlarmClock` class in Listing 5.17 does not facilitate asynchronous notification. After all, during the delay period, the client is blocked while waiting for the wakeup call and can't do anything. In other words, the behavior just illustrated is synchronous and not asynchronous. It would be similar to phoning a friend and then waiting on hold for a couple of hours until he or she got home.

To provide truly asynchronous behavior, the `RequestWakeup()` method should return immediately to the client and then invoke the delegate at some point after that. This is a more involved procedure that requires either using a thread in the `AlarmClock` class to return to the client immediately or utilizing *asynchronous delegates,* whereby the CLR uses threads implicitly to accomplish the same thing. For the sake of brevity we have omitted these more complex approaches; however, a truly asynchronous `AlarmClock` class can be found at ⌁CS050008. (Note that there are several Timer classes in the BCL that will wake you up at regular intervals, and so there is really no need to write your own `AlarmClock`.)

Delegate Chaining

One of the most powerful features of delegates is that they can wrap a "chain" of methods, all of which will be called when the delegate is invoked. In most .NET languages, delegate chains are constructed by means of the `Combine()` method of the `Delegate` class found in the BCL library. In C#, however, the construction of delegate chains is syntactically cleaner because the compiler overloads the + operator for the delegate class (operator overloading is covered in Chapter 6). The partial code listing below illustrates delegate chaining in C#. The full version can be found at ⌁CS050009.

```
static void Wakeup1(DateTime mTime)
{
  Console.WriteLine("W1: I got my wakeup call at:");
  Console.WriteLine(mTime.ToString());
}

static void Wakeup2(DateTime mTime)
{
  Console.WriteLine("W2: I got my wakeup call at:");
  Console.WriteLine(mTime.ToString());
}

public static void Main()
{
  AlarmClock.WakeMeUp WakeUpCalls = null;
  WakeUpCalls = new AlarmClock.WakeMeUp(Wakeup1);
  WakeUpCalls += new AlarmClock.WakeMeUp(Wakeup2);
  mClock.RequestWakeup(WakeUpCalls,3);
}
```

Listing 5.20 Delegate chaining in C#

You can, if you want, use the `Chain()` and `Combine()` methods to construct delegate chains in C#, as is required by other .NET languages. In fact, this is what the C# compiler is doing behind the scenes when you use the + operator. Inspecting the IL code of the program above using

ILDASM confirms this. Just as you can add a method to a delegate chain by means of the + operator, you can remove methods using the minus (–) operator.

Because the delegate now wraps two methods (`Wakeup1` and `Wakeup2`), if you compile and run the code in Listing 5.20, you will see the following output:

```
W1: I got my wakeup call at:
5/3/2002 2:18:28 PM
W2: I got my wakeup call at:
5/3/2002 2:18:28 PM
```

Listing 5.21   Delegate chaining output

Keep in mind that the `AlarmClock` class that actually invokes the delegate has no idea it is calling a chain of methods. As you will recall from our earlier discussion, the C# compiler is calling the delegate's `Invoke()` method behind the scenes. At this point the CLR intercedes, determines that the delegate wraps a chain of methods, and calls them accordingly.

Events

The event concept is closely related to the asynchronous nature of delegates. An event is a block of code that is executed when something occurs. VB6, for example, is an event-driven programming language; a large portion of VB development consists of writing code to handle events that are raised by the objects in one's application. To display a message box when a button is clicked, for example, you insert the following code in the Button's click event within the VB6 IDE:

```
Private Sub Button1_Click()
  MsgBox("Button was clicked.")
End Sub
```

Listing 5.22   Responding to a button click in Visual Basic 6

`Button1_Click()` is called an *event handler* because it handles the Button's click event. It is important to realize that you rarely call the Button's event handler directly from your application; rather, the VB runtime automatically invokes `Button1_Click()` when the button is clicked.

It is not uncommon for classes to expose their own events. For example, a class responsible for stock pricing may expose an event named `PriceChanged()`, which triggers when an underlying stock price changes. In C#, events are exposed by means of the `event` keyword.

However, before we can leverage this keyword, we must understand how events and delegates are related.

Events and Delegates

Events and delegates function in a similar manner: They both allow a component to asynchronously notify a client that something important has occurred (a stock price was changed, a database was updated, etc.). What is interesting is that delegates are the underlying architecture behind events in the .NET Framework. That is, when a class exposes an event, it is really using delegates as the callback mechanism. Furthermore, whereas other languages such as VB.NET and JScript abstract this fact, C# does not afford such abstraction, and you must use the two concepts in conjunction in order to expose events. To this end we will demonstrate how we would write an event-enabled class in C#.

Example: Events in C#

In this example we will write a class called StockInfo that exposes an event called PriceChanged(). Predictably, this event should fire when a stock price changes (although in our example it will fire repeatedly in two-second intervals). To write an event in C# (or, more accurately, to write a class that exposes an event), you must first give the class a delegate that takes two parameters.

```
public delegate void PriceChangedDelegate(Object o, Price
EventArgs p);
```

Listing 5.23   Event syntax in C#

A description of these parameters follows:

1. Object: The first parameter of the delegate contains the object that invoked the event (usually this is the class itself, StockInfo in our case).
2. A class that inherits from System.EventArgs: The second parameter is a class that contains any information the event must communicate. In this example our event must communicate a double parameter called price, and even though price is simply a double, we will nonetheless need to construct an entire class that will house the double as a public member variable.

The important thing to understand when using events in C# *is that the parameters of an event are communicated by means of a single class that contains public member variables corresponding to the event parameters.* If, for example, we want an event that communicates two parameters—a stock symbol and a stock price—then we would need a class with two public members: a double for price and a string symbol. Because we need to communicate only one parameter, however, all we need is a class that inherits from System.EventArgs, with a public member variable called Price.

Building the EventArg Class
Create a new source file (call it StockInfo.cs) and add the code in Listing 5.24 to it.

```
public class PriceEventArgs : System.EventArgs
{
  public double Price;
  public PriceEventArgs(double StockPrice)
  {
    Price=StockPrice;
  }
}
```
Listing 5.24   The PriceEventArgs class

Having written a class that inherits from System.EventArgs, we now declare a delegate that accepts this class as its second parameter, as illustrated in Listing 5.23. Note that the second method is a constructor, which we will discuss in Chapter 6.

Think about what a client could do if it was called back with such a delegate. First, it could determine who invoked the delegate by inspecting the Object parameter. Second, it could scrutinize the PriceEventArgs class, which happens to contain a member variable called Price. (That is why the Price variable has to be public in Listing 5.24, so that clients can retrieve the stock price.)

Writing an Event-Enabled Class
We are now in a position to write an event-enabled class in C#. The main point is that the event declaration is prefixed with the PriceChangedDelegate we just created. This is in contrast to languages such as VB where an event is declared in a method-like fashion with parameters (e.g., public event PriceChanged(ByVal price as double)). To raise (or fire) the event from the class, we simply call the delegate using the same technique we used in Listing 5.17. These points are highlighted in Listing 5.25.

```
public class Stockinfo{
  public delegate void PriceChangedDelegate(Object o,
```

```
      PriceEventArgs p);
  public event PriceChangedDelegate PriceChanged;
  public void Start()
  {
    PriceEventArgs price = new PriceEventArgs(100.00);
    // Continually loop and call the PriceChanged() event
    while (true) {
      PriceChanged(this,price);
      Thread.Sleep(2000);
      price.Price++;
    }
  }
}
```

Listing 5.25   The StockInfo class

The `StockInfo` class in Listing 5.25 exposes an event called `PriceChanged()` that is continually invoked when the class's `Start()` method is called. Before we demonstrate how to use this event from C#, compile this class into a Class Library assembly by means of csc.exe.

Using Events from C#

To catch an event in C# you must first declare a method that handles the event (that is, the method that gets called when the class triggers the event). This method must match the method signature of the delegate in the underlying class, which for our example is a method with two parameters: `Object` and `PriceEventArgs`. Next, you must subscribe to the event, which is similar to subscribing to a delegate. Listing 5.26 outlines the process.

```
public class UseEvents
{
  // Method that will handle the event:
  static void MyPriceChanged(Object o, PriceEventArgs p)
  {
    Console.WriteLine("The stock is now: ${0}",p.Price);
  }

  static void Main()
  {
    // Declare an instance of the StockInfo class:
    Stockinfo s = new Stockinfo();
```

```
  // Subscribe to the event
  // (similar to subscribing to a delegate).
  s.PriceChanged +=  new Stockinfo.PriceChangedDelegate
    (MyPriceChanged);
  s.Start();
  }
}
```

Listing 5.26 Using events in C#

After declaring the method that handles the event (`MyPriceChanged`), the preceding code creates an instance of the `StockInfo` class. Next, it subscribes to the `PriceChanged()` events by utilizing the delegate-chaining syntax we illustrated in Listing 5.20. In effect, this line, which is highlighted in Listing 5.26, says the following to the C# compiler:

> "Please call the `MyPriceChanged()` method when `StockInfo` fires its `PriceChanged()` event."

The similarity in using delegates and events from C# is reflective of an important fact: An *event in C# is simply a delegate with a standard method signature*. Such standardization allows events to propagate across languages. For example, a VB client could very easily use our C# `StockInfo` class by means of VB's `WithEvents` keyword; doing the same with delegates would require more work. A VB client application that illustrates both approaches can be found at ⟨CN⟩CS050010.

HOW AND WHY

Why should I use events over delegates?
Both delegates and events have their respective advantages. (As we learned, an event is, in fact, a delegate with a standard method signature.) Because events are standardized, they integrate more cleanly with other .NET languages such as VB.NET; a C# event is recognized natively by the VB compiler and is exposed through user-friendly features such as IntelliSense.

Because the method signature for a delegate is completely within your jurisdiction, it can be used in custom situations where events fall short. And unlike events, delegates can be used in situations other than callback scenarios where their multicasting capabilities may be of use. Finally, as will be discussed in Chapter 7, delegates are also used to pass function pointers to native APIs such as the Win32.

What is the System.MulticastDelegate.GetInvocationList() method used for?

In our example, the WakeMeUp() delegate did not have a return value. Consider what would happen if it did. The RequestWakeup() method would invoke the delegate as follows:

```
someResult = WakeMeUp(SomeTime);
```

The delegate would invoke the method it wrapped and propagate whatever value the method returned to someResult. If the delegate wrapped a set of chained methods, however, the return value of the last method in the chain would be stored in someResult, while the rest of the return values would be discarded. This behavior is not always desirable. It could be that we would want someResult to store some combination of the values returned by the methods wrapped by the delegate. GetInvocationList() is designed to address this situation.

The GetInvocationList() method can be used to retrieve the chain of methods that a delegate wraps. Once retrieved, each method can be called individually, and its return value can be manipulated as desired. An example illustrating the GetInvocationList() method can be found at ⁿCS050011. (Note that GetInvocationList() is also useful when a delegate is wrapping multiple methods and one of these methods throws an exception; by using GetInvocationList() you can trap the exception and still call the other methods that were wrapped by the delegate.)

Are there any alternatives to delegates?

If you come from a Java background, you may realize by now that a delegate is roughly equivalent to an anonymous inner class (particularly in Swing or AWT). Both mechanisms are typically used to provide a class reference that can be handed back and forth between programs. In fact, you could replace the C# delegate mechanism with your own "callback interface." C# interfaces are discussed in detail in Chapter 6. Although using interfaces instead of delegates requires significantly more code in C# and prevents you from taking advantage of the built-in event and delegate mechanisms, it does offer some advantages in terms of guaranteeing method functionality. For more information on using interfaces instead of delegates, see ⁿCS050012.

SUMMARY

Delegates are classes that inherit from System.MulticastDelegate, and they encapsulate one or more class methods. The functions wrapped by a delegate must match the return value and arguments of the delegate signature. The += and -= operators of a delegate class can be used to add and remove the methods it wraps. When you invoke a delegate, you implicitly invoke its contained methods.

Delegates are used in the .NET Framework in place of callback functions (function pointers in C++, `AddressOf()` in Visual Basic). By acting as a buffer between functions and their callers, delegate classes can ensure that callbacks are performed in a type-safe manner. The ability of delegates to be used for callbacks and to wrap multiple methods allows for a phenomenon known as multicasting, whereby one source notifies numerous functions of a given event.

Finally, delegates are now the underlying mechanism behind events in the .NET Framework. In C#, classes can expose events by means of the `event` keyword. Events in the .NET Framework are really an abstraction for a special type of delegate that accepts two parameters: an `object`, which represents the invoker of the delegate, and a class that derives from `System.EventArgs`. The class variable contains any information that the event must communicate (usually by means of public member variables). This convention allows events to span across multiple languages in the .NET Framework.

Topic: Garbage Collection

Like a Java Virtual Machine, the CLR removes the burden of memory management from developers by destroying objects when they are no longer being referenced. For years Visual Basic programmers were usually protected from memory leaks by the VB runtime, and this luxury is now inherent in any language that targets the CLR, including C#.

Before we proceed, it is important to keep in mind that garbage collection applies only to variables that reside on the heap, that is, reference types (classes). As we learned in the previous chapter, local value types, which include primitive types such as integers, chars, and floats, as well as enumerations and structures, are placed on the stack and are immediately removed from memory when they go out of scope.

CONCEPTS

The Finalize() Method
Before an object is removed from memory, it must free any resources that it has allocated during its lifetime. In C++ this "cleanup code" is

usually housed in the object's destructor, and in VB it is placed within a method called `Class Terminate()`. Under the .NET Framework the convention is similar to Java: Cleanup code is placed within an object's `Finalize()` method, which is called just before the object is garbage collected by the framework. `Finalize()` is a method in the `System.Object` class from which all other .NET classes derive.

Given this convention, it may seem odd that you do not write `Finalize()` methods in C#, but instead utilize a destructor syntax similar to that of C++. A destructor is denoted by placing a tilde character (~) in front of the class name. For example, given a class named `Foo`, a destructor would look as follows:

```
public class Foo
{
   ~Foo ()
   {
      // Place cleanup code here.
      Console.WriteLine("I'm being destroyed!");
   }
}
```

Listing 5.27   Destructors in C#

Behind the scenes, however, the compiler has taken the code inside the destructor and placed it within the class's `Finalize()` method (something you can verify by using the ILDASM tool to examine the resulting assembly). Nevertheless, the intended behavior is the same: The cleanup code within the destructor is called just before the object is destroyed by the CLR. The C# compiler will also mimic C++ destructor behavior in one other respect: If the class inherits from another class, the compiler will insert code to call the base class's `Finalize()` method after your cleanup code has executed. This would be equivalent to having a class's destructor call its parent destructor once it had executed, a service provided automatically by C++ compilers.

When should I write a destructor?

Given the simplicity of the destructor syntax in Listing 5.27, you may be tempted to write destructors for all your classes. Certainly, freeing a class's resources seems like a necessary and responsible task to perform. However, if we consider the issue for a moment, we find an interesting paradox: How do we "free" a class's resources, given that everything in the .NET Framework (including the class's resources) is garbage collected for us? The following code demonstrates this concern more clearly.

```
public class Foo
{
  private int[] myList;
  Foo()
  {
    // Allocate an array of 5000 strings:
    myList = new int[5000];
  }
  ~Foo ()
  {
    // We should destroy the array here, but how?
  }
}
```

Listing 5.28   Freeing resources in C#

The class in Listing 5.28 has a private array of integers named myList. Within the class's constructor we dimension the array, which reserves space for five thousand integer elements on the heap. (Note that a constructor in C# is denoted via a method with the same name as the class and runs when the class is instantiated.) Accordingly, within the class's destructor we should release the resources of the class, which requires that we destroy the array. But how exactly do we do this? Unlike C++, C# does not have a delete operator to reclaim memory on the heap.

As you might have guessed, there is no way to explicitly delete entities in C# because, like our class itself, reference types are also garbage collected. In other words, when the Foo class in Listing 5.28 is garbage collected, the CLR will also destroy any internal resources onto which it is holding, because, like the class, they are no longer being referenced. The by-product of this behavior is that a class's resources are also garbage collected, which shields class authors from the complexities of resource release to begin with. Why, then, would we ever write a class destructor, given that the CLR does our work for us?

The answer is that numerous cleanup operations fall outside the realm of garbage collection and are therefore not performed automatically by the CLR. The closing of a database connection is a good example. If our Foo class in Listing 5.28 opened a database connection upon instantiation, we would want to close it before the class was destroyed. Because the CLR does not know how to close database connections (there are different data access models with differing conventions), it is appropriate to place this operation within a destructor. In other words, *resources that cannot be tracked by garbage collection, such as data-*

base connections, device handles, and communication objects (socket connections, etc.), should be released explicitly by means of a destructor. (Of course, you may include this cleanup code in a try-catch-finally block within your main class methods, in which case you would never have to write a destructor.)

Nondeterministic Finalization

Although it is true that objects are destroyed when they are no longer being referenced, under the .NET Framework there is no guarantee as to when this actually happens. In other words, the time between when an object is last referenced and its destruction can vary. If the processor's workload is heavy, the garbage collector may not get around to destroying an object until long after it has no longer been referenced. If the object has allocated expensive resources, it will hold on to them unnecessarily for this extended period of time. This unpredictable behavior is referred to as *nondeterministic finalization*. An illustration of this phenomenon is given in Listing 5.29.

```
using System;

public class Foo {
  ~Foo () {
    // Print out a message when the class is destroyed
    Console.WriteLine("I was garbage collected!");
  }
}

class Class1
{
  static void SomeMethod()
  {
    Foo f = new Foo();
  }

  static void Main()
  {
    // Call the following method that creates
    // an instance of the class:
    SomeMethod();

    // Start printing out numbers 0-10000
    for (int k=0; k<=10000;k++)
```

```
    {
      Console.WriteLine(k);
    }
  }
}
```

Listing 5.29   An illustration of nondeterministic finalization

The code in Listing 5.29 illustrates the unpredictable timing of the CLR's garbage collector. The first line in Main() calls SomeMethod(), which creates an instance of the Foo class named f and then returns back to Main(). Because f has gone out of scope, it is no longer being referenced and must be destroyed the next time the CLR's garbage collector runs. In the meantime, Main() starts printing out numbers 1 to 10,000.

Save the code in Listing 5.29 in a file called GCollect.cs and compile it using the C# compiler. Next, run the application by executing the following line at the command prompt:

```
GCollect >numbers.txt
```

The preceding syntax may be unfamiliar to some developers. By appending >numbers.txt to our execution command, we are telling our application that any screen output is to be redirected to a file called numbers.txt. This technique is referred to as *piping* to a file and can be very useful when you want to trap screen output to a text file.

If you examine the numbers.txt file that was created (using a text editor such as Notepad), you will see it contains a list of numbers. If you do a search for "garbage," however, you will find something like the following:

```
1933
1934
1935
I was garbage collected!
1936
1937
1938
```

Listing 5.30   Application output

To understand what is happening, let's consider Listing 5.29 once again. After Main() calls SomeMethod(), it begins outputting numbers to the screen (it really writes them to numbers.txt because we have piped the application's output to this file). Remember, however, that the f variable must still be garbage collected. When the CLR's garbage collector runs, it calls the Foo.Finalize() method, which interrupts the stream of numbers that Main() is printing. In the output in Listing 5.30, the Finalize() method interrupted Main() between printing numbers 1935 and 1936.

If you execute GCollect.exe numerous times and examine the numbers.txt file it produces, you will see that the CLR's garbage collector interrupts Main() at different points on each run (in five iterations we got values of 1935, 3766, 2172, 1661, and 2186). This exercise demonstrates that you can never be certain as to when an unreferenced object will be destroyed; it all depends on when the CLR's garbage collector next executes. In other words, the execution of the garbage collector is *nondeterministic*.

Dispose() and SuppressFinalization()

Nondeterministic finalization may not seem particularly noteworthy. After all, what does it matter that an object is unnecessarily kept alive for some period of time as long as it is eventually destroyed? The answer is that objects which have allocated expensive resources (database connections and communication channels) should be able to release them in a more timely manner.

Microsoft's solution is to have classes expose a method that clients must call explicitly when they are finished using objects. By placing cleanup code within this method as opposed to Finalize(), resources can be freed immediately and do not depend on the next execution of the garbage collector. Under the .NET Framework, the convention is for a class to implement a special interface called IDisposable.

We will cover interface implementation in Chapter 6, but basically by implementing this interface a class agrees to provide a special method called Dispose(), which frees resources. When clients are finished using a class, they call this method to explicitly release resources, rather than relying on the unpredictable timings of garbage collection.

The problem with this approach is that you are left in the precarious situation of hoping that clients call your Dispose() method. If they do not, expensive resources will never be freed, which can be as problematic as the original dilemma of having them freed in an untimely fashion. The solution to this problem requires using the SuppressFinalization() method found in the System.GC class.

Under this approach, objects have two methods that free resources: Dispose() and Finalize(). Depending on the client's actions, resource release can proceed in one of two ways:

1. The client calls Dispose(), and the Dispose() method releases the object's resources and calls GC.SuppressFinalization(), informing the CLR that Finalize() should not be called.
2. The client forgets to call Dispose(), and when the object is garbage collected, the CLR calls Finalize(), which releases the object's resources.

In the best case, a client calls Dispose() after using your object, and resources are freed immediately. In the worst case, a client forgets to call Dispose(), and the garbage collector eventually calls Finalize(). The following code demonstrates this hybrid approach.

```
// Note the syntax for implementing an interface.
// We'll explain this concept in Chapter 6.
public class Foo : IDisposable
{
  private void CleanUp()
  {
    // Cleanup resources (database connections, etc) here.
  }
  public void IDisposable.Dispose()
  {
    // Free resources:
    CleanUp();
    // No need for CLR to call Finalize, so don't let it:
    GC.SuppressFinalize(this);
    Console.WriteLine("Client called Dispose!");
  }
  ~Foo ()
  {
    // Client did not call Dispose!, free resources:
    CleanUp();
    Console.WriteLine("Client didn't call Dispose().");
    Console.WriteLine("So I was garbage collected.");
  }
}
```

Listing 5.31   Dispose() and garbage collection

The GC.SuppressFinalize(this) line informs the CLR that the object has released its resources and that the CLR should not call

Finalize(). As with C++ and Java, the this construct in C# refers to the current object instance on which the method is executing (equivalent to me in VB).

In addition to guarding against a client's failure to call Dispose(), you should also handle clients who might call a Dispose() method multiple times. In Listing 5.31 this would translate into determining whether resources have already been freed in the CleanUp() method.

Performance Issues

Keep in mind that you only have to implement Finalize() when an object requires explicit notification of its destruction. Implementing Finalize() unnecessarily can significantly degrade performance. If a client instantiates a five thousand–element array of "finalizable" objects, for example, the CLR must call Finalize() explicitly against every element. Because of this behavior, finalizable objects are destroyed later than their nonfinalizable counterparts, an implementation detail of the framework that we discuss at ᴄɴCS050013. As a result of their demoted status, finalizable objects can unnecessarily prolong the destruction of other objects to which they have references.

Using Disposable Objects in C#

Clients that use disposable objects (i.e., objects that have implemented the IDisposable interface) should call Dispose() on the object after they have finished using it. In C# this task can be performed automatically by means of the using statement (not to be confused with the using *directive,* which references namespaces).

The using statement defines a block of code and declares an object (or objects) that can be used within that block. When the block finishes executing, the C# compiler automatically calls Dispose() on all the objects that were declared in the using statement. Code that employs this technique against our Foo class from Listing 5.31 is given below.

```
class Class1
{
  static void SomeMethod()
  {
  using (Foo f = new Foo())
  {
    // Do operations with Foo()
  }
  // f.Dispose() is called here.
}
```

```
static void Main()
{
  SomeMethod();
  for (int k=0; k<=10000;k++)
  {
    Console.WriteLine("{0}", k);
  }
}
}
```

Listing 5.32 C#'s using statement

Listing 5.32 overhauls our garbage collection example in order to take advantage of Foo's new functionality. By placing our declaration of Foo within the using statement, we let the C# compiler worry about calling Dispose(), which it does immediately after the using code block finishes executing. Thus, if you compile and run the code in Listing 5.32, the class's resources will always be released in a timely manner at the same point. Compile and run the application, and you will discover that Dispose() is called before any numbers are printed in the Main() method.

Similar to Value Types
The characteristics behind the using statement—that objects are released once they go out of scope—is very similar to the properties of a value type variable. The following code illustrates the similarity.

```
using (Foo f = new Foo())
{
  int a;
  // Do operations with a and f
  // both a and f are released here.
}
```

Listing 5.33 Similarities between Dispose() and value types

Like the integer value type a, the reference type f will be destroyed once the code block finishes executing. Remember, however, that Dispose() does not destroy the class itself; it simply releases any resources that the class is holding on to. The class itself (Foo, in this case) still has to undergo garbage collection by the CLR.

Declaring Multiple Objects in a Using Block
It is also possible to declare multiple objects of the same type within a using statement:

```
using (Foo f1 = new Foo(), f2=new Foo())
{
  // Do operations with f1 and f2
}
// both f1.Dispose() and f2.Dispose() are called here
```

Listing 5.34   Declaring multiple objects in Dispose()

The `using` construct in Listing 5.34 declares two objects, `f1` and `f2`, which can be used within the code block. Outside the block, both their respective `Dispose()` methods are called. Unfortunately, the `using` construct supports only one type at a time. In other words, the following code is not permissible in C#:

```
using (Foo f1 = new Foo(), Calc c1=new Calc())
{
    // Error, cannot use different types in one using statement
}
```

Listing 5.35   Limitation of the using statement.

However, this limitation is easily rectified by employing two `using` statements before the code block, as illustrated in Listing 5.36.

```
using (Foo  f1 = new Foo())
using (Calc c1 = new Calc())
{
   // Use f1 and c1
}
// Both f1.Dispose() and c1.Dispose() are called here
```

Listing 5.36   Multiple types with the using statement

Remember that the luxury of the `using` statement—the fact that `Dispose()` is invoked automatically for you by the compiler—is specific to C#. When you develop in other .NET languages, such as VB and managed C++, you must make this call manually. In Chapter 1 when we claimed that C# was the native language of the CLR because of its syntactical amenities specific to .NET, this is one of the reasons we had in mind.

Advance Garbage Collection

Although our explanation of garbage collection accurately reflects the workings of the CLR underneath the hood, matters are more complex. For example, exactly how and when does the CLR determine that an object is no longer being referenced? Although we have alluded to the concept of nondeterminism, whereby an object's time of destruction can fluctuate, what is the algorithm that drives the CLR's memory-release mechanism?

Furthermore, during this uncertain period when an object's destruction is pending, can we "rescue" and utilize the object if desired? Understanding these matters suddenly plunges developers into the intricate details of CLR, such as generations, f-queues, weak references, and so on. For a more involved discussion of garbage collection under the .NET Framework, see ⚙CS050014.

HOW AND WHY

Can I prevent an object from being destroyed in its Finalize() method?
The CLR garbage collects objects when they are no longer being referenced. It is possible (although unlikely) for one to establish a reference to the object in its own Finalize() method. This could involve setting some static variable to the object instance, as demonstrated by the following code:

```
~Foo() {
  someGlobalVariable = this;
}
```

Listing 5.37 *Establishing a reference to an object inside of Finalize()*

As a result of this assignment, a reference to the object now exists, and it can no longer be collected. Thus, the object has gone through the unique cycle of having been alive, deemed okay to be destroyed (dead), and then being alive again. This fortunate change in the object's fate is called *Resurrection*. Information on this advanced and rarely used technique can be found at ⚙CS050015.

Can I force the garbage collector to destroy outstanding objects?
Although the CLR will run the garbage collector automatically from time to time, you can run it explicitly by using the GC.Collect() method found in the BCL. However, there are some side effects to calling this method, such as the suspension of any other threads that are running within the application. For details see ⚙CS050016.

SUMMARY

Automatic memory management in the .NET Framework is performed by the CLR, which destroys objects when they are no longer being referenced by periodically running its garbage collector. C# classes that require explicit notification of their destruction must implement a class destructor, which is translated into a `Finalize()` method by the compiler behind the scenes.

Although the garbage collector will call an object's `Finalize()` method after it has last been referenced, it makes no guarantee as to the time between these two events. As a result, objects that have allocated resources might hold on to them well after the object is no longer being used. To remedy this situation you should implement an interface called `IDisposable`, which exposes a method named `Dispose()` that a client can call explicitly when it has finished utilizing the object.

Dealing with `IDisposable`-enabled objects in C# is made easy by means of the `using` statement. This statement can be utilized to declare objects in conjunction with a code block. Once the code block finishes executing, C# will automatically call the `Dispose()` methods on relevant objects.

Chapter Summary

In this chapter we examined the various language features in the .NET Framework. We looked at attributes, which are nonprogrammatic code statements that influence application behavior by embedding additional metadata into an assembly. An assembly's metadata can be retrieved by means of reflection, the second topic of this chapter. Reflection can be used when you have no prior knowledge of an assembly and wish to call its classes dynamically at runtime.

Delegates are the .NET equivalents of C/C++ function pointers and are most often used to facilitate asynchronous notification between a component and a client. Delegates are also used in conjunction with the `event` keyword in C#, which allows classes to expose custom events that the client can plug into.

The final topic of this chapter, garbage collection, is a service afforded to all programs executing within the CLR. Garbage collection presents some new issues for developers, most notably for C and C++ programmers who were previously burdened with the responsibility of memory management. C# classes that wish to release resources before they are garbage collected must do so through a class destructor, which the compiler translates into a special method called `Finalize()`.

In the following chapters we will see some of these language features in practice. Attributes, for example, will be used in Chapter 7 to call Win32 DLL functions from the managed environment.

Chapter 6

OBJECT-ORIENTED PROGRAMMING (OOP)

C# applications draw upon the Base Class Libraries (BCL) for functionality. The name of the BCL reflects its contents, for it consists primarily of *classes*. Virtually anything you do in .NET—from writing a desktop application to constructing a web service—involves the use of a class in some fashion. Moreover, for more advanced .NET operations, such as the construction of a custom exception or attribute, you must leverage object-oriented programming (OOP) features such as class and interface inheritance.

In this chapter we examine the class and OOP features exposed by C#. As we stated at the beginning of this book, C# is a component-based language that makes it easy to write and extend classes in the .NET Framework. Like C++ and Java, C# exposes standard OOP features such as inheritance (the ability for a class to extend another class), polymorphism (the ability to separate an interface from its implementation), and encapsulation (the ability for objects to hide certain methods and instance variables from other objects). Developers not familiar with these concepts may want to consult the quick refresher at ⌖CS060001.

In addition to requisite OOP features, C# exposes some advanced class constructs that may be new even to seasoned C++ and Java developers. New features in the C# world include class indexers, cast overloading, and native syntax elements for class properties.

This chapter also examines the nonclass types available in C#. These include interfaces, which form contracts between clients and components by prescribing the methods that an implementation class must expose, and structures, which are similar to classes except that they are value types and are stored on the stack.

Topic: Classes and Objects

A *class* encapsulates data and defines the operations that can be performed on the data. An *object* is an instance of a particular class. The System.String class, for example, is a class that defines behavior for handling character data. On the other hand, the object name defined by System.String name="Rob"; is an instance of the String class.

Usually, you cannot use a class without first creating an instance of the class. The exceptions, as we saw in Listing 1.4, are static methods defined by the static keyword, which can be applied to methods so that they are callable on the class name as opposed to an object instance. For example, because the Console.WriteLine() method is static, we can say Console.Writeline("simple") without creating a Console class.

CONCEPTS

Members

A class consists of *members*. In C# there are four primary types of members that a class can house:

1. *Methods,* such as WriteLine(), which allow a sequence of instructions to be invoked against the class. Usually, a method provides a service that is useful to a client application, such as outputting information to the screen or performing a computation.
2. *Fields,* which a class uses to store information. Most often, fields are not accessible to client applications. As we will see, their visibility is often set to *private*. We will revisit visibility in the next concept.
3. *Properties,* which allow clients to retrieve useful information about the class. Although properties are analogous to fields, as we will see, they allow for a better encapsulation of data.
4. *Constructors,* which are methods that are invoked the first time the class is created. Constructors are useful for performing initialization operations on the class.

In this topic we will examine each of these member types in turn, along with the options that C# makes available when you write them. Before we do this, however, we must understand the important concept of visibility.

Visibility

The members of a class can be declared with varying levels of visibility. The visibility of a member determines which code can and cannot access that member. In C# there are five levels of visibility, which are listed in Table 6.1.

public	Member is accessible to everyone.
internal	Member is accessible only to callers within the same assembly.
protected	Member is accessible only to derived classes.
internal protected	Member is accessible to callers in the assembly and derived classes.
private	Member is accessible only to the class itself.

Table 6.1   C# visibility modifiers

The visibility modifiers in Table 6.1 can be applied to methods, fields, properties, and constructors. In the absence of a modifier, all C# members default to `private`. Thus, in the following code, the `Bar` field can be called only by the class itself, whereas the `Foo()` method can be called by any class that derives from `Fruit` (as well as the `Fruit` class itself).

```
class Fruit
{
  int Bar;
  protected void Foo() {}
}
```

Listing 6.1   Visibility modifiers

The `internal` and `public` modifiers can also be applied to a class itself, but the other modifiers are reserved for class members only. In the absence of one of these modifiers, a C# class defaults to `internal` visibility. Thus, in Listing 6.1 the `Fruit` class is accessible only to callers within the same assembly.

As we will see, visibility modifiers permit *encapsulation* by allowing you to prescribe which aspects of a class are accessible to clients. Furthermore, they have special uses when applied to constructors, which we will now examine.

Constructors

A constructor is a method that is executed when a class is instantiated. As we saw in Listing 5.24, a constructor is simply a method with the same name as the class itself. A constructor does not have to take any parameters, as shown in the following code.

```
class Fruit
{
  private string fType;
  public Fruit()
  {
    fType="Pear";
  }
}
```

Listing 6.2 A class constructor

As a result of the constructor in Listing 6.2, anytime the Fruit class is instantiated, the fType field is initialized to "Pear." Constructors often house initialization code, such as the creation of database connections, sockets, etc.

Parameterized Constructors

It is also possible to pass information to a constructor by means of a *parameterized constructor*. The following code illustrates such a constructor.

```
class Fruit
{
  private string fType;
  public Fruit(string fruitType)
  {
   fType=fruitType;
  }
}

Fruit f = new Fruit(); // WILL NOT WORK!
Fruit f = new Fruit("Apple"); // That's better
```

Listing 6.3 A class constructor

The constructor in Listing 6.3 stipulates that an instantiation of the Fruit class must be accompanied by a string variable. A subtle by-product of parameterized constructors is that you lose the default no-argument constructor, which C# gives the class implicitly. (We will revisit the default constructor in a following concept.) In other words, by writing a parameterized constructor you force the client to instantiate your class according to a certain convention. For example, as depicted in Listing 6.3, instances of Fruit must be created with a string variable.

Multiple Constructors

To make the initialization process more versatile, a class will often have both parameterized and no-argument constructors:

```
class Fruit
{
  private string fType;
  public Fruit() {
    fType="Pear"
  }
  public Fruit(string fruitType)
  {
    fType=fruitType;
  }
  public Fruit(int fruitType)
  {
    if (fruitType == 1) fType = "Apple";
    if (fruitType == 2) fType = "Orange";
  }
}

Fruit f = new Fruit();
Fruit f = new Fruit("Banana");
Fruit f = new Fruit(1);
```

Listing 6.4 Numerous constructors in a class

The Fruit class in Listing 6.4 has multiple constructors. Thus, the class can be instantiated without any arguments or can be provided with a string or integer upon creation. At compile time C# matches the provided arguments with the appropriate constructor (and raises an error if no matching constructor is found). Notice that all of our constructors thus far have been marked public, an occurrence that we will revisit in a moment. Also note that it is not possible to specify a return value for a constructor.

Destructor

Whereas a constructor is called when an object is created, a *destructor* is invoked when the object is destroyed. In C++, destructors are denoted by prefixing the class name with the tilde character (e.g., ~Fruit()). Although this naming convention is still employed in C#, as we saw in Chapter 5 (Listing 5.27), destructors translate into Finalize() methods behind the scenes. This method is invoked before the object is destroyed, thus simulating destructor-style behavior. Since destructors were discussed in Chapter 5, we will not reexamine them here.

Tangent: Restrictions on Static Members
As we saw in Chapter 1 (Listing 1.4), applying the static modifier to a member of a class allows access to that member without instantiating the class. An important rule governing the use of the static keyword is that *static methods cannot modify non-static variables (fields)*. Phrased alternatively, a static method can only modify a class's static variables. This restriction is illustrated in Listing 6.5.

```
class Fruit
{
  private string fType;
  static private string Color;
  public static void MakeAPear()
  {
    Color = "yellow";   // O.K.
    fType="Pear";       // Problem!
  }
}
```

Listing 6.5 *Restrictions on static types*

Because the MakeAPear() method is static, it cannot modify non-static members such as fType, but it can modify static members such as Color. This limitation is important when you consider the more esoteric topic of *static constructors* (and is obviously important when you write normal static methods). If you try to write a method like Listing 6.5, the C# compiler will generate an error message: "An object reference is required for the non-static field, method, or property 'Fruit.fType' ". In other words, you need to create an instance of the Fruit class before the fType field has any meaning.

Static Constructors
Like their "normal" counterparts, static constructors can be used for initialization operations. Unlike a normal constructor, a static one cannot modify non-static variables (which makes sense, given the rule governing static members). Another difference is that a static constructor is only called the *first* time an instance of the class is created or when the

class is referenced in a static fashion. The following code clarifies this behavior.

```
class Fruit
{
  public static string fType;
  static Fruit()
  {
    fType="Pear";
    Console.WriteLine("Static constructor called");
  }
  public static SomeMethod() {}
}

// Below, when does the static constructor fire?
Fruit f1= new Fruit();
Fruit f2= new Fruit();
Fruit f3= new Fruit();
```

Listing 6.6   Static constructors

Even though three instances of the Fruit class are created in Listing 6.6, the static constructor only fires when the first instance is created; therefore, the message "Static constructor called" appears only once. The static constructor will also fire (if it has not already done so) when a static member of the class is referenced. Thus, the code Fruit.SomeMethod() will also invoke the static constructor. *Note that if a class has both a static and an instance constructor, the static one will always fire first and then the instance constructor will be called.*

To recap, *a static constructor fires only once*, when the first instance of the class is created or one of its static members is referenced. A static constructor cannot accept parameters (i.e., *static parameterized constructors* are not allowed), and you cannot apply a visibility modifier to a static constructor (note the absence of a public modifier in Listing 6.6).

Private Constructors

You may wonder why you would ever make a constructor anything but public. Indeed, the benefit behind the private constructor is not always obvious. Recall from Table 6.1 that a private member can only be accessed by the class itself. When a constructor is denoted private, clients are prevented from calling it. The creation of a class, however, requires a call to the class's constructor. Therefore, by placing the private keyword in front of a constructor, you prevent a class from ever being initialized. Why would you ever want to do such a thing?

Many utility classes expose only static members. Consider the following `Calculator` class.

```
class Calculator
{
  public static int Add(int a, int b) {/*Imp omitted*/}
  public static double Cos(float angle) {/*Imp omitted*/}
  public static double Random() {/*Imp omitted*/}
  private Calculator(){}
}
```

Listing 6.7   Private constructors

All the methods in this class must be called in a static fashion (e.g., a=Calculator.Add(1,2);). Therefore, there is no reason for a client to instantiate this class, and the `private` constructor makes this clear by actively preventing instantiation. Attempts to instantiate the class raise the following compile-time error:

> 'Calculator.Calculator()' is inaccessible due to its protection level

If we did not explicitly create a `private` constructor, then C# would have added a default no-argument constructor, and users could create an instance of the class.

An example of a class that leverages the `private` constructor technique is the `Console` class in the BCL. Attempts to instantiate this class elicit the aforementioned error. The class can only be accessed statically, as we have illustrated throughout this book.

```
Console c = new Console(); // Error!
Console.WriteLine("Easy");
```

Listing 6.8   A private constructor cannot be referenced

Another common use for internal constructors is the "factory pattern" used throughout the Java classes. A "factory class" will expose a static method called getInstance() (or something similar). Internally, the factory class will create an instance of the desired class, perhaps using a `private` constructor to initialize itself, and return a reference to the calling class. This pattern abstracts object creation and can be very useful for creating certain architectures. See ⤴CS060002 for more details.

The Default Constructor

If you do not explicitly write a constructor for your class, the C# compiler will automatically create a no-argument constructor marked with `public` visibility. The constructor won't actually contain any implementation code. In fact, it's simply a convenience that allows the class to be instantiated. However, as illustrated in the `private` constructor concept previously, this "hidden" constructor can cause some unexpected headaches.

Fields

A field, sometimes called an instance variable or member variable, allows a class to store data (often referred to as storing "state"). For example, the `fType` variable in Listing 6.2 is a field that stores the type of fruit being represented by the `Fruit` class. Fields can also be `static` (Listing 6.6), which means that all instances of the class will share the field (effectively allowing them to communicate with one another). Most often, fields are marked `private` because they store information internal to the class. If a field is made nonprivate, then it can be accessed by clients.

```
class Calculator
{
  public int Sum;   // Accessible to clients
  public void AddNumber(int num)
  {
      Sum+=num;
  }
}

// Client application:
Calculator c = new Calculator();
c.AddNumber(5);
c.AddNumber(3);
Console.WriteLine("Sum is:{0}",c.Sum);
```

Listing 6.9   Public fields

Because the `Sum` variable in Listing 6.9 is `public`, it is accessible to application programs. Although fields can certainly be exposed in this manner, properties (examined next) offer a better alternative. First, a property can be configured to be read-only or write-only, in contrast to a field that is both readable and writable by clients. In Listing 6.9, for example, a client can set the `Sum` variable to an incorrect value (ideally, this variable would be read-only to clients). Second, as we will see, properties allow for a better abstraction of data.

Constant Fields
A constant field is used to store a fixed data value. By prefixing a variable with the const modifier, you can supply it with an initial value that cannot be changed thereafter.

```
class Calculator
{
   public const double PI=3.141592653589;
}

// Application program:
Console.WriteLine("PI={0}",Calculator.PI);
```

Listing 6.10   Declaring constant fields

Note that constant fields are implicitly static, which means that they must be accessed through the class name, as opposed to an object instance. There are some notable limitations with the const modifier. First, the value of a constant variable must be provided during the declaration of that variable. Second, the constant value provided must be resolvable at compile time. For example, the following declaration is not permissible:

```
class Calculator
{
   public double approx=22/7;
   public const double PI=approx;
}
```

Listing 6.11   Incorrect const usage

Because approx is a nonconstant variable (it can be changed), C# disallows the assignment. A subtle by-product of this rule is that const can only be used with value type variables (strings being the exception).

The Readonly Keyword
Because of these limitations, a more versatile version of const is exposed by way of the readonly modifier. Unlike const, readonly can be used for reference types. Furthermore, readonly variables can be initialized in the class's constructor, allowing for a more versatile initialization scheme.

```
class Calculator
{
   public readonly ArrayList fib;
   public Calculator() {
      // Initialize the ArrayList with the first 30
      // numbers in the fibonacci sequence:
      fib = new ArrayList();
      fib.Add(1); fib.Add(1);
      for (int k=2; k<=30;k++)
         fib.Add((int)fib[k-2]+(int)fib[k-1]);
   }
   public void AddNumber()
   {
      fib = new ArrayList();    // Error!
      fib.Add(1);               // O.K, but why?
   }
}
```

Listing 6.12   Creating readonly fields

The `readonly` variable in Listing 6.12 is more capable than `const`; it can be used on classes such as `ArrayList` and can be initialized in the class's constructor. Thereafter, the variable cannot be modified. It may seem odd, therefore, that we can add a number to this variable within the `AddNumber()` method.

Recall from Chapter 4 that a reference type is really a pointer to an object on the heap. Although outside the constructor you cannot modify where a `readonly` variable points, *you can modify the object to which it is pointing.* Thus, within the `AddNumber()` method we are forbidden from pointing `fib` to a new `ArrayList` object, but we can modify the `ArrayList` object to which it is already pointing (such as adding a number to it). For a contrast of the `const` and `readonly` modifiers, see CS060003.

Properties

A property is accessed in a similar manner to a `public` field. Whereas a `public` field is simply a class variable that is exposed to the client, a property value can be obtained and set by means of executable code. In C# a property is manipulated via the `set` and `get` keywords, as illustrated in the following code.

```
public class Fruit
{
```

```
    private string fType="Pear";
    public string typeOfFruit
    {
      get
      {
        return fType;
      }
      set
      {
        fType = value.ToUpper();
      }
    }
}

// Application program:
Fruit f = new Fruit();
f.typeOfFruit = "Apple";   // calls set
Console.WriteLine("Type = {0}",f.typeOfFruit); // calls get
```

Listing 6.13 Declaring C# properties

As with our previous implementations of the Fruit class, the underlying type of fruit is maintained by means of a private string field. Because it is private, this field is not accessible to clients. Instead, a client must use the typeOfFruit property to determine the type of fruit being represented. When the client references the property (that is, when he obtains its value), the code within the get block executes; in this case we simply return the value of the private field. Conversely, when the user updates the property, the code within the set block executes. The special value keyword represents the value to which the client wishes to set the property (think of it as an implicit argument on the set method call). In our implementation we convert this value into uppercase, so that if the user sets the property to "apple," the private field is set to "APPLE."

The indirection provided by properties can be very useful. First, there is no stipulation that a property must operate against a private field; its value can be computed when it is referenced (perhaps it is retrieved from a database). You can also make a property read-only by writing a get block and simply omitting a set code block. Both these characteristics are illustrated in the following Calculator class.

```
class Calculator
{
  private int []a = new int[1000];
  private int numbers=0;
```

```
public void AddNumber(int num)
{
  a[numbers]=num;
}
public int Sum
{
  get
  {
    // Compute the sum when the property
    // is accessed
    int sum=0;
    for (int k=0;k<=numbers;k++) sum+=a[k];
    return sum;
  }
}
}
```

Listing 6.14   Executable logic and properties

Anytime the `Sum` property is referenced by a client, the code within the `get` block executes and the property's value (a sum of numbers in this case) is computed in real time. Properties are also useful for performing bounds checking. For example, some data values should never be negative (e.g., age, weight, and salary). The code within a property `set` block can enforce such constraints. Also note that a property can be made write-only by means of a `set` block without an associated `get`.

Methods

The convention for writing methods in C# is virtually identical to that in C++ and Java; the method return type precedes its name (or is `void` if the method does not return a value). What is different however, are some new (optional) keywords that prescribe the manner in which a parameter is passed to a method. Most programming languages allow you to pass a variable *by reference* or *by value*. When a variable is passed by reference, modifications to the variable within the method persist when the method finishes executing. When passed by value, a variable retains its original contents after the method executes.

The Ref Keyword

In C#, value types are passed by value, and reference types are passed by reference (an easy rule to remember). To pass a value type by reference you must use the `ref` keyword (similar to the `Byref` keyword in VB).

```
class Calculator
{
  public static void Increment(ref int number)
  {
    number++;
  }
}

// Application program:
int a = 5;
Calculator.AddOne(ref a);
// a now equals 6.
```

Listing 6.15 Passing variables by reference

When a variable is passed by reference, modifications to the variable propagate outside the method. Thus, after a call to Increment(), the integer parameter is increased by one. Note that the ref keyword *must be applied on both the method and calls to the method*. The latter requirement makes it clear to a client that the variable parameter may change within the method. Also bear in mind that *a reference type cannot be passed by value*. As a result, changes to reference types within a method will always be reflected outside the method.

The Out Keyword

Usually, a variable must be initialized before it can be passed to a method. You can forgo this requirement by means of the out keyword, which informs the compiler that a method is not interested in the contents of a parameter and will only set its outgoing value. The following code illustrates this keyword.

```
class Calculator
{
  public static int SetToOne(out int number)
  {
    number = 1;
  }
}

// Application program:
int a;
```

```
Calculator.SetToOne(out a); // No error
// a now equals 1.
```

Listing 6.16   The out keyword

As a result of the `out` keyword, uninitialized variables can be passed to the `SetToOne()` method (try removing this keyword and observing the results).

C# has a number of more rarely used keywords relating to parameters and variables. These include `params`, which is used to define methods that accept a variable number of parameters (see ⌐CN⌐CS060004), and `volatile`, which is used to give multiple threads access to a single unsynchronized resource (see ⌐CN⌐CS060005).

SUMMARY

A class contains members, which may be fields, properties, or methods. Each class and its members have an associated visibility, which indicates how the class or members can be used. For example, the `public` keyword indicates that a class or member can be accessed by any code in any assembly. In contrast, the `private` keyword indicates that the member can be accessed only by the class itself.

Constructors are special methods that are used to initialize settings inside a class. A class can have zero or more constructors, each of which may take zero or more arguments. If you omit a constructor, then the C# compiler will automatically add a zero-argument public constructor to your class.

In the next topic we will look at how to extend the basic class definition.

Topic: Class Inheritance

Class inheritance is the cornerstone of object-oriented programming. Quite simply, inheritance is code reuse. Almost every nontrivial project will involve situations where two or more classes have overlapping functional requirements. Rather than repeat identical code in all the classes (increasing maintenance), you can create a class with the common functionality, often called the *base* class. Specialized classes can extend (inherit from) the base class, thus inheriting the common functions. If the common code has to change, it can be changed in the base class without modifying the specialized classes. You can further specialize a class by replacing (overriding) some functionality of the base class.

When you create an instance of a class in C#, the CLR actually creates an instance of every class from which your class derives. These "invisible" classes provide access to inherited methods and fields. For example, when you call a class's `GetType()` method to utilize the process of reflection that we examined in Chapter 5, you are actually calling the method provided by the `System.Object` class, from which all .NET classes ultimately derive. This behind-the-scenes indirection may not seem intuitive, but it is actually a very efficient mechanism for allowing access to the base class definition. This process also has some interesting side effects, as you will see later in this topic. In particular, you should pay special attention to constructors.

Inheritance is used throughout the Base Class Libraries. For example, as we saw in Chapter 4, errors in the .NET Framework are communicated through exception classes. Although the `DivideByZeroException` and `FileNotFoundException` classes represent different errors, they both inherit from the base `System.Exception` class. By treating each subclass as if it were the base class, you do not have to write separate functions to handle each type of error (i.e., you can trap any type of error by catching a generic `System.Exception`).

CONCEPTS

Inheritance in C#

In C# you can inherit from any class by using conventions similar to C++. Consider the following `Calculator` class.

```
class Calculator
{
  public int Multiply(int x, int y)
  {
    return x*y;
  }
}
```

Listing 6.17   The Calculator class

This trivial class exposes one method named `Multiply()`. We can leverage this functionality and write a more capable class called `SciCalc`, which inherits from `Calculator`. This process is illustrated in Listing 6.18.

```
class SciCalc : Calculator
{
  public int Factorial(int x)
  {
    int z=1;
    for (int k=1;k<=x;k++) z = Multiply(z,k);
    return z;
  }
}
```

Listing 6.18   Inheritance in C#

C#'s inheritance syntax is straightforward. To inherit from a class, simply append the class declaration with a colon and the name of the class from which you want to inherit. Because SciCalc inherits from Calculator, the Factorial() method in Listing 6.18 automatically has access to the Multiply() method of its parent. The SciCalc class does not have to implement this method because it is included through inheritance. (Note that C# does not support the C++ notion of protected and private inheritance or inheriting from two classes at once. For a fuller explanation and compensating ideas for C++ developers, see CS060006.)

Inheritance and System.Object
When a class does not inherit from another class (as is the case with the Calculator class in Listing 6.17), the C# compiler implicitly inherits the class from System.Object. You can make this relationship more explicit by writing class Calculator : System.Object, but the effect is the same. You should now understand what we mean when we say that every C# class eventually derives from System.Object. Remember that when the CLR constructs a class in memory, it also creates the parent class from which that class derives. Therefore, when a user instantiates the SciCalc class from Listing 6.18, an instance of Calculator is created. Similarly, when Calculator is created, an instance of its base class, System.Object, is constructed. SciCalc thus exposes the methods of its parent (Multiply()) as well as the methods of its parent's parent (ToString(), Finalize(), etc.).

As this example illustrates, the class creation process is like a line of falling dominoes; the creation of each class triggers the creation of its base, and so on. Eventually, the last domino to fall will be System.Object.

Overriding Methods in C#

In some situations the base class method isn't exactly appropriate for the derived class. The derived class may need to override (i.e., replace) the base class's methods. In C# a derived class can replace the methods of its parent by using the `new` keyword. For example, the SciCalc class from the previous example may want to replace the Calculator.Multiply() method with a more rigorous implementation. To this end it simply provides its own Multiply() method, which is declared by means of `new`.

```
class SciCalc : Calculator
{
  public new int Multiply(int x, int y)
  {
    try {
      return x*y;
    }
    catch {
      // Error during multiply (maybe overflow)
      // So return 0:
      return 0;
    }
  }
}
```

Listing 6.19   Overriding methods in C#

As a result of the new method definition, SciCalc will rely on its own Multiply() implementation instead of using its parent's. If you omit the new keyword when you override a method, C# will raise a compile-time error. In other words, the new keyword is an explicit notification to the compiler that a base class method is being replaced.

Keep in mind that the overridden method signature must match the one defined in the parent. If the parameters differ, then override is not taking place and a new method is created for the child class. For example, if the Multiply() method in Listing 6.19 accepted two longs parameters (instead of ints), SciCalc would simply house two different multiplication methods: one that multiplied integers and one that multiplied longs. The former would be implemented in the base, and the latter would be implemented in the child. Because method overriding would no longer be taking place, the second Multiply() would not be declared with the new keyword. (Incidentally, the ability of a class to house numerous methods with the same name but different parameters is called *function overloading,* a topic we investigate more thoroughly at CS060007).

Class Casting

Recall from Chapter 4 that casting is the conversion of one type into another type. For example, you can explicitly cast a long variable into an integer through the following syntax:

$$\text{MyInt = (int)MyLong;}$$

Casting can also be applied to class hierarchies. Specifically, you can cast a derived class into any one of its parents. Thus, from our previous example we could cast a `SciCalc` class into a `Calculator`.

```
SciCalc s = new SciCalc();
Calculator c = (Calculator) s;
```

Listing 6.20   Casting classes in C#

The casting of class instances—the fact that a derived cast can be treated as one of its parents—raises an interesting question. If a derived class has been cast to one of its parents and has also overridden a method of that parent, which method gets called against the casted instance? This question is more clearly demonstrated in the following code.

```
class Calculator
{
  public int Multiply(int x, int y) {
    Console.WriteLine("Calc's Multiply");
    return x*y;
  }
}

class SciCalc : Calculator
{
  public new int Multiply(int x, int y)
  {
    Console.WriteLine("SciCalc's Multiply");
    return x*y;
  }
}

// Application program
Calculator myCalc = (Calculator) new SciCalc();
int a = myCalc.Multiply(5,5);
```

Listing 6.21   Casting and method overriding

Notice that the `Multiply()` method for each class in Listing 6.21 prints out a different message to the console. After creating an instance of `SciCalc`, we assign (and cast it) to a `Calculator` variable. Finally, we call `Multiply()` on the `Calculator` variable, `myCalc`. In this case, which version of `Multiply()` gets called and, hence, what will be the output on the console? There are two lines of reasoning:

1. Because `Multiply()` is being called against a `Calculator` class, `Calculator`'s implementation gets executed and the program prints "Calc's Multiply."
2. Even though `myCalc` is a `Calculator` class, it really refers to an instance of `SciCalc`, and so `SciCalc.Multiply()` is called, and the program outputs "SciCalc's Multiply."

Those of you who reasoned (or guessed) at the first answer are correct. Since `myCalc` was declared as a `Calculator` class, the C# compiler calls `Calculator`'s implementation of `Multiply()`. In other words, *under method overriding via the new keyword, a derived method is called only against references of the derived class type*. Thus, if we wish to invoke `SciCalc.Multiply()`, we must declare a `SciCalc` variable explicitly.

```
SciCalc s = new SciCalc();
int a = s.Multiply(5,5);
```

Listing 6.22   Calling SciCalc's multiply method

Note that this mechanism is in sharp contrast to Java, where the derived class's functionality is always called.

Virtual Functions

The behavior depicted in Listing 6.21 is not always desirable. Under some (in fact, many) circumstances we would want the method of the underlying instance to be called. For example, even though `myCalc` is a `Calculator` class, it is really storing an instance of a `SciCalc` class, and thus we would want `SciCalc`'s method to be called regardless of how `myCalc` has been cast. In other words, we want calls to overridden methods to always result in the derived implementation, regardless of how the class is referenced. This behavior is accomplished by means of the `virtual` and `override` keywords as illustrated in Listing 6.23.

```
class Calculator
{
  public virtual int Multiply(int x, int y)
  {
```

```
    Console.WriteLine("Calc's calculator");
    return x*y;
  }
}

class SciCalc : Calculator
{
  public override int Multiply(int x, int y)
  {
    Console.WriteLine("SciCalc's Calculator");
    return x*y;
  }
}

// Application program
Calculator myCalc = (Calculator) new SciCalc();
int a = myCalc.Multiply(5,5); //SciCalc's multiply is called
```

Listing 6.23   The virtual and overrides keywords

The effect of the `virtual` keyword in C# is similar to that of C++. Calls to a `virtual` function result in the implementation of the underlying type that a variable is storing, as opposed to the type of class that the variable was cast to. To replace a `virtual` method in a derived class you must use the `override` keyword, as illustrated in Listing 6.23. By adding the `virtual` and `override` keywords in the preceding code, we guarantee that `SciCalc`'s multiply method gets called against the `myCalc` variable. (As a side note, if you use the `virtual` and `override` keywords, your C# classes will behave like normal Java classes.)

Polymorphism
The behavior provided by virtual functions—that calls to an overridden method will always result in the derived implementation—falls under the OOP concept of polymorphism. Polymorphism (which means "many forms") is the *dynamic binding of method invocations to a particular class.* All this definition says is that in Listing 6.23, C# determines which `Multiply()` gets called at runtime. This is because the compiler can only establish at runtime whether `myCalc` points to a `Calculator` class or a derived class, `SciCalc`.

Polymorphic behavior can be extremely useful when you are interacting with the BCL or writing classes in general. In Chapter 5, for example, we saw that a sequence of bytes in .NET is abstracted via classes such as `FileStream` and `MemoryStream`. In fact, all stream classes in .NET derive from the base `Stream` class found in the `System.IO` namespace.

Using polymorphism you can write a method that accepts a generic Stream class to manipulate a sequence of bytes. Because the method has been coded against this generic class (and because of polymorphism), it can accept as a parameter any of the Stream's children. Thus, if the user provides the method with FileStream class, the sequence of bytes will be written to disk. Conversely, if a NetworkStream class is supplied, the sequence of bytes will be sent over a communication channel. The point is that because polymorphism binds method invocations at runtime, you can code generically against a base class and still leverage the specialized functionality of the base's children.

Inheritance and Constructors

As we have stated, when you instantiate a derived class, the CLR actually creates an instance of every class in the class hierarchy. For the most part you can safely ignore these extra objects and let the C# compiler worry about implementing polymorphic or nonpolymorphic behavior based on your use of the virtual and override keywords. An exception to this rule arises when you consider the role of constructors in the world of inheritance. Specifically, you must consider how the constructors of derived classes are invoked.

By default the C# compiler calls the base class's no-argument constructor before it calls the child's constructor. Consider Listing 6.24.

```
class Fruit {
  public Fruit() {
    Console.WriteLine("Fruit's Constructor");
  }
}
class Apple : Fruit {
  public Apple(){
    Console.WriteLine("Apple's Constructor");
  }
}
class Macintosh : Apple {
  public Macintosh(){
    Console.WriteLine("Macintosh's Constructor");
  }
}

// Application program:
Macintosh m = new Macintosh();
```

Listing 6.24 Constructor chains in C#

Because each constructor prints information on the screen, when you create an instance of the `Macintosh` class, the program will output what is given in Listing 6.25.

```
Fruit's Constructor
Apple's Constructor
Macintosh's Constructor
```

Listing 6.25 Output of constructor chain

Notice that the constructors are triggered in the order of inheritance: `Fruit`, `Apple`, and, finally, `Macintosh`.

Inheritance and Parameterized Constructors
The automatic constructor behavior in Listing 6.24 works well for no-argument constructors. Unfortunately, the same behavior is not provided for parameterized constructors. Thus, the following code, although seemingly errorless, does not compile in C#.

```
class Fruit
{
  public Fruit(int i) {
    Console.WriteLine("Fruit's Constructor");
  }
}

class Apple : Fruit
{
  public Apple(int i)
  {
    Console.WriteLine("Apple's Constructor");
  }
}
```

Listing 6.26 Problematic constructor chains in C#

Attempts to compile Listing 6.26 result in the following error:

```
No overload for method 'Fruit' takes '0' arguments.
```

At first glance the source of this error may not be apparent. Recall from the constructor section in the previous topic that when you give a class a parameterized constructor, you lose the free no-argument constructor that C# gives you implicitly. We also know that when C# creates a derived class, it calls the no-argument constructor of its parent. Thus, when an Apple class is created in the preceding code, C# looks for a parameterless (no-argument) constructor for Fruit. The compiler does not find such a method, however, because we gave Fruit a parameterized constructor (and thus lost the free no-argument one). As a result, the aforementioned error is generated.

The Base Keyword
One way to overcome this problem is to simply give the Fruit class a default no-argument constructor. However, it would be preferable if we could map Apple's parameterized constructor to Fruit's. In other words, it would be nice if a = new Apple(5); called Fruit's constructor with 5 as a parameter. In essence, what we want is for parameterized constructors to be triggered in a hierarchical fashion. We can do this by means of a special keyword called base, which allows us to invoke the base class's constructor (base is roughly equivalent to the Java super keyword). As illustrated in Listing 6.27, this keyword is placed directly after the declaration of the constructor.

```
class Apple : Fruit
{
  public Apple(int i) : base(i)
  {
    Console.WriteLine("Apple's Constructor");
  }
}
```

Listing 6.27   The base keyword

Because of this small modification, Apple's parameterized constructor will successfully call Fruit's parameterized equivalent.

A stipulation enforced by some languages (but not C#) is that when a base class exposes only a parameterized constructor, the child class must expose a constructor of the same type. Listing 6.28 illustrates this requirement.

```
// The following code DOES NOT compile
class Fruit
{
  public Fruit(int i) {}
}

class Apple : Fruit
```

```
{
  public Apple() {}
}
```

Listing 6.28   Parameterized constructor rules

Because `Fruit` has only a parameterized constructor, it must be instantiated with an integer variable. Unfortunately, this code does not compile because the `Apple` class, from which `Fruit` derives, does not house an identical constructor. To fix this code we would have to give `Apple` an integer constructor equivalent to `Fruit`'s.

Another option in C# is to direct `Apple`'s no-argument constructor to `Fruit`'s parameterized version.

```
class Apple : Fruit
{
  public Apple() : base(5000)
  {}
}
```

Listing 6.29   Directing constructors

Now, anytime an `Apple` is created, `Fruit` will be implicitly initialized through its integer constructor with a parameter of 5,000.

Other Uses for the Base Keyword
Note that the `base` keyword can also be used to invoke methods on the base class. Typically, an overriding method takes advantage of the implementation provided by the base class by invoking the base method either at the beginning or end of the overriding method. For example, if you had a derived database connection class, it might make sense for its `Close()` method to call the base class implementation of the `Close()` method.

```
class SpecialDbConnection : StandardDBConnection
{
  public void Close()
  {
    // Perform close operations
    // Also close the base clase's connection:
    base.Close();
  }
}
```

Listing 6.30   Other uses for the base keyword

Thus, both Close() methods will be called (parent and child), ensuring that resources are released correctly.

Inheritance Notes
Before we dispense with the topic of inheritance, there are a few points we should make:

1. Unlike C++, in C# you are limited to inheriting from one class only (i.e., the language does not support multiple implementation inheritance).
2. The base class *does not* have to reside in the same source file as the child class. For example, it can reside in a class library assembly file (.DLL), which should be referenced prior to inheritance.
3. Because the base class can reside in an external *language-neutral* assembly, *you can inherit from classes written in other .NET languages.* As we learned in Chapter 3, this technique is referred to *as cross-language inheritance* and is a fundamentally new feature made available by the .NET Framework. For information and examples on this capability, see ⟲CS060008.
4. Class inheritance is an intrinsic part of the BCL. For example, exception classes, attributes, ASP.NET, and Windows Form classes are all built on inheritance. As we saw in Chapter 3, VS.NET will often perform inheritance on your behalf when you write various .NET applications (e.g., Windows Forms).

HOW AND WHY

How do I prevent a class from being inherited?
To prevent a class from being inherited you can declare it with the sealed modifier:

```
public sealed class Fruit {}
```

Listing 6.31 Preventing inheritance

As a result of this modifier, C# will prevent classes from deriving from Fruit. The converse of the sealed keyword is the abstract modifier, which stipulates that a class cannot be instantiated directly but must *always* be derived by other classes. Examples of both these modifiers can be found at ⟲CS060009. Note that you can also prevent a method from being inherited by declaring it with the private modifier. As we saw at the beginning of this topic, private methods are visible only to the class and cannot be accessed by derived classes or clients.

How do I disable polymorphic behavior for a virtual function?
Consider the Calculator class in Listing 6.23. Because the Multiply() method is declared with the virtual keyword, it exhibits polymorphic behavior when a child class overrides it. In some situations you may wish to nullify this behavior in the child class. In other words, even though the method has been declared virtual, you may want to replace its polymorphic properties with the normal (nonpolymorphic) behavior that you get by means of the new keyword. This is accomplished by using the virtual and new keywords in the base and child classes, respectively, as illustrated at ⚓CS060010. In essence, you end up overloading the function rather than overriding it.

How do I change the visibility of an inherited method?
When you override a method from a base class, you can change the visibility of the method provided that you follow certain rules, specifically:

1. If you used the virtual and new keywords, you cannot change visibility.
2. If you simply overrode a method, you can make the visibility wider but not narrower. For instance, if you override a private method, you can give it a visibility of internal. However, you cannot assign a visibility of private to a method that is public in the base class.

SUMMARY

Class inheritance is the ability of a class to inherit the methods and implementation code of another class, and is a fundamental concept in the C# language and the BCL. Inheritance is useful in situations where two or more classes have intersecting functionality. By placing common code in one class (called the base class) and inheriting it across other classes (called derived classes), changes to the base class are immediately reflected in the derived ones.

Inheritance can become tricky when a derived class replaces the methods in the base class. C# has two ways of dealing with this situation:

1. Method overriding by means of the new keyword. In this situation the new implementation is called only if the method is exe-

cuted directly on the derived class. If the derived class is cast to the base class, the original implementation gets called.
2. The `virtual` and `override` keywords—the former being used in the base, and the latter being used in the child. These keywords prescribe that calls to overridden methods will always result in the derived implementation, regardless of how the class is referenced. Thus, the new implementation is called even if the derived class has been cast to one of its parents. This type of behavior is based on the OOP concept of *polymorphism*, and is an important principle in C# and the BCL.

Topic: Interfaces and Structures

In this topic we examine two of the major nonclass types in C#: interfaces and structures. Interfaces form contracts between clients and components by prescribing which methods a class must expose. Structures are similar to classes except that they are value types that are stored on the stack for fast instantiation and destruction. Both entities play important roles in the world of C# and the BCL.

CONCEPTS

Interfaces

Interfaces are best understood against the concept of class inheritance, which we examined in the previous topic. Consider the `Calculator` class that we wrote in Listing 6.17. Because this class contains a method called `Multiply()`, we are guaranteed that the derivatives of the class will also expose a `Multiply()` method. A child class will either inherit `Calculator`'s implementation, or it will override it and provide its own implementation. In a sense the process of inheritance prescribes a "structure" on the child class; the contents of the base class (its methods) are enforced on the child (the class inherits the methods).

The purpose of an interface is to impose a certain structure (requirements) on a class. The difference between an interface and class inheritance is that by inheriting from an interface, a class *must* provide implementations for all the methods defined in the interface (it cannot override them *optionally* as is the case with class inheritance).

By itself, an interface is useless; its methods do not contain any implementation code, and it cannot be instantiated. Instead, its sole purpose is to define a set of methods that classes must implement. Consider the following definition of an interface named `IFoo` (by convention, interfaces usually begin with a capital I).

```
interface IFoo
{
   void Bar();
}
```

Listing 6.32   The IFoo interface

Any class that inherits this interface must implement a method called `Bar()`. In a very real way the `IFoo` interface functions as a contract between a client and the class; by implementing this interface, a class guarantees to clients that it supports the `Bar()` method. And as we will see in the following example, the benefits of interfaces go beyond a simple guarantee.

Detour: A Short Word on Visibility
Before looking at the example, we have to take a detour to talk about interface visibility. An interface, like a class, may be declared with either `public` or `internal` visibility. By default, as with classes, `internal` visibility is applied. This visibility has a significant impact because the methods of the interface automatically inherit the visibility of the class. You cannot assign specific visibility to individual methods inside the interface. In other words, all the methods in an interface are either `internal` (default) or `public`.

Example: Interfaces
Our example in this topic is based on the following interface definition:

```
interface ICalc
{
  int Add(int a, int b);
  int Subtract(int a, int b);
}
```

Listing 6.33   The ICalc interface

Again, note that an interface does not house any implementation code (the compiler will prevent you from adding any). In addition, the methods have not been marked with visibility modifiers such as `public` because the inheriting class decides on method visibility. (In addition to methods, an interface can also contain definitions for properties, events, and indexers. The last construct is covered in the next topic.)

Implementing the Interface

In order to implement an interface in C#, we use the same syntax that we employed in the previous topic on inheritance; that is, we append the declaration of the class with a colon and the interface name. However, there are two ways in which the actual interface methods can be declared within the class. Both variations are given in the following code.

```
// Variation 1 (Implicit declaration)
public class Calc : ICalc
{
   public int Add(int a, int b) {return a+b;}
   public int Subtract(int a, int b) {return a+b;}
}

// Variation 2 (Explicit declaration)
public class Calc : ICalc
{
   int ICalc.Add(int a, int b) {return a+b;}
   int ICalc.Subtract(int a, int b) {return a-b;}
}
```

Listing 6.34 *Implementing an interface in C#*

Note that with both techniques the method signatures in the class must match the signatures in the interface.

The first technique, called *implicit declaration,* declares all the methods of the interface as `public` methods in the class. When you use implicit declaration, you must use the `public` modifier for visibility on the methods, regardless of whether the interface is declared `internal` or `public`.

The second technique, termed *explicit declaration,* prefixes each method name with the name of the interface being implemented. Note that if you employ the second technique, then you cannot apply visibility modifiers such as `public` and `private` (the compiler will generate an error if such a keyword is present). As we will see, explicitly declared methods must be accessed through the interface definition, which means that their visibility is the same as the interface itself (either `internal` or `public`).

Although both techniques are satisfactory, the first variation is usually preferable (for reasons we will explain momentarily). The less-often-used explicit format is generally reserved for situations when a class is implementing numerous interfaces, a process we will now examine.

Multiple Interfaces

A single class can implement multiple interfaces. However, the class must provide an implementation for each method in each interface. We might, for example, create a second calculator interface that defined additional scientific methods.

```
interface IScientific
{
  double Cosine(double a);
}
```

Listing 6.35   The IScientific interface

We can then increase the functionality of the Calc class by implementing both the ICalc and IScientific interfaces.

```
public class Calc : ICalc, IScientific
{
  public int Add(int a, int b) {return a+b;}
  public int Subtract(int a, int b) {return a-b;}
  public Cosine(double a) {return Math.Cos(a);}
}
```

Listing 6.36   Multiple interface inheritance

You may wonder what happens when two interfaces contain the exact same method definition. In this case, the explicit declaration technique becomes important. For example, if IScientific also contained an Add() method, the Calc class could contain two implementations of an addition method.

```
public class Calc : ICalc, IScientific
{
  int ICalc.Add(int a, int b) {return a+b;}
  int IScientific.Add (int a, int b) {return a+b;}
  // Other methods...
}
```

Listing 6.37   Interface name collisions

Because we can differentiate between interfaces by means of the added prefix, we can provide two different Add() methods for each interface. In contrast, if we relied on the implicit technique, we could provide only one method for addition, which would provide the Add() implementation for both interfaces (which may or may not be desirable).

```
public class Calc : ICalc,IScientific
{
  public int Add(int a, int b) {return a+b;}
  public int Subtract(int a, int b) {return a+b;}
  public double Cosine(double a) {return 4.3;}
}
```

Listing 6.38   Multiple interfaces and implicit declaration

As you can see, the explicit approach is better for multiple interface situations when name collisions are involved. However, how can a class expose two Add() methods (Listing 6.37)? Furthermore, are there any other differences between the two declaration techniques other than this admittedly esoteric situation?

Explicit and Implicit Declaration

The primary difference between explicit and implicit declaration is the manner in which you must invoke the methods of the implementing class. When implicit declaration is used, interface methods are directly callable on the class. However, *when explicit declaration is employed, the class must first be cast to the interface before methods can be invoked*. This important difference is illustrated below.

```
public class Calc1 : ICalc
{
  public int Add(int a, int b) {return a+b;}
  public int Subtract(int a, int b) {return a+b;}
}

public class Calc2: ICalc
{
  int ICalc.Add(int a, int b) {return a+b;}
  int ICalc.Subtract(int a, int b) {return a+b;}
}

Calc1 c1 = new Calc1();
int x=c1.Add(1,2);

Calc2 c2 = new Calc2();
ICalc c = (ICalc)c2;
int y = c.Add(1,2);
```

Listing 6.39   Differences between implicit and explicit casting

Listing 6.39 contains two classes: Calc1, which relies on implicit declaration, and Calc2, where the declaration is explicit. As a result, the Add() method can be called directly against instances of Calc1. To do the same on Calc2, however, we must first cast it to an ICalc interface. Because of this added step, interfaces are usually implemented by means of the implicit technique.

At first glance the rule governing explicit declaration might seem pointless. However, it accounts for the situation whereby a class may have two interface methods with the same name and signature. Consider Listing 6.37 in which the class houses two Add() methods. Because of this rule, we can specify which Add() method we wish to call by first casting to the appropriate interface.

```
Calc c = new Calc();
ICalc x  = (ICalc)c;
IScientific s=(IScientific)s;
x.Add(); // Calls ICalc.Add()
s.Add(); // Calls IScientific.Add()
```

Listing 6.40   Calling interface methods with the same name

As Listing 6.40 demonstrates, the version of Add() that is invoked depends on the interface to which that class has been cast. For this reason it is preferable to use the explicit technique in special multi-interface situations. In fact, it is possible to use both techniques in combination, a process we outline at ⚓CS060011.

Interfaces and Polymorphism

The value of interfaces goes beyond a simple guarantee that a class exposes certain methods (although this is their primary purpose). Most notably, interfaces allow the implementing class to be treated in a polymorphic manner (the concept of polymorphism was covered in the previous topic). As the following code illustrates, a class that implements an interface can be treated as an instance of that interface.

```
Calc c = new Calc();
c.Add(); // Invoke the class directly

ICalc i = (ICalc)c;
i.Add(); // Invoke through the casted interface
```

Listing 6.41   Casting a class to an interface

Listing 6.41 illustrates two ways to call the Add() method. The first code block simply calls the Add() method against an instance of Calc, whereas the second casts `Calc` to an `ICalc` interface before the method is invoked.

The second technique may not seem especially useful. After all, why not simply call methods against an instance of the class itself and avoid the extra step of casting to an interface? The answer is that by casting to an interface we can access only the methods defined in the interface; we cannot access other methods that the class may have defined. This is important for two reasons.

First, an interface can serve as a protection mechanism. We might, for example, append a method to the `Calc` class called `BeCareful()`, which is intended only for privileged clients. By giving unauthorized clients an `ICalc` interface instead of `Calc`, we prevent them from calling `BeCareful()` while still allowing them to call `Add()` and `Subtract()`.

A second, more practical use of interface casting is illustrated in the following code. This listing contains a method called `SumNumbers()`, which accepts an `ICalc` interface as a parameter.

```
public class FooBar
{
  public void SumNumbers(ICalc c)
  {
    // Sum numbers 1 to 100, using any class
    // that implements ICalc:
    int Sum=0;
    for (int k=1; k<=100;k++)
      Sum=c.Add(Sum, k);
  }
  static void Main()
  {
    FooBar f = new FooBar();
    Calc c = new Calc();
    f.SumNumbers((ICalc)c);
  }
}
```

Listing 6.42 Interfaces and polymorphism

In Listing 6.42 we call `SumNumbers()` by passing it an `ICalc` interface, which is obtained by casting an instance of `Calc` to `ICalc` (alternatively, you can simply pass the class itself to the method, and C# will cast it to the interface *implicitly*). The main point of this demonstration is that `SumNumbers()` does not care about the underlying class; it will accept *any* class that implements the `ICalc` interface. We could just as easily replace the `Calc` class with the scientific calculator we created in Listing 6.36; `SumNumbers()` method will still work because the class in Listing 6.36 also implements `ICalc`. Remember, however, that because `SumNumbers()` accepts an `ICalc` interface, it can only call `Add()` and `Subtract()`. It cannot call `Cosine()` even though the scientific calculator class implements this method.

The purpose of interfaces is closely related to the class inheritance concepts we discussed in the previous topic. Both interfaces and class inheritance let you program against a generic entity (an interface or base class) and still leverage specialized functionality (the interface-implementing class or the child class). Each technique has its respective advantages. With class inheritance a child class can *optionally* override methods, in contrast to interfaces where method implementations are required. On the other hand, a class can implement multiple interfaces but can inherit only from one base class. There are some other subtle differences between interfaces and base classes, that make them appropriate for certain OOP situations. A discussion on these differences can be found at ᴄɴ→CS060012.

Interfaces and the BCL

Interfaces are used throughout the Base Class Libraries. Oftentimes, to write a class that takes advantage of certain runtime operations (such as sorting or serialization), the class must implement interfaces exposed in the BCL. Some of the popular ones are listed below.

1. `ICollection`, `IDictionary`, and `IList` are implemented by a class to store a collection of objects in various ways. Most of the classes in the `System.Collections` namespace that we examined in Chapter 4 implement these interfaces.
2. `IComparable` and `IComparison` allow a class to compare itself to other objects (which is required by certain sorting methods in the BCL).
3. `IDisposable` is implemented by a class for garbage collection efficiency, as we saw in Chapter 5.
4. `IEnumerable` allows a class to be traversed by means of the `foreach` construct we saw in Chapter 5.
5. `ISerializable` allows a class to perform custom serialization, which was covered in Chapter 5.

For a closer look at some of these interfaces as well as other interfaces exposed by the BCL, see ᴄɴ→CS060013.

STRUCTURES

A structure is similar to a class in that it allows developers to create custom data types. (However, a C# structure is very different from its C++ counterpart; see CS060014 for details.) Unlike a class, a structure is a *value type,* which means that it resides on the stack for efficient access (value types were covered in Chapter 4). A structure in C# is denoted by means of the struct keyword, as depicted in Listing 6.43.

```
struct Age
{
  public int years;
  public int AgeInMonths ()
  {
    return years*12;
  }
  public int AgeInDays()
  {
    return years*365;
  }
}
```

Listing 6.43   Structures in C#

Because the Age structure in the preceding code is a value type, it does not have to be instantiated via the new keyword:

```
Age a; // no new keyword!
a.years = 25;
Console.WriteLine("Your age in days is: {0}",a.AgeInDays());
```

Listing 6.44   Using structures in C#

Structures are best understood by considering how they are similar to and different from classes. Like a class, a structure can expose fields, methods, properties, indexers, and operators with varying levels of visibility (the last two are covered in the following topic). Another similarity is that a structure itself can be marked with the internal and public modifiers. However, a structure is different from a class in the following ways:

1. A structure is a value type that resides on the stack. Usually, the size of the stack is much smaller than the heap (where classes are stored). Thus, although structures may be more efficient

than classes with respect to memory usage, their footprint sizes (the amount of data they store) should be closely considered.
2. A structure cannot be given a no-argument (parameterless) constructor. Instead, the C# compiler gives all structures such a constructor implicitly, which initializes the structure's fields to 0 (or `null` for strings).
3. Following from the previous rule, you can give a structure parameterized constructors. However, these constructors must initialize all the fields of the structure.
4. A structure cannot inherit from another class or structure, and therefore cannot contain `abstract`, `virtual`, or `sealed` methods (though a structure can implement interfaces).

Because a structure is a value type, it can also be used with the pointer operations we will examine in the next chapter; as we will see, C# pointers can only be used with value types. C++ developers should also note that they cannot use bit fields within a C# structure, although the framework does provide the `BitArray` class, which offers bit-level access. For details on this class see ☞CS060015.

HOW AND WHY

Can an interface inherit from another interface?
It is possible for an interface to inherit another interface. Consider the `ICalc` interface in Listing 6.33.
We could write a second interface called `ICalc2`, which inherits from `ICalc`.

```
interface ICalc2 : ICalc
{
    int Multiply(int a, int b);
}
```

Listing 6.45   Interface inheritance in C#

If a class implements `ICalc2`, it must implement the methods of both `ICalc2` (`Multiply`) and `ICalc` (`Add` and `Subtract`). Interface inheritance can raise some interesting implementation issues, which are discussed at ☞CS060016.

How do I determine whether a class implements a certain interface?
The easiest way to determine whether a class implements an interface is to use the `is` keyword. This construct is used in a straightforward manner.

```
if (SomeClassVariable is IEnumerable) {
   // iterate using a foreach loop
}
```

Listing 6.46   The is keyword

Note that the `is` keyword can also be used to determine whether a child class is a derivate of a certain base class (i.e., `if (FileStreamVar is Stream)`). A construct closely related to the `is` keyword is the as construct, which is a safer way to perform casting in C#. For details see ᴄɴ▸CS060017.

SUMMARY

Structures and interfaces represent two powerful nonclass types in the C# language. An interface is a collection of function prototypes that serves as a contract between a client and a class. By implementing an interface, a class guarantees to a client that it supports certain methods. Interfaces allow for polymorphism, whereby a class can cast itself to one of the interfaces that it has implemented. This polymorphic behavior allows C# clients to use interfaces without regard for the class that implements them. The .NET Framework exposes several interfaces that allow a class to integrate itself with common operations performed by the BCL.

Like a class, a structure can expose properties, fields, and methods. The primary difference between a class and a structure is that the latter is a value type that is stored on the stack. For this reason, structures are allocated and released more efficiently than classes.

Topic: Class Infrastructure

The C# language was designed with component-based development in mind. The features we covered in the first topic of this chapter—inheritance techniques, visibility modifiers, and class member types such as properties, fields, and methods—allow you to construct classes to represent virtually any type of data.

In addition to the boilerplate features we saw in the previous topics, C# offers some additional class-based features. These features, some of which are recognizable from C++, are listed below.

1. *Operator overloading,* which allows you to prescribe what occurs when a certain operator is used with a class. For example, by overloading the addition operator (+) you can determine what occurs when two instances of your class are added.
2. *Cast overloading,* whereby you can determine what occurs when a class is cast into a given type. For example, you can prescribe what occurs when a class is cast into an integer (i.e., determine how the class converts itself into an integer).
3. *Indexers,* which allow instances of a class to be accessed in an array-like fashion. Indexers are useful when a class is storing a collection of data.

As the following examples demonstrate, these features allow C# classes to be accessed and manipulated in very powerful ways.

CONCEPTS

Example: Operating Overloading
Operator overloading allows you to determine how operators affect classes. (It also works with structures, but we will limit our discussion to classes since the procedure for structures is identical.) Consider a class called Age, which stores the given age of a person in years and days. By overloading the addition operator for this class, we allow users to add two instances of an Age class. The following code illustrates an Age class that is so enabled.

```
public class Age
{
  public int years;
  public int days;
  public static Age operator + (Age x, Age y)
  {
    Age a = new Age();
    a.years = x.years + y.years;
    a.years += (x.days + y.days)/365;
    a.days = (x.days + y.days) % 365;
    return a;
  }
}
```

Listing 6.47   Operator overloading in C#

To overload an operator in C# you must write a method that gets invoked when the operator is applied against the class. This method must take on the special signature depicted in Listing 6.47: It must be static, return an instance of the class itself, and specify which operator is being overloaded. The operator is specified by means of the operator keyword followed by the operator itself, in this case addition (+).

Observe that this method accepts two Age classes, which represent the objects that are being added. Thus, within this method it is our job to add two Age objects in a meaningful way and return an Age object as the result. An important point is that the manner in which we add two instances of our class is completely up to us. For this example, we add the respective year and day fields of each class and also account for the situation where the combined day field may exceed 365. The overloaded addition allows our class to be used in the following fashion:

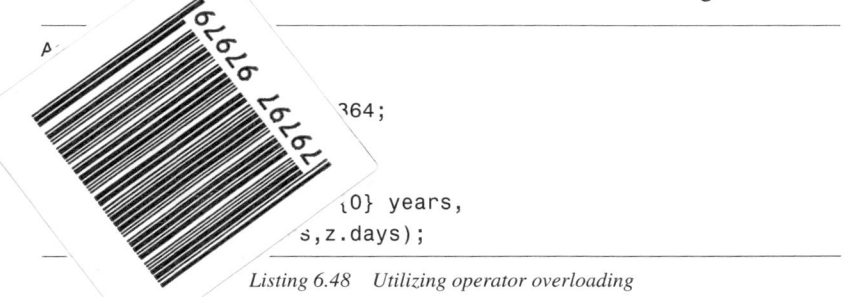

Listing 6.48 *Utilizing operator overloading*

The line in Listing 6.48, which adds two instances of the Age class, has been highlighted. Normally we cannot add instances of a class together (C# only knows how to add primitive types and strings), but we can now carry out this operation because the addition operator has been overloaded. Upon reaching the highlighted line, C# transfers execution to our method in Listing 6.47, and the classes are added together.

Operator Overloading Guidelines
A natural question regarding operator overloading is which operators can be overridden. The following tables list those operators that can and cannot be used with overloading.

Operators That Can Be Overridden in C#	
+, -, !, ~, ++, --	Unary—takes one argument
+, -, *, /, %, &, |, ^, <<, >>	Binary—takes two arguments
==, !=	Binary, must override these as a pair

<, >	Binary, must override as a pair
<=, =>	Binary, must override as a pair

Table 6.2   *Operators that can be overridden*

Operators That Cannot Be Overridden in C#	
=, ., ?:, ->, new, is, sizeof, typeof	
&&, ||	
+=, -=, *=, /=, %=	However, x+=y is the same as x=x+y
&=, |=, ^=, <<=, >>=	Same as above

Table 6.3   *Operators that cannot be overridden*

Table 6.2 and Table 6.3 list the rules that govern operator overloading in C#. The distinction between unary and binary operators in the first table may seem confusing. Recall from Chapter 4 that a unary operator functions against only one variable, whereas a binary functions against two. For example, the minus operator can be used in one of two ways.

```
Age z = x - y;   // binary
Age z = -x;      // the "negative of y"
```

Listing 6.49   *Unary and binary operators*

In C# you can overload the minus operator under both conditions, but you must do so separately. To overload a binary operator the underlying method must accept two parameters (as in Listing 6.47); to overload a unary operator the method accepts one parameter. A class that overloads both flavors of the minus operator can be found at ᶜᴺ⮕CS060018.

Overloading == and !=
Table 6.2 stipulates that if you overload the equals operator (==), you must also overload not equals (!=). The ability to overload these operators is extremely useful because, as we learned in Chapter 4, reference types cannot be compared automatically for equality in terms of *content*. (Instead, the equals operator returns true if two reference types refer to the same location on the heap.) To overload the == and != operators you must also overload the Equals() method that is inherited from System.Object. Listing 6.50 illustrates the manner in which you typically overload the comparison operators.

```
public class Age
{
  public int years;
  public int days;
  public override bool Equals(Object o) {
    Age a = (Age)o;
    return (this.years == a.years && this.days == a.days);
  }
  public static bool operator == (Age x, Age y)
  {
    return Equals(x,y);
  }
  public static bool operator != (Age x, Age y)
  {
    return !Equals(x,y);
  }
}
```

Listing 6.50   Overloading == and !=

The Equals() method determines whether two instances of a class are the same; for our example this equates to comparing the years and days fields of each Age class. Next, we utilize this method to override the == and != operators; the former returns the result of Equals(), whereas the latter returns the inverse of Equals(). Unfortunately, Listing 6.50 does not compile because it is also necessary to implement another system method called GetHashCode(). This method is a complement of Equals() and is necessary to establish a unique identity for the class instance. An Age class that implements this method can be found at ⟳CS060019.

Operator Overloading and the CLS
In Chapter 3 we discussed the Common Language Specification (CLS), which allows other .NET languages to communicate with C# components. Unfortunately, operator overloading is not defined in the CLS. Thus, overloaded operators may not function correctly in languages other than C#. For example, instances of our Age class cannot be added in VB.NET. Therefore, it is a good idea to provide standard methods that expose the same functionality as the operators you are overloading (e.g., Add(), Subtract(), etc.). A discussion of overloading and the CLS can be found at ⟳CS060020.

Cast Overloading

Whereas operator overloading allows you to prescribe what occurs when a certain operator is used against a class, cast overloading can be used to determine what happens when a class is cast into a specific type. By overloading the cast operator for a specific type, you provide C# with instructions on how to convert your class to that type. For example, we can determine how the Age class in Listing 6.50 should convert itself into an integer if it happens to be cast into one. Furthermore, we can specify whether the class must be explicitly or implicitly cast into the target type. For example, the following code allows the Age class to be explicitly cast into an integer, in which case the person's age in days is returned.

```
public class Age
{
  public int years;
  public int days;

  // Explicit casting to an integer:
  public static explicit operator int(Age a)
  {
    return a.years*365+a.days;
  }
}
```

Listing 6.51   Explicit cast overloading

The process behind cast overloading is similar to operator overloading: You must write a static method that performs the appropriate conversion. In Listing 6.51 we stipulate that we are allowing the class to be converted explicitly into an integer (note the highlighted keywords). Thus, users can manipulate the class as follows:

```
Age a = new Age();
a.years = 24;
a.days = 100;
// Print out the person's age in days:
Console.WriteLine("Age in days = {0}",(int)a);
```

Listing 6.52   Employing explicit casting

Remember that the manner in which a class is converted to the target type is completely up to you. In this case the Age class converts itself into an integer representing the person's age in days; we could just as easily have returned the person's age in years or minutes. Thus, with casting, the underlying cast implementation is not especially clear to the user, and, hence, providing a method such as `ConvertToDays()` is usually the preferred approach. Also note that the cast will only compile if it performed explicitly, as is the case in Listing 6.52. We can remove this requirement by replacing the `explicit` keyword in Listing 6.51 with `implicit`. This change allows the class to be cast in an implicit fashion.

```
Age a = new Age();
a.years = 24;
a.days = 100;
int days1 = a;          // implicit casting
int days2 = (int)a;  // explicit still works
```

Listing 6.53   Employing implicit casting

If you implement implicit cast overloading, then you get explicit overloading for free. Thus, as illustrated in Listing 6.53, we can cast the class to an integer either implicitly or explicitly. In case you are wondering, you cannot write separate implementations for implicit and explicit overloading. In other words, you can't have one method for an implicit cast and another for an explicit cast. Instead, cast overloading in C# must proceed along one of two lines:

1. You use the `explicit` keyword (as in Listing 6.51), in which case the class must be cast explicitly to the target type.
2. You use the `implicit` keyword, in which case the class can be cast implicitly or explicitly.

Note, however, that you *can* overload the cast operator for numerous types. For example, we can allow the Age class to be cast to an integer, string, or ArrayList class. To do so we would have to write three methods, each of which would convert an Age class to the respective type. An Age class that is so equipped can be found at ⟳CS060021.

Casting to Bool
One useful aspect of cast overloading is the ability to override the bool type, which allows the class to be used in an if statement. Listing 6.54 illustrates this technique.

```
public class CAge
{
  public int years;
  public int days;
  public static implicit operator bool(CAge a)
```

```
    {
        // return true if the person is 18 or older
        return (a.years >=18);
    }
}

//Application program:
Age a = new Age();
a.years = 21;
if (a) {
    // Implicitly casts the class to bool
    // Person can vote...
}
```

Listing 6.54   Overloading bool

Because we have provided an implicit cast overload for the Boolean data type, we can very quickly determine whether someone is old enough to vote.

Indexers

Indexers allow a class to be accessed in an array-like fashion. In a sense you can think of indexers as the overloading of C#'s array subscript characters ([ ]). However, whereas the argument to an array subscript is a number (the element of the array), the argument to an indexer can be any type of variable. The following class illustrates the versatility of indexers.

```
class DaysOfWeek
{
    private string[] dow =
    new string[]{ "monday", "tuesday","wednesday",
        "thursday", "friday","saturday", "sunday" };

    // Indexer by integer that returns a string:
    public string this[int n]
    {
        get { return dow[n]; }
    }

    //Indexer by string that returns a bool:
    public bool this[string day]
    {
        get {
```

```
      // return true if they have specified a valid day:
      return ((IList)this.dow).Contains(day);
    }
  }
}
```

Listing 6.55   Array indexers

The syntax for indexers is similar to a property in that you must use the `get` and `set` keywords that determine how an indexer value is retrieved and set, respectively. Because we have omitted the `set` keyword in Listing 6.55, our indexers are *read-only*. In addition, the indexer syntax must specify (1) the return type of the indexer, and (2) the type that is used to reference the indexer. Thus, the `DaysOfWeek` class in Listing 6.55 exposes two indexers: one that returns a string when the class is array-referenced by integer, and another that returns a Boolean when the class is array-referenced by string. These indexers would be used in the following fashion:

```
DaysOfWeek d = new DaysOfWeek();

//Print out the days of the week:
for (int k=0; k<=6;k++) Console.Write("{0},",d[k]);

// Determine if "saturday" is a valid day:
if (d["saturday"])
{
  Console.WriteLine("Thank goodness for saturday");
}
```

Listing 6.56   Utilizing indexers

Note that indexers are a part of the Common Language Specification (CLS). Thus, the indexers in Listing 6.55 will work correctly in languages such as VB.NET and JScript.NET. Additional examples of indexers can be found at ⟲CS060022.

HOW AND WHY

Can I override the assignment (=) operator?
As we saw in Chapter 4, the assignment operator copies pointer values when it is used with reference types. For example, after the following code executes, both the `Foo` and `Bar` variables refer to the same instance of an `ArrayList` class on the heap. Thus, changes to `Bar` affect `Foo`.

```
ArrayList Foo, Bar;
Foo = new ArrayList();
Bar = Foo;
```

Listing 6.57   The assignment operator and reference types

It would be ideal if we could override the assignment operator to perform a content copy instead of a pointer copy. Under this type of behavior the = operator would create a new instance of the target class and physically replicate its contents (what is known as a *deep copy*). Thus, at the end of Listing 6.57, both Foo and Bar would refer to separate but equivalent instances of ArrayList.

Unfortunately, as Table 6.3 stipulates, this operator cannot be overridden. However, the .NET Framework allows a class to perform deep copies by means of the IClonable interface. This interface, as well as subtleties that arise when it is used with class hierarchies, is discussed online at ᶜᴺ⇨CS060023.

SUMMARY

The component-based nature of the C# language is best illustrated by the features in this topic: operator overloading, cast overloading, and indexers. Together these three features allow C# classes to be accessed and manipulated very intuitively. Operator overloading allows instances of a class to be used with operators such as multiplication and addition as well as equals (==) and not equals (!=). By overloading operators you can allow instances of a class to be added together, compared, bit-shifted, etc. The underlying implementation of these operations (e.g., the manner in which two classes are added) is completely up to the developer.

Cast overloading enables instances of a class to be converted into other types such as integers and strings. There are two types of cast overloading in C#: implicit, whereby a class can be converted to other types implicitly, and explicit, in which case the cast must be performed explicitly in order for the conversion to work. A final point regarding overloading is to use it only where it makes sense, that is, for mathematical or simple utility classes where the expected behavior of + or * is obvious. In most cases well-named methods are more appropriate.

Indexers allow a class to be accessed in an array-like fashion by means of C#'s subscript characters ([]). Like properties, indexers are written via the get and set keywords, which prescribe whether the indexer can be read or written, respectively. Like properties, an indexer can be made read-only or write-only by omitting the `set` and `get` keywords, respectively. Indexers are more flexible than standard arrays, as the array subscript can be a noninteger (e.g., `MyClass["Brent"] = 4`).

Chapter Summary

The OOP features described in this chapter are an integral part of the C# language and the Base Class Libraries. Like its predecessors, C# supports standard features such as inheritance, polymorphism, and interfaces.

Virtually any type of .NET application that you write will leverage the concepts illustrated in this chapter. Almost every significant project requires the use of inheritance or interfaces in some fashion since both entities are heavily utilized throughout the BCL. Indeed, object-oriented programming (OOP) is an integral part of C# and the .NET Framework. Fortunately, the C# language does a very good job of implementing OOP concepts in a fashion that is intuitive to the developer.

Chapter 7

NATIVE AND UNSAFE CODE

A natural question for developers given the advent of .NET is the impending status of widespread technologies such as COM and Win32 DLLs. Unlike applications produced by .NET language compilers, these older frameworks generate native code that runs outside the CLR. The .NET Framework and C# would be of little value if developers were forced to abandon their existing components and technologies. Clearly, there must be some way to integrate code from these two different worlds.

In this chapter we examine three technologies that allow C# developers to step outside the managed execution of the CLR. The first, called Platform Invocation Services (*PInvoke* for short), allows C# applications to call functions exposed by Win32 DLLs. The second, termed *COM Interop,* allows these same applications to use native COM components from .NET. The third technology consists of special *unsafe* features in the C# language, which allow developers to leverage C-style constructs such as pointers and unchecked array access.

In addition to allowing native code to be invoked from the managed environment, the .NET Framework also permits the reverse to occur by allowing managed code to be called from the native realm. This is accomplished by means of a technology called *Reverse COM Interop,* whereby a .NET assembly can masquerade as a COM component to a "pre-.NET" application (such as a VB6 or traditional ASP code). We illustrate this technology at ⊶CS070001.

CORE CONCEPTS

Native Code Cautions
Calling native components from .NET applications is undesirable. Remember that unlike C# applications, native code executes outside the boundaries of the CLR. Invoking native components from within a C# application forces the CLR to suspend its execution and give way to code that operates outside its boundaries. This process is further compounded because the CLR must translate data between both sides of the fence by means of a process called *marshaling*. For example, if you call a Windows API function that accepts a string, the CLR must convert your managed System.String into a native equivalent, and reverse the process when the function returns.

For performance reasons it is good practice to avoid the use of native code wherever possible. As we saw in Chapter 3, the .NET Framework offers a strong set of features through the Base Class Libraries, which contain evolved versions of many technologies that you have used in the past. For this reason it is advantageous to use the BCL instead of native APIs that offer the same functionality. (Nevertheless, porting is a thorny issue that involves numerous trade-offs and considerations; see o^{CN}CS070002 for a more involved discussion on the topic.)

Native Code Versus Unsafe Code
Before we proceed with the topics in this chapter, there is an important distinction to be made. As we will see in the last topic, C#'s unsafe keyword allows the use of "low-level" features such as pointers and gives rise to something called "unsafe code." You might imagine that these "unsafe" regions consist of native code blocks that execute outside the CLR. This, however, is not the case. To understand why requires making a subtle distinction in the .NET terminology that can be confusing.

Native code is machine code which exists in a binary format that can be executed directly by the processor (hence the term *native*). Win32 DLLs and COM components are compiled into this type of code. Native code is said to run in the "unmanaged" environment because it executes outside the boundaries of the CLR. Unsafe code, on the other hand, is still translated into IL code by the C# compiler and operates within the managed environment. Unlike regular IL code, however, unsafe code blocks are not verified by the CLR for type safety or memory access before they are JIT compiled. As a result, unsafe IL code may run faster than its "safe" counterpart, but it is *not* to be confused with native machine code.

Confusion arises because the Microsoft documentation frequently makes references to "unmanaged" code, without differentiating between native machine code and unsafe IL code. To clarify, code in the .NET Framework can be classified into one of three types:

1. *Managed code:* This is the default type of code that is generated by .NET language compilers such as VB.NET and C#. Code of this type exists as IL and is fully verified by the CLR for memory access, type safety, and security before it is JIT compiled into native machine code. All the C# applications we have written thus far have compiled to managed code.
2. *Unsafe code:* Code of this type can only be generated by means of C#'s special unsafe language features. Code is still compiled to IL, but it is not verified before it is translated into native machine code. Thus, unsafe code must still undergo JIT compilation by the CLR before it can execute.
3. *Native/unmanaged code:* Code of this type does not have to be JIT compiled because it has already been translated into processor-specific instructions (e.g., x86 assembly for Intel processors). COM components and Win32 DLLs exist in this format. Native code can also be produced directly from .NET in one of two ways: (1) by means of the NGEN.EXE utility, which "pre-JITs" assemblies, and (2) by using the managed C++ compiler, which allows one to write applications that compile directly to native code.

Topic: PInvoke and DllImport

In many respects standard Win32 DLLs are still the backbone of the Windows Operating System. A quick glance at the *windows\system32* directory reveals the hundreds of DLLs that provide applications with services such as compression, encryption, the ability to create and maintain windows, and communication. For years Windows developers have relied on such DLLs to obtain OS-specific information. For example, the GetSystemDirectory() function in kernel32.dll allows one to ascertain the full path of the aforementioned Windows system directory, which is often useful in installation and deployment scenarios.

CONCEPTS

DLLImport Attribute

Calling a function that resides in a Win32 DLL from C# is accomplished by means of the DllImport attribute located in the System.Runtime.InteropServices namespace (attributes are covered in Chapter 5). You simply declare the function prototype and the DLL in which it is contained, and then call the function as if it were any other function in your source code. DllImport informs the CLR that the function exists in a DLL and must be accessed by means of the CLR's PInvoke services.

Example: Calling the Win32 from C#

The following code demonstrates calling the Sleep() function found in kernel32.dll, which delays program execution for a number of milliseconds.

```csharp
using System;
using System.Runtime.InteropServices;

public class NativeExample
{
  [DllImport("kernel32.dll")]
  public extern static void Sleep(uint msec);

  public static void Main()
  {
    Console.Write("Delaying 1 second...");
    Sleep(1000);
    Console.WriteLine("done.");
  }
}
```

Listing 7.1   Calling a Win32 function from C#

The extern keyword in the declaration of the Sleep() method informs the compiler that we will not be providing an implementation for the method but that it is instead found in the specified DLL. Thus, whenever the Sleep() function is called by our program, the CLR will look in kernel32.dll for a function with the corresponding name and call it if it finds one. If the function cannot be found, then a runtime exception will be thrown.

The Entrypoint Parameter

As is often the case with Win32 API calls, the DLL may contain an unfriendly name for the method. We may want to create a shorter, more usable alias for our program. For example, we may wish to call our `Sleep()` function `Snooze()` (perhaps we already have a `Sleep()` method within our class). In this case we can use the `Entrypoint` parameter of the `DllImport` attribute to tell the CLR that our `Snooze()` function really maps to `Sleep()` in the underlying DLL.

```
[DllImport("kernel32.dll", Entrypoint="Sleep")]
public extern static void Snooze(uint msec)
```

Listing 7.2   Using Entrypoint

As a result of this indirection, our program can now `Snooze()` instead of `Sleep()`. Note that you can also specify functions by their *ordinal numbers,* as illustrated at ᶜᴺ⇒CS070003.

Parameter Marshaling

Whenever the CLR calls a Win32 function, it must translate (marshal) the function's parameters between the managed and native realms. For example, if a function returns a "native" string, the CLR must translate it into a managed `System.String` before it can be used with a .NET application. Likewise, before a `System.String` is given as a parameter to a DLL function, it must be converted into a native equivalent. The complexity of this process is compounded because there are several flavors of strings in the native world. Developers familiar with the Win32 will attest to the difficulties of having to deal with ANSI and Unicode strings, as well as newer COM BSTRs. Although the CLR can guess as to the native target string type to which it must convert, it can very well guess incorrectly, producing undesirable results.

The Charset and MarshalAs Options

The .NET Framework exposes two facilities to assist the CLR in dealing with these various string types. The first is the `DllImport Charset` option, which allows you to control whether strings should be marshaled using ANSI or Unicode conventions. The second option is a similar form of assistance called the `MarshalAs` attribute, which can specify exactly how the string should be marshaled to the native Win32 world. As shown in Listing 7.3, both of these attributes are applied when the Win32 function is declared.

```
[DllImport("MyDll.dll")]
public extern static void I_EXPECT_A_BSTR(
```

```
[MarshalAs(UnmanagedType.BStr)] String s1);

[DllImport("MyDll.dll")]
public extern static void I_EXPECT_A_LWStr(
  [MarshalAs(UnmanagedType.LPWStr)] String s2);

[DllImport("MyDll.dll", CharSet=CharSet.Unicode)]
public extern static void I_EXPECT_UNICODE(String s1);

[DllImport("MyDll.dll", CharSet=CharSet.Ansi)]
public extern static void I_EXPECT_ANSI(String s2);
//remaining imports omitted
```

Listing 7.3 The MarshalAs and CharSet attributes

In addition to giving marshaling advice on strings, the MarshalAs attribute can be used on other types such as bools and arrays. It can also be used to define the marshaling conventions for the individual fields in a structure, as shown below.

```
public struct STOCK
{
  [MarshalAs(UnmanagedType.BStr)]
  public String ticker;
  [MarshalAs(UnmanagedType.VariantBool)]
  public bool available;
  //and so on
}
```

Listing 7.4 Applying the MarshalAs attribute on a structure

StructLayout and FieldOffset

Two other attributes, StructLayout and FieldOffset, are also used with structures to control the physical layout of the structure in memory (they are detailed on-line at CS070004). These attributes are especially useful since several Win32 DLL functions accept structures as parameters. One such function is GlobalMemoryStatus(), which allows you to ascertain the memory characteristics of the underlying machine. As illustrated in Listing 7.5, this function accepts a structure as a parameter and populates it with relevant information.

```
using System;
using System.Runtime.InteropServices;
```

```csharp
// We must manually define this structure in code:
public struct MEMORYSTATUS
{
  public int dwLength;
  public int dwMemoryLoad;
  public int dwTotalPhys;
  public int dwAvailPhys;
  public int dwTotalPageFile;
  public int dwAvailPageFile;
  public int dwTotalVirtual ;
  public int dwAvailVirtual ;
}

class CallNative {
  [DllImport("kernel32.dll")]
  public static extern void GlobalMemoryStatus(
    out MEMORYSTATUS buffer);

  public static void Main()
  {
    // Determine the amount of RAM on the system:
    MEMORYSTATUS m;
    GlobalMemoryStatus(out m);
    Console.WriteLine("Total RAM = {0}",m.dwTotalPhys);
  }
}
```

Listing 7.5 Calling GlobalMemoryStatus() from C#

Keep in mind that it is your responsibility to determine and declare the structure(s) that a Win32 function is expecting. In the preceding code, for example, we had to consult the MSDN in order to determine the layout of the MEMORYSTATUS structure that was given to `GlobalMemoryStatus()`.

Listing 7.5 illustrates one of the few situations where you must resort to native means for functionality. Surprisingly, there is no class in the BCL that allows you to directly obtain the amount of memory on the system. Also keep in mind that PInvoke can be used against any Win32 DLL (such as third-party components), although in our examples we have used it against Microsoft "system" DLLs that house the Windows API.

Error Handling
A special class of Win32 functions that must be considered are those that return HRESULTs. COM developers will recognize HRESULT as the return value used to propagate error information between components and clients. Several DLL functions, especially those found in ole32.dll (used for COM automation), are designed in this manner. The `PreserveSig` parameter of the `DllImport` attribute determines whether the CLR should throw a .NET exception when an error occurs or whether error information should be returned by the function itself so that it can be checked explicitly.

It helps to realize that `PreserveSig` stands for "Preserve Signature," which preserves the manner in which the function is prototyped in the underlying DLL. This parameter is demonstrated on-line at CS070005. Note that the `PreserveSig` parameter *applies only to COM-style error handling*. The CLR cannot automatically handle errors for functions that use their return values to indicate success or failure in a format other than HRESULT.

HOW AND WHY

When should I use the `MarshalAs` attribute?
Types that can be marshaled by the CLR without assistance are called *isomorphic* types. (These are also known as *blittable* types. The word *blitt* was borrowed from the computer graphics world and refers to the manipulation of a large array of bits. Therefore, to be "blittable" a data type must contain members that can easily be represented in an array of bytes.) These include numerical types such as integers, singles, and doubles. Types that require marshaling assistance are referred to as *nonisomorphic* types. These include Boolean, string, and array types. A list of nonisomorphic types and marshaling hints can be found at CS070006.

How do I handle Win32 DLL functions that use callbacks?
Many functions in the Win32 API utilize callback functions. They accept a C-style function pointer (`AddressOf` in Visual Basic) and call this function to notify you that something has occurred. For example, the `CopyFileEx()` function found in kernel32.dll will copy a file and call your function repeatedly after a certain number of bytes have been copied.

To leverage a callback Win32 function from C# you must use the .NET equivalent of function pointers—delegates (which were examined in Chapter 5). An example of using a delegate with the `CopyFileEx()` function can be found at ⚓CS070007.

SUMMARY

The `DllImport` attribute found in the `System.Runtime.InteropServices` namespace allows C# applications to call functions that reside in Win32 DLLs. When a DLL function is invoked from .NET, the CLR marshals its parameters and return values between the managed and native worlds. Functions that use strings require special attention due to the different types of Win32 strings that exist. The `DllImport` attribute exposes numerous parameters such as `Charset` and `MarshalsAs`, which allow one to assist the CLR in its string conversion efforts. The `PreserveSig` parameter allows you to control how error information is propagated from functions returning COM HRESULTS.

Topic: COM Interop

With COM Interop, developers can invoke COM components directly from C#. Like the PInvoke mechanism examined in the previous topic, this technology relies on attributes to precisely describe the characteristics of the native (in this case COM) component being called. This helps the CLR construct a Runtime Callable Wrapper (RCW), which acts as a proxy between the COM component and your C# application. The RCW is responsible for invoking the COM component, marshaling parameters between the managed and native domains, and controlling the COM component's lifetime.

A utility called TLBIMP.EXE, which is provided with the .NET Framework, greatly simplifies COM integration by masking many of the conversion details from developers. TLBIMP.EXE is a conversion tool: Given a COM component, it will emit an "Interop" assembly that can be referenced directly by a C# application. The application uses this assembly as it would any other, completely unaware that the assembly has constructed an RCW behind the scenes and that it is secretly communicating with a COM component. When you make method calls against the assembly, it ferries them to the underlying COM object that does the real work.

The TLBIMP.EXE utility is designed to work with COM components that have type libraries. Recall from Chapter 3 that type libraries are COM's equivalent of metadata and that they fuel features such as Intelli-

Sense in VB6. Although type libraries are optional in COM, the majority of existing COM technologies such as VB6, ATL, MFC, and even Visual J++ produce type-library-enabled components. Accessing the small minority of components without type libraries relies on the reflection technique we examined in Chapter 5. An example of calling COM components using reflection can be found at ⚓CS070008.

CONCEPTS

Example: Calling a COM Component from C#
In this example we illustrate how to call a COM component named StockInfo from C#. The source code for this component as well as the component itself (the .DLL file) can be downloaded at ⚓CS070009.

StockInfo exposes two methods: GetCurrentPrice(), which returns the current price of a stock given a stock symbol, and GetSymbolList(), which returns an array of strings representing valid symbols. Assuming that our component was named StockInfo.DLL, we would create an Interop assembly by using the TLBIMP utility as follows:

```
TLBIMP.EXE StockInfo.dll /out:StockNet.dll
```

If everything proceeds smoothly, TLBIMP will generate an assembly named StockNet.DLL. It is important to realize that this assembly *is not a functional substitute for the COM component* because it doesn't contain executable code for either method. Rather, it contains metadata that the CLR uses to construct a Runtime Callable Wrapper (RCW), which acts as a bridge between our C# application and the native COM object.

Differences Between the Interop Assembly and the COM Component
If you examine the resulting assembly with the ILDASM utility we introduced in Chapter 3, you will find that (as expected) it exposes two methods: GetCurrentPrice() and GetSymbolList(). During the conversion process, however, the TLBIMP tool converts the native parameters of the COM component into .NET equivalents. For example, although GetSymbolList() returns an array of COM BSTR elements to a client, the Interop assembly converts the return value into an array of System.Strings. This conversion is especially nice for C++ developers, who no longer have to concern themselves with the deallocation of BSTRs.

Another difference between the COM component and the Interop assembly is that the new methods do not return HRESULTS, the COM-specific method by which errors are returned from components to their calling client. Visual Basic developers may be unfamiliar with HRESULTs since the Visual Basic runtime abstracts the details of COM error checking. HRESULTs are used by VB behind the scenes, however, and failures communicated to the client via HRESULTs are what trips VB's `On Error Goto` mechanism. The COM Interop service offers a similar form of simplification by trapping errors from COM components and delivering them to your programs as .NET exceptions that can be trapped by means of try-catch clocks. For example, a COM method that returned an HRESULT of E_OUTOFMEMORY would manifest itself as an `OutOfMemoryException` in your C# application.

Namespaces and Interop Assemblies

A question that arises when employing COM Interop concerns the namespace that is used to access the classes within the Interop assembly. By default the classes of an Interop assembly are placed within a namespace equal to the file name of the assembly. Thus, in our example the `StockInfo` class is placed within the `StockNet` namespace. This behavior can be overridden by means of the `/namespace` option of the TLBIMP utility.

Writing a C# application that leverages the Interop assembly is straightforward:

```
using System;
using stockNet;

class CallNative
{
  public static void Main()
  {
    StockInfoClass s = new StockInfoClass();
    System.Array sym = s.GetSymbolList();
    foreach (string x in sym)
      Console.WriteLine("Price of:
        {0}={1}",x,s.GetCurrentPrice(x));
  }
}
```

Listing 7.6   Calling the StockInfo component from C#

Compile and run the preceding code using the C# compiler (don't forget to reference the Interop assembly: `/r:stockNet.dll`), and it will produce the following output:

```
Price of: AAA = 10.1
Price of: BBB = 20.2
Price of: CCC = 30.3
Price of: DDD = 40.4
```

Listing 7.7   Program output

As Listing 7.6 illustrates, calling a COM component from C# is simple once the Interop assembly has been generated. In fact, there is nothing COM-specific about Listing 7.6—the Interop assembly is used like any "normal" assembly in the .NET Framework.

VS.NET and COM Support

Calling components from C# is made even simpler by the built-in facilities of Visual Studio.NET. When you write applications within the development environment, you can forgo the use of the TLBIMP utility and simply use the menu options exposed by the IDE. Go to Project → Add References, click the COM Tab, and VS.NET will allow you to select the COM component you wish to use, as illustrated in Figure 7.1.

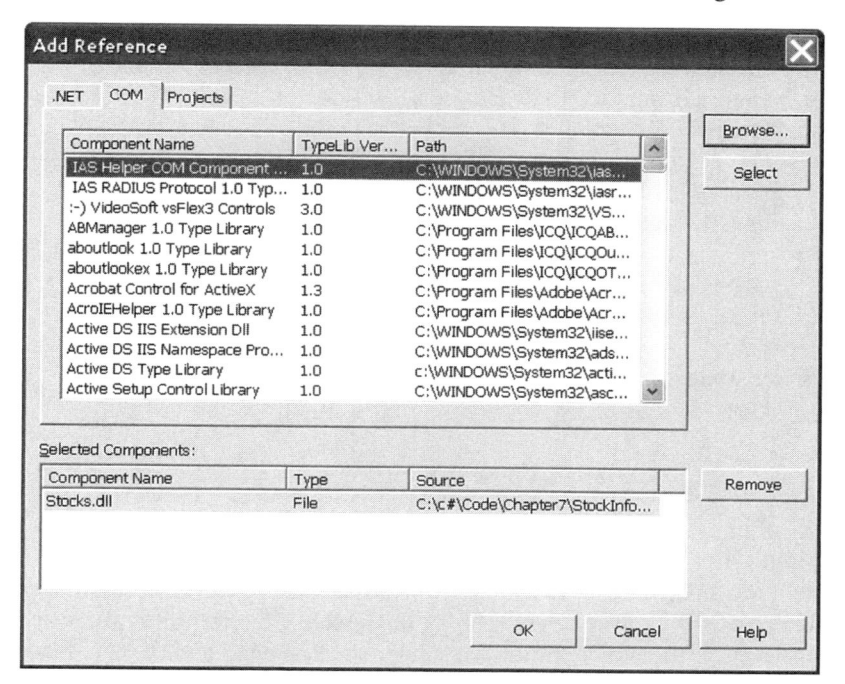

Figure 7.1   Using COM components in VS.NET

Once you have selected the COM component(s) that you wish to use and click OK, the environment will call TLBIMP on your behalf to generate the appropriate Interop assemblies. In addition, the IDE will reference these assemblies from the current project so that their classes can be accessed directly from the project's source code. As you can see, the combination of VS.NET's design-time COM support and the Interop technology on which it is based make leveraging COM components from C# as simple as using regular class library assemblies.

COM Interop Caveats

Although calling COM components from C# is straightforward, there are a few caveats to bear in mind. Most notably, you must account for behavioral changes that result when a COM component is converted into an Interop assembly. Consider the following line of ADO code (recall that ADO is exposed through COM), which changes the cursor type for a `Recordset` (i.e., it alters the manner in which its records can be viewed):

```
myADORecord.CursorType = adOpenDynamic
```

This line, which works perfectly with pre-.NET clients such as VB6 and ASP, will not compile under C#. This is not a shortcoming of C# but, rather, a difference between the visibilities of types in COM components versus assemblies. The adOpenDynamic constant is part of the CursorType enumeration, and although COM makes enumeration members globally visible to clients, assemblies require that you fully qualify the constant value:

```
myADORecord.CursorType = CursorTypeEnum.adOpenDynamic
```

It is small hiccups such as this that will complicate using COM from C#. For some other COM/assembly caveats, see CS070010.

HOW AND WHY

Why didn't the TLBIMP utility convert my component into an Interop assembly?

There is a small category of components that will not work successfully with TLBIMP. Conversion will fail if TLBIMP encounters difficulties in translating a method's parameters into managed equivalents. This occurs when your COM component is using non-OLE data types, such as custom-defined structures. (Visual Basic does not permit such data types, and thus VB components will convert without a problem.) If you do have a C++ COM component that is utilizing such special types, you must write a *managed wrapper* in either C# or managed C++ to use your component from the .NET environment. An example of a managed wrapper that allows access to such a COM component can be found at ⚙CS070011.

How will COM threading models affect my managed program?

Unlike the .NET Framework, COM can synchronize access to a component by using an entity called an *apartment*. Before a thread uses a COM component, it must inform the COM subsystem as to the manner in which the component will be accessed from that thread. This declaration allows COM to determine whether or not the component requires protection.

Although a complete discussion of COM threading models is beyond the scope of this book, you should be aware that all .NET threads will declare Multithreaded Apartment (MTA) affiliation by default. If a thread will be using Single Threaded Apartment (STA) components (such as those produced by VB6), this setting may adversely affect performance. You can declare a thread's concurrency model explicitly by using the ApartmentState field found in the System.Threading namespace.

Another way to influence COM's apartment model is to apply the STAThread attribute on a particular method; it forces COM objects accessed within that method to utilize STA conventions. Recall from Chapter 1 that this attribute is automatically applied on the Main() methods of Console and Windows applications created in VS.NET. You may wonder why VS.NET defaults to the less capable STA model on application programs. The reasons are largely rooted in the architectural details of COM and Windows. For more information see ⚙CS070012.

SUMMARY

COM Interop allows C# applications to use COM components as if they were regular .NET assemblies. This process is facilitated by the TLBIMP utility, which emits an Interop assembly by examining the COM component with which one wishes to communicate. Once generated, the Interop assembly can be used like a regular .NET assembly. Behind the scenes the Interop assembly instructs the CLR to construct a Runtime Callable Wrapper (RCW), which communicates with the actual COM component. The RCW takes care of marshaling parameters between the managed program and the unmanaged component.

Topic: Unsafe Code

Unsafe code allows C# developers to leverage some of the "low-level" language features of C and C++. Most notably, these features include pointers, which allow you to inspect and modify memory directly, outside the watchful eye of the CLR. The increased latitude that is provided by unsafe code, however, comes at a cost. First, the pointer features in C# are as versatile (and hence as unsafe) as those found in C and C++. In addition, applications with unsafe code blocks must be granted a higher level of security by the CLR's Code Access Security (CAS) system in order to execute.

Recall the distinction that we established at the beginning of this chapter: Unsafe code still executes within the CLR, but it is not verified for safety during the JIT compilation phase (i.e., unsafe code is *not* native code). Although unsafe code blocks are not subject to security checks, the decision as to whether an unsafe application will be allowed to execute in the first place is still made by the CLR. Specifically, unsafe applications must be *fully trusted* in order to execute. The concept of fully trusted code and its security implications are discussed on-line at o━CN➤CS070013.

Because this topic assumes knowledge of pointers and pointer syntax, developers unfamiliar with pointers or C++ pointer notation should consult the on-line explanation at o━CN➤CS070014.

CONCEPTS

When to Use Unsafe Code

In general, unsafe code features should only be used in the following situations:

1. When a section of code must be as fast as possible and the use of pointers will significantly increase its execution speed.
2. To interact with native components (Win32 DLLs and COM components) that accept pointers as parameters.

The second point is based on the native elements that we examined in the previous two topics. Oftentimes, native components accept pointers as parameters. An example is the Win32 `WriteFile()` function, which writes a sequence of bytes onto disk. One of the parameters this function expects is a pointer to the data that is to be written. By using unsafe code in combination with the `DllImport` attribute we examined in the first topic, this function is easily callable from C#. (See ^{CN}CS070015 for a C# application that utilizes `WriteFile()`).

The first point—that unsafe code is appropriate for performance-critical operations where pointers might be beneficial—is harder to define. When exactly do pointers increase performance? Although there is no definitive answer to this question, computationally intense operations such as matrix and image manipulations are generally good candidates for pointers. Operations involving arrays (copying, modifying, etc.) can also be sped up by means of pointers. In other words, operations that require the manipulation of large blocks of memory are potential applicants for unsafe code.

Keep in mind that using pointers often results in cryptic code that is difficult to debug. Furthermore, it is the developer and not the CLR who is responsible for keeping track of the memory that is modified by pointers. In other words, pointers can be very easy to misuse.

C# Unsafe Code Features

C# exposes four unsafe code elements; these are listed in Table 7.1. In this topic we will concentrate on the first two constructs and relegate a discussion of the lesser-used `sizeof()` and `stackalloc()` operators to ^{CN}CS070016.

Unsafe Keyword	Purpose
`int *a;`	A pointer (denoted by '*'), in this case a pointer to an integer.
`fixed`	Prevents a reference type from being garbage collected within a code block so that it can be pointed to.
`sizeof`	Returns the amount of memory a given type occupies.
`stackalloc`	Reserves a given amount of memory on the stack for the developer.

Table 7.1 C# unsafe code features

To use any of the keywords in Table 7.1 you must apply the `unsafe` keyword to any method that houses unsafe code. This keyword can be applied to methods, properties, and constructors (but not static constructors). Listing 7.8 illustrates its usage.

```
class Unsafe
{
   unsafe static void Main( )
```

```
    {
        int a;
        int *b;
        b = &a;  // b now "points" to a
    }
}
```

Listing 7.8   The unsafe modifier

In addition to applying the `unsafe` modifier to the appropriate methods, you must also instruct the C# compiler to produce unsafe code. This requires either using the `/unsafe` option with the command-line compiler (csc.exe) or configuring your project within VS.NET to permit unsafe code blocks, as illustrated in **Error! Reference source not found.** (To navigate to this screen go to Project → Properties and click the Build tab under Configuration Properties.)

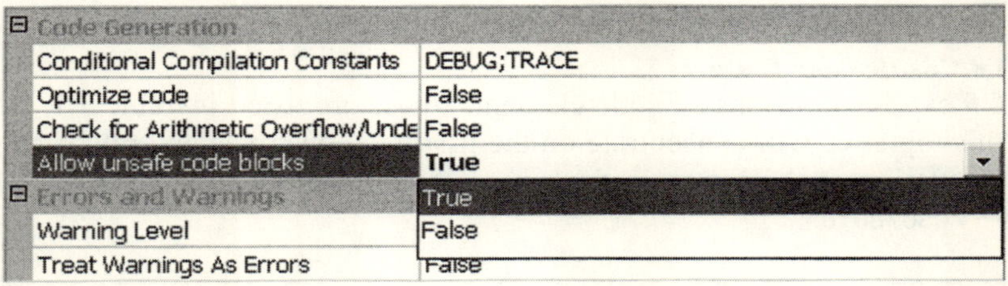

Code Generation	
Conditional Compilation Constants	DEBUG;TRACE
Optimize code	False
Check for Arithmetic Overflow/Unde	False
Allow unsafe code blocks	True
Errors and Warnings	True
Warning Level	False
Treat Warnings As Errors	False

Figure 7.2   Enabling unsafe code in VS.NET

Employing either option allows you to utilize the unsafe code features we now discuss.

Pointers

Pointers are powerful mechanisms that permit the direct manipulation of memory. A pointer variable stores a memory address, and when you manipulate the pointer, you are really modifying the contents of that address. The use of pointers in C# revolves around two operators: the asterisk (*), which is sometimes called the indirection operator, and the ampersand (&), which is commonly referred to as the address-of operator.

A pointer is declared by prefixing the variable name with an asterisk. Thus, in the following code `foo` is a pointer to an integer. It is important to understand that `foo` does not store an integer but, rather, points to the memory location where an integer is being stored. After declaring `foo` we must point it to a valid memory location. To do this we assign it to the memory location of an integer variable, which is accomplished by means of the address-of operator (&). Listing 7.9 outlines the process.

```
unsafe public static void Main()
{
  int bar = 5;
  int star = 10;
  int *foo;
  foo = &bar;    // point to the "bar" variable
  (*foo)++;      // increment the contents of bar by 1
  foo = &star;   // point to the "star" variable
  (*foo)+=5;     // increment the contents of star by 5
  Console.WriteLine ("{0}",bar);
  Console.WriteLine ("{0}",star);
}
```

Listing 7.9 C# pointer manipulation

After the third line in Listing 7.9 executes, foo points to the memory location of bar. Thereafter, we can modify the contents to which foo is pointing by using the asterisk operator. Thus, (*foo)++ is identical to bar++ because foo is actually pointing to the same memory space as bar. The important point is that when you manipulate a pointer via the asterisk operator, you are manipulating the memory to which it points. Thus, the second pointer manipulation in Listing 7.9 operates on a memory location that is different from the first one because foo now points to star.

Why Bother with Pointers?
At this point developers not familiar with pointers might wonder why they would ever use them. In Listing 7.9, for example, it would be easier to modify the variables themselves (bar and star) instead of employing the roundabout pointer technique. Pointers may seem even less attractive when you consider the following restrictions that C# places on them:

1. By default a pointer can only point to variables located on the stack (primitives, structures, enumerations, etc.).
2. A pointer is not seamlessly interchangeable with an array, as is the case in C and C++. You cannot, for example, pass an array to a method expecting a pointer. (See ᴄɴCS070017 if you are not familiar with the relationship between pointers and arrays in C and C++.)

The true value of pointers lies in their ability to manipulate large blocks of memory quickly. In order to do this we must understand the concept of *pinning*, which is accomplished by means of the fixed statement.

The Fixed Statement (Pinning Memory)

Pointers are useful to manipulate large blocks of memory, most notably array structures. In Chapter 4 we learned that arrays are stored on the heap. As we saw in Chapter 5, elements on the heap are garbage collected at periodic intervals by the CLR. During the process of garbage collection, the CLR rearranges the contents of the heap to "fill" the space that was left by the objects that were destroyed. Unfortunately, the "cleaning up" of the heap in such a manner raises a problem for pointer operations.

Remember that a pointer stores an address. Because the address (memory location) of a heap variable can change during garbage collection, it is possible that after a collection operation the address stored by a pointer will be invalid. Thus, in order to point to a variable on the heap, you must prevent the variable from being garbage collected by using the fixed statement. This statement is used to declare a code block wherein a heap variable is *pinned* (prevented from being collected) during the execution of that block. Because the variable cannot be garbage collected, you can utilize pointers within the block to manipulate the variable. The following code leverages the fixed statement to increment each element in an array by one.

```
unsafe static void IncArray(int []arr, int size)
{
  fixed (int *pArr=arr)
  {
    // Declare a second pointer:
    int *pEle=pArr;
    for (int k=0;k<size;k++)
    {
      // Increment the current element by one:
      *pEle = (*pEle)+1;
      // Move to the next element in the array:
      pEle++;
      // Print out the hex address of the pointer:
      Console.WriteLine("pEle now points to: {0:x}",
        (uint)pEle);
    }
```

```
    }
}

unsafe static void Main(string[] args)
{
  int []a = new int[100];
  IncArray(a,100);
}
```

Listing 7.10   The fixed statement

The IncArray() method in Listing 7.10 uses the fixed statement to pin the array so that it can be modified by means of pointers. Observe that the fixed statement declares a pointer (in this case pArr) to the element that is being pinned. (It might seem odd that we can assign an array to a pointer without the address-of (&) operator; again, see CS070017 to understand the relationship between pointers and arrays.) A pointer declared within a fixed statement, however, is *read only*. For this reason we must declare a second pointer (pEle) within the fixed block, which actually performs the manipulation. After incrementing the first element in the array by one, we modify the pointer to point to the next element in the array by means of the following line:

                    pEle++;

At first glance this line may seem confusing. What does it mean to increment a pointer by one? The output code in Listing 7.11, which prints out the memory address to which pEle is pointing, should shed some light on this question. Compile and run the application, and you will see output similar to the following:

```
pEle now points to: c41af0
pEle now points to: c41af4
pEle now points to: c41af8
pEle now points to: c41afc
//and so on
```

Listing 7.11   Application output

First, note that the address being pointed to is printed out in hexadecimal format by means of the {0:x} token of the WriteLine() method (memory addresses are usually presented in hex notation). Second, note that the address of the pointer increases successively by four. Based on Table 4.1, we know that an integer occupies 4 bytes of memory. As you may have guessed, these two occurrences are related: *When you increment a pointer in C#, the compiler actually increments the memory address to which it points by an amount equal to the size of the type being pointed to.*

Thus, by incrementing pEle by one, we are in fact incrementing its memory address by four, so that it points to the *next* integer element in the array. If pEle had been a pointer to a long, then incrementing it would have increased its memory address by eight—the size of a long variable.

The remaining code in Listing 7.10 is straightforward since each element in the array is increased by one. Remember that an element pinned by a fixed statement cannot be garbage collected until the code block that follows finishes executing. It is a good idea, therefore, to keep fixed code blocks as short as possible.

Like our first pointer example, Listing 7.10 may seem complex and unnecessary. Why should we use pointers to modify the elements of an array when we can do it directly? The answer, in a word, is s*peed*. Whereas standard nonpointer array manipulations (such as a[4]=4) are subject to *bounds* checking, manipulation via pointers is not. In other words, with pointers you are directly modifying the heap, whereas without them your operations are first checked for safety by the CLR. For complex operations such as the replication of large arrays and matrices, the speed-up offered by pointers can become significant. However, you always have to consider the trade-off of decreased safety. For example, you have to perform your own array bounds checking. More pragmatic examples of C# pointer usage can be found at CS070018.

Restrictions of the Fixed Statement

Because the fixed construct prevents variables on the heap from being garbage collected, you might reason that it can be used to point to any reference type variable since all reference types are stored on the heap. This concept is illustrated in the following code, which declares a pointer to an ArrayList class.

```
// This won't compile!
ArrayList a = new ArrayList();
fixed (ArrayList *p=&a)
{
    // Do something here...
}
```

Listing 7.12 Pointing to a reference type

Unfortunately, attempts to run Listing 7.12 generate the following compile-time error:

```
Cannot take the address or size of a variable of a
    managed type ('System.Collections.ArrayList')
```

As the compiler reports, it is not possible to point to a "managed" type. This is a somewhat confusing proclamation, since *all* data types in .NET are managed. What the compiler is really saying is that *you cannot point to an instance of a class*. This being the case, a natural question to ask is, What exactly can one point to in C#? The answer is given by the following convoluted rule:

You can point to anything that is capable *of being stored on the stack.*

Carefully reflect on this statement, and you should see why you can declare a pointer to an integer and not to an ArrayList. An integer is a value type that can be stored on the stack, whereas an ArrayList is a class that must be stored on the heap. Thus, whenever you are unsure as to whether or not a variable can be pointed to, ask yourself this question. You should immediately recognize that stack-bound types such as primitives (integers, chars, etc.) as well as structs can be used with pointers.

An important and subtle point with our given rule is the word *capable*. Although you can point to anything *capable* of being stored on the stack, it is possible for that type to reside on the heap. Consider the integer array in our previous example. By themselves, integers reside on the stack (and hence can be pointed to). When they are members of an array, however, they reside on the heap. Thus, a clarified version of our rule can be stated as:

Any data type capable of being stored on the stack can be pointed to, although it may not reside on the stack during the pointer operation. If the variable resides on the heap, then it must be pinned by means of the fixed *statement.*

Another example of this phenomenon is given in the following definition of the Foo class.

```
class Foo
{
    public ArrayList list = new ArrayList();
```

```
    public int size=5000;
}
```

Listing 7.13   Pointing to integers

Since `Foo` is a class, all instances of it are stored on the heap. This includes its member variables, `size` and `list`. Although integers are usually placed on the stack, in this case the integer variable `size` resides on the heap (since it is a part of the `Foo` class). According to our rule, if we wish to point to `size`, we must use the fixed statement:

```
Foo f = new Foo();
fixed (int *p=&f.size)
{
    // Do some operations...
}
```

Listing 7.14   Pointing to a class's member variables

Note that we are still forbidden from pointing to the `list` member variable. Because it is an `ArrayList`, it cannot be stored on the stack and is thus disqualified from pointer operations.

HOW AND WHY

Why can't I point to a class?

You may wonder why C# allows you to point only to those variables capable of being stored on the stack. Remember that with pointers you are interfacing with memory directly. In order for pointer operations to be useful, the underlying memory that is being manipulated must be interpretable by the developer. The in-memory representation of stack-type variables (integers, chars, bytes, etc.) consists of only their values. For example, an integer, regardless of whether it is stored on the stack or the heap, is simply 4 bytes of memory that represent the value of the integer itself.

Consider an `ArrayList` class, however. From Chapter 4 you know that this class acts like an array that can resize itself dynamically. But what does this class "look" like in memory? In addition to the elements it stores, an `ArrayList` consists of IL code, runtime information about the list it is storing (the number of elements, etc.), and so on. In order to use pointers with an `ArrayList`, we would have to understand how .NET constructs a class instance in memory, which is proprietary and subject to change. Thus, C# wisely does not allow one to point to a class directly.

However, for those with a penchant for the "nuts and bolts," there is an *indirect* way to obtain a pointer to a class. Consider the Foo class in Listing 7.13. Although we cannot point to the Foo.list member variable, because it is an ArrayList class, we can obtain a pointer to the size integer variable. Using intricate pointer arithmetic we can traverse the class's *vtable* (the virtual function table, which is an in-memory representation of the class) to obtain a pointer to list. Once this pointer has been obtained, we can peek at the managed heap to see what an ArrayList "looks" like in memory. This laborious approach is demonstrated on-line at ᴄɴCS070019.

SUMMARY

The use of pointers in C# is accomplished by means of the language's unsafe code facilities. Unsafe code in C# is enabled by either the /unsafe command-line compiler option or by configuration options exposed by VS.NET. Pointers allow developers to manipulate memory outside the auspices of the CLR, and they are useful in performance-critical situations as well as in interoperating with native COM components and DLLs. Pointers can only be used with types that are *capable* of being stored on the stack, such as primitive types and structs. To point to a stack-capable type that resides on the heap (such as integers within an array), you must use the fixed statement.

Chapter Summary

The .NET Framework exposes two technologies to call native code from C#. Platform Invoke (PInvoke) Services allow functions residing in Win32 DLLs to be called using the DllImport attribute. PInvoke exposes additional attributes that assist the CLR in marshaling data to such functions, particularly string types, which can be problematic. PInvoke also has facilities for handling functions that return error information in the form of HRESULTs.

COM Interop allows developers to invoke COM components from C#. This integration is facilitated by the TLBIMP utility, which generates an Interop assembly from a COM type library. The Interop assembly can then be used as a genuine assembly in C# applications. An associated technology called Reverse COM Interop allows .NET assemblies to be used by native COM clients.

To use pointers in C# you must use the language's "unsafe" code features. Unsafe code does not compile to native machine code but, rather, results in nonverifiable IL that must still be translated by the CLR. In addition to easing integration with DLL functions that accept pointers as parameters, unsafe code blocks can improve code efficiency by allowing developers to modify memory on the stack and heap directly.

Index

abstract modifier, 199
accessibility, 7
Active State, 8
ADO.NET, 21–22
advanced reflection, 144–47
AlarmClock class, 150–51
AppDomain, 46, 72
arithmetic operators, 96–97
arrays, 14, 122–31
  ArrayList class, 128–30, 219–20, 243–45
  collections, 127–30
  Hashtable class, 129–30
  initialization, 123–24
  jagged, 125–27, 130
  limitations, 125–28
  multidimensional, 124–26, 130
  new keyword, 122–23
  pinning, 240–41
  pointers, 237, 239–44
  searching, 129–30
  System.Collections class, 128, 130–31
as construct, 211
ASP.NET, 20–21, 35–36
assemblies, 18–19, 40, 56–65, 72
  COM Interop, 232–35

Dynamic Link Library (DLL) files, 56–62
  metadata, 57–58, 62–64, 65
  namespaces, 54–55
  private *vs.* shared, 58
  reflection, 141–42
  registries, 57–58
  security, 58
  type libraries, 57
  WhoAmI application, 64–65
assignment operator, 128–30, 219–20
asynchronous schemes, 149, 153–55, 172
attributes, 15, 69, 132–41, 172
  CLS Compliant, 69
  conditional, 134–37, 140
  custom, 134, 140–41, 147–48
  DllImport, 134, 225–26, 230
  FieldOffset, 227–28
  MarshalAs, 226–27, 229, 230
  predefined, 134, 140
  serializable, 137–40, 208
  Tangent, 69

base classes, 188–201
Base Class Libraries (BCL), 6–7, 11–12, 40, 49–56, 174
  ADO.NET, 22

Base Class Libraries (BCL) (cont'd)
  assemblies, 54–55, 64
  classes, 19–20, 72
  directory, 53–54
  inheritance, 189
  interfaces, 208
  location, 53–54
  namespaces, 49–53, 60, 72
  references, 60–62
  sorting, 32–33
  static members, 26, 179
  user accounts, 64
  Windows Forms, 51–53
base keyword, 197–99
BinaryFormatter class, 138
binary operators, 96–99
bitwise complement operator, 96
blittable types, 229
Boolean casting, 79–80, 217–18
Boolean operators, 96–100
bool type, 217–18
boxing/unboxing, 15, 88–91, 101
brackets, 13–14
break statement, 105
buttons, 51–53

C++, 9–10, 12–13, 43
callback function, 229
  See also delegates
case sensitivity, 14
casting, 78–80, 192–93
cast overloading, 15, 174, 212, 216–18, 220
catch block, 109–10, 113, 118
chaining, 154–55
character data types, 75
CharSet option, 226–27, 230
checked exceptions, 15
classes, 72, 174–88
  AlarmClock, 150–51
  ArrayList, 128–30, 219–20, 243–45
  attributes, 134
  base, 188–201
  BinaryFormatter, 138
  casting, 192–93
  cast overloading, 174, 212, 216–18
  constructors, 177–82
  destructors, 162–64, 172, 178–79
  events, 155–60
  exception, 111–15, 118, 189
  factory, 181

fields, 182–84
function overloading, 191
Hashtable, 129–30
hierarchies, 192
indexers, 174, 212, 218–20
infrastructure, 211–21
inheritance, 174, 188–201
inner, 16, 160
interfaces, 210–11
members, 175–76
methods, 186–88
namespaces, 49–50
native syntax elements, 174
Object-Oriented Programming (OOP), 19–20, 175–88
operator overloading, 212–15
pointers, 244
properties, 184–86
reflection, 141–42, 144
serialization, 139–40
SoapFormatter, 138
StringBuilder, 121–22
System.Array, 125, 129
System.Collections, 76, 128, 130–31
System.MulticastDelegate, 150, 151–52, 160
System.String, 7, 119
System.Text, 121
visibility, 175
  See also Base Class Libraries (BCL); methods; namespaces; nonclass types
Class Library files. *See* Dynamic Link Library (DLL) files
cleanup operations, 163
client applications, 152–53
CLS Compliant attribute, 69
code
  blocks, 84–86, 118
  managed, 6, 41–42, 224, 243
  native, 222–24, 226
  unmanaged, 6, 223–24
  unsafe, 236–45
  See also Intermediate Language (IL) code
Code Access Security (CAS), 42, 236
collections, 127–30
COM+, 19, 35–36
COM (Component Object Model), 18–19, 56, 222

error handling, 229
Interop technology, 18–19, 42
registries, 57–58
type libraries, 57
unsafe code, 236–37
COM HRESULTS, 229–32
COM Interop, 222, 230–35
  apartments, 235
  assemblies, 232–34
  calling a component, 231–32
  namespaces, 232–34
  Runtime Callable Wrapper (RCW), 230, 235
  threading models, 235
  TLBIMP utility, 230–31, 234–35, 245
comments, 73–74
Common Language Interface (CLI), 41
Common Language Runtime (CLR), 6, 11, 13, 40–49, 72
  AppDomain, 46, 72
  application domain protection, 46
  attributes, 133–34
  cleanup operations, 163–64
  data types, 43–44
  delegates, 150
  garbage collection, 45, 72
  Just-In-Time (JIT) compilation, 42
  location, 46
  managed code, 41–42, 224, 243
  memory management, 45
  native code, 223–24
  .NET executables, 27
  `serializable` attribute, 137
  serialization, 139–40
  Win32DLLs, 224–29
Common Language Specification (CLS), 215
Common Language System (CLS), 67–71
Common Type System (CTS), 42, 46–48, 72, 75–76, 131
`compare( )` method, 119–20
comparing data types, 86–88
comparisons, 208
compiler tools, 7–8, 24, 134–35
components, 4–5, 18–19, 56–65
`conditional` attribute, 134–37, 140
condition statements, 106–9
console application, 24–30
  from the command line, 24–27

`static Main ( )` method, 27
  using Visual Studio .NET, 27–30
constant fields, 183
`const` modifier, 183–84
constructors, 175, 177–82
  `as`, 211
  inheritance, 195–99
  `readonly` modifier, 183–84
  structures, 210
containers, 76
`continue` construct, 105–6
converting between data types, 88–89
copying data types, 83–84, 124–25
cross-language inheritance, 40, 66–67, 71, 199
cryptography, 58
curly brackets, 13
custom attributes, 134, 140–41, 147–48

Dataset, 21
data types, 74–95, 131
  Boolean, 80
  boxing/unboxing, 88–91
  byte, 118
  `char`, 118
  character, 75
  Common Type System (CTS), 43–44, 75–76
  comparing, 86–88
  containers, 76
  converting between, 88–89
  copying, 83–84
  `DateTime` structure, 94–95
  destruction, 84–85
  explicit casting, 78–80
  floating point, 75–76
  integral, 75
  libraries, 230–31
  miscellaneous, 76
  names, 14
  narrowing conversions, 78–80
  reference, 80–91, 101
  scope, 84–85
  strings, 77, 118–22
  `System.Object` types, 44–45, 75
  `System.ValueType` object, 91
  `TimeSpan` structure, 94–95
  transferring between, 78–80
  user-defined value types, 91–94
  value, 80–94, 101, 169
  value type declaration, 81–82, 119

data types (*cont'd*)
  ValueType objects, 75, 91
  variable declaration, 76–78
  variable ranges, 13, 26, 77–78
  visibility, 84–85
  See also metadata
DateTime structure, 94–95, 150–51
debug statements, 115–16
declarations
  explicit, 203, 205–6
  implicit, 203, 205–6
  of value types, 81–82, 119
  of variables, 76–78
decrement operators, 95
deep copying, 84, 124
default code, 223–24
default constructors, 182
#define directive, 115–16, 118, 134
delegates, 133, 149–61, 172, 229–30
  chaining, 154–55
  client applications, 152–53
  events, 155–60
  GetInvocationList ( ), 160
derived methods, 193, 195
destruction of data types, 84–85
destructors, 162–64, 172, 178–79
development environment, 7
directives, 115–17
disconnected data, 21
Discovery Files (DISCO), 22
Dispose ( ) method, 166–70, 172
DllImport attribute, 134, 225–26, 230
DllImport CharSet option, 226–27
documentation-generation, 15
Dynamic Link Library (DLL) files, 56–62, 65, 224
  DllImport attribute, 134, 225–26, 230
  reflection, 146–47

ECMA-262 script, 10
#else directive, 115–16
else if statements, 106–7
encapsulation, 174, 175
#endif directive, 115–16
Entrypoint parameter, 226
enumerations, 91–93
equality operator, 86–87, 119, 214–15
error handling, 109–15, 118
  attributes, 140
  unsafe code, 237

Win32DLLs, 229, 230
escape characters, 77
European Computer Manufacturers Association (ECMA), 3
  Common Language Interface (CLI), 41
ECMA-262 script, 10
events, 155–60, 172
Evidence Base Security, 42
exception classes, 111–15, 118, 189
exception handling, 109–15, 118
executable (EXE) files, 27, 56–57, 65
explicit casting, 78–80
explicit declarations, 203, 205–6
Extensible Markup Language. *See* XML (Extensible Markup Language)

FieldOffset attribute, 227–28
fields, 175, 182–84, 183–84
Finalize ( ) method, 161–62, 166–68, 171, 172
finally block, 109–10
fixed keyword, 237
fixed statements, 240–45
floating point types, 75–76
flow constructs, 101–18, 131
  break statement, 105
  condition statements, 106–9
  continue construct, 105–6
  directives, 115–17
  exception handling, 109–15, 118
  foreach construct, 104–5
  for loop, 102–3
  looping, 102–6, 117
  preprocessor, 115–17
  structured exceptions, 109–11
  while/do while construct, 103–4
Foo ( ) method, 44
foreach construct, 104–5, 125, 208
for loop, 102–3
formatters, 138
Fujitsu Software, 8

garbage collection, 45, 72, 133, 161–72, 208
  Dispose ( ) method, 166–70, 172
  Finalize ( ) method, 161–62, 166–68, 171, 172
  forced, 171
  GC.Collect ( ) method, 171

Index · 251

IDisposable interface, 166–70, 172
nondeterministic finalization, 164–66
piping to a file, 165–66
pointers, 240–42
referencing, 161, 171
SuppressFinalization ( ) method, 166–68
using statement, 168–70, 172
GetInvocationList ( ), 160
Global Assembly Cache (GAC), 58–59
GlobalMemoryStatus ( ), 227–28
goto statements, 15, 108–9, 117, 131
Graphics Device Interface (GDI), 20
GUI development, 19–20

Hashtable class, 129–30
the heap, 80–81
    fixed statement, 240–44
    garbage collection, 161
    pointers, 240
    See also reference types
HTTP, 6, 22–23

IDisposable interface, 166–70, 172, 208
#if directive, 115–16
if/else statements, 106–7, 131, 217–18
ILDASM utility, 62–65
implicit declarations, 203, 205–6
increment operators, 95
indexers, 15, 174, 212, 218–20
inheritance, 174, 188–201
    casting, 192–93
    constructors, 195–99
    function overloading, 191
    interfaces, 201–2, 208, 210
    new keyword, 191, 200, 201
    overriding, 191, 201
    polymorphism, 194–95, 201
    prevention, 199–200
    structures, 210
    virtual keyword, 193–95, 200–201
    visibility, 200
    Visual Inheritance, 20
initializing a variable, 76, 104
    arrays, 123–24
    out keyword, 187–88
inner classes, 16, 160
installation, 35–39
instance constructors, 180
instance variables, 182–84

int *a keyword, 237
integral data types, 75
Integrated Development Environment (IDE), 7
IntelliSense, 57, 65
interfaces, 160, 174–75, 201–8
    Base Class Libraries (BCL), 208
    Common Language Interface (CLI), 41
    explicit declarations, 203, 205–6
    implicit declarations, 203, 205–6
    inheritance, 208, 210
    ISerializable, 139–40
    is keyword, 210–11
    multiple, 204–5
    polymorphism, 206–8, 211
    visibility, 202
    Win32 API (Applications Programming Interface), 17–18
Intermediate Language (IL) code, 6, 7, 42, 57, 65
Internet Information Server (IIS), 22
Internet standards, 6
ISerializable interface, 139–40
isomorphic types, 229

J#, 10
jagged arrays, 125–27, 130
Java, 14–16, 50
    anonymous inner class, 160
    data types, 43
    GDI+, 20
    J#, 10
    Java Class Libraries (JCL), 7
    Java Language Conversion Assistant, 10
    Java User Migration Path (JUMP), 10
    Just-In-Time (JIT) compilation, 42
    Virtual Machine, 6
JScript.NET, 10
Just-In-Time (JIT) Compilation, 42, 236

keywords, 15, 186–88
    base, 197–99
    fixed, 237
    int *a, 237
    is, 210–11
    methods, 186–88
    new, 122–23, 130, 191, 200–201
    out, 187–88

252 · Index

keywords (*cont'd*)
  override, 193–95, 201
  params, 188
  ref, 186–87
  sealed, 199
  sizeof, 237
  stackalloc, 237
  unsafe, 223–24, 237
  using, 50
  virtual, 193–95, 200–201
  volatile, 188

languages, 4–5, 6–7, 16, 131
  Component Object Model, 56
  cross-language inheritance, 66–67
  interoperability, 66–72
  J#, 10
  JScript.NET, 10
  Managed C++, 9–10
  Microsoft Intermediate Language (IL), 6, 7
  .NET framework, 8–10
  neutrality, 11–12, 56
  SOAP, 22
  Visual Basic.NET, 8–9
  web services, 22
  See also keywords; syntax
Linux, 4, 41
logical operators, 97–99
looping, 102–6, 117, 131
  break statement, 105
  continue construct, 105–6
  foreach construct, 104–5
  for loop, 102–3
  while/do while construct, 103–4

Managed C++, 9–10, 13
managed code, 6, 41–42, 224, 243
MarshalAs attribute, 226–27, 229–30
marshaling, 223, 226–29
members, 25–26, 175–76, 179, 183
memory management, 13, 45
  data types, 78
  fixed statement, 240–44
  GlobalMemoryStatus ( ), 227–28
  pointers, 236–40, 245
  See also garbage collection
metadata, 57–58, 65, 132
  attributes, 69, 133, 137, 140–41, 147–48, 172
  extending, 147–48

ILDASM utility, 62–64
reflection, 141, 144, 147–48, 172
methods, 24–25, 175
  derived, 193, 195
  keywords, 186–88
  members, 26
  metadata, 63–64
  namespaces, 49–50
  out keyword, 187–88
  strings, 119–20
Microsoft, 4
  ADO.NET, 21–22
  Component Object Model (COM), 18–19
  Intermediate Language (IL), 6, 7
  Internet Information Server (IIS), 22
  Java User Migration Path (JUMP), 10
  Microsoft Development Network (MSDN), 14
  See also .NET framework; Visual Studio .NET (VS.NET)
modulus operator, 96–97
multiple constructors, 178
multiple interfaces, 204–5

namespaces, 49–53, 60, 72
  assemblies, 54–55
  COM Interop, 232–34
  System.Collection, 76
  System.Diagnostic, 134–35
  System.Reflection, 144, 146, 149
  System.Reflection.Emit, 148, 149
  System.Runtime.InteropServices, 225, 230
naming attributes, 140
narrowing conversions, 78–80
native code, 222–24, 226
native syntax elements, 174
nested code blocks, 86
nested exception handling, 110–11, 114–15
NetCOBOL, 8
.NET Framework, 3–10, 40–72
  ADO.NET, 21–22
  ASP.NET, 20–21
  compiler tools, 7–8
  executables, 27
  GUI development, 19–20
  installation, 35–39
  J#, 10
  JScript.NET, 10

language accessibility, 7
Managed C++, 9–10
manipulating strings, 7
utilities, 8
Visual Basic.NET, 8–9
web services, 22–23, 35
Windows Forms, 19–20
See also Base Class Libraries (BCL);
    Common Language Runtime
    (CLR)
.NET Remoting, 23
new keyword, 122–23, 130, 191,
    200–201
nonclass types, 174–75
  interfaces, 174–75, 201–8
  structures, 175, 201, 209–11
nondeterministic finalization, 164–66
nonisomorphic types, 229

Object-Oriented Programming (OOP),
    5, 14–15, 174–221
  cast overloading, 216–18, 220
  classes, 19–20, 175–88
  class infrastructure, 211–21
  constructors, 177–82, 195–99
  destructors, 178–79
  encapsulation, 174–75
  inheritance, 174, 188–201
  interfaces, 201–8
  operator overloading, 212–15, 220
  polymorphism, 174, 194–95, 201,
      206–8, 211
  structures, 209–11
operator overloading, 15, 95, 212–15,
    220
operators, 74, 95–101, 131
  as ( ), 100
  arithmetic, 96–97
  binary, 96–99
  checked ( ), 101
  decrement, 95
  increment, 95
  is ( ), 100
  logical, 97–99
  modulus, 96–97
  relational, 97
  shortcut, 95–96
  sizeof ( ), 100
  ternary, 100
  typeof ( ), 100
  unary, 95–96

unchecked ( ), 101
OS requirements, 35–36
out keyword, 187–88
override keyword, 193–95, 201

parameter marshaling, 226–29
parametized constructors, 177–78,
    196–97, 210
params keyword, 188
performance enhancement
  boxing, 89–91
  Finalize ( ) method, 166–68
persistable objects, 137
piping to a file, 165–66
Platform Invocation Services
    (PInvoke), 18, 42, 224–30, 245
platforms, 35–36, 41, 222
pointers, 236–42
polymorphism, 174, 194–95, 200–201,
    206–8, 211
predefined attributes, 134, 140
preprocessor, 15, 115–18
PreserveSig parameter, 229–30
primitive types, 14–15, 245
private assemblies, 58
private constructors, 180–81
private key, 59
private modifier, 199
properties, 14, 175, 184–86

readonly modifier, 183–84
reference types, 80–91, 101
  arrays, 124
  boxing/unboxing, 88–91
  comparing types, 86–88
  converting between types, 88–89
  copying types, 83–84
  destruction, 84–85
  equality operator, 119, 214–15
  explicit casting, 78–80
  garbage collection, 161, 163
  narrowing conversions, 78–80
  readonly modifier, 183–84
  scope, 84–85
  transferring between types, 78–80
  type declaration, 81–82
  visibility, 84–85
referencing, 55, 60–62, 76, 161, 171
ref keyword, 186–87
reflection, 132, 141–49, 172
registry components, 57–58

254 · Index

relational operators, 97
remote components, 23
resurrection, 171
Reverse COM Interop, 222, 245
Runtime Callable Wrapper (RCW), 230, 235

scope, 84–85
searching arrays, 129–30
security, 42, 236
semi-colons, 13
serializable attribute, 134, 137–40, 208
set-up options, 38
shallow copying, 84, 124
shared assemblies, 58
short circuit evaluation, 98–99
shortcut operators, 95–96
simple reflection, 142–44
sizeof keyword, 237
slowdowns, 89–91
SoapFormatter class, 138
SOAP (Simple Object Access Protocol), 22
software components, 56–65
　See also Dynamic Link Library (DLL) files
Solution Explorer, 55
sorting example, 32–33
special characters, 77
square brackets, 14
the stack, 80–81, 209, 239
　pointers, 240–44
　See also value types
stackalloc keyword, 237
stack walk concept, 110–11
standards
　COM, 56
　Common Language Interface (CLI), 41
　Common Language System, 67–69
　Internet, 6
　Win32DLLs, 56
statement delimiters, 13
static constructors, 179–80
static/nonstatic members, 25–26, 179, 183
storage, 131
　fields, 182–84
　interfaces, 208
　See also arrays

streams, 138, 195
strings, 7, 87–88, 118–22, 245
　declaration, 77
　DLL functions, 226, 230
　immutability, 120
　StringBuilder class, 121–22
StructLayout attribute, 227–28
structures, 93–94, 175, 201, 209–11
SuppressFinalization ( ) method, 166–68
switch statements, 107–8, 117, 131
syntax, 4, 73–131
　arrays, 122–31
　comments, 73–74
　data types, 74–95
　destructor, 162–64
　inheritance, 190
　interfaces, 203
　native syntax elements, 174
　operators, 95–101
　program flow, 101–18
　strings, 118–22
　See also data types; operators
System.Array class, 125, 129
System.Collections class, 76, 128, 130–31
System.Diagnostic namespace, 134–35
System.Exception, 111–15
System.MulticastDelegate class, 150, 151–52
　GetInvocationList ( ), 160
System.Object types, 44–45, 75, 131, 190
System.Reflection.Emit namespace, 148, 149
System.Reflection namespace, 144, 146, 149
System.Runtime.InteropServices namespace, 225, 230
System.String class, 7, 119
System.Text class, 121
System.ValueType object, 91

Tangent attribute, 69
ternary operators, 100
threading, 133
TimeSpan structure, 94–95
TLBIMP utility, 230–31, 234–35, 245

`ToString( )` method, 44
`try` block, 109–10, 114, 118
type declarations, 81–82
type libraries, 230–31
types. *See* data types

unary operators, 95–96
unboxing, 15
uniformity, 66–71
UNIX, 41
unmanaged code, 223–24
unsafe code, 222–24, 236–45
 `fixed` statements, 240–45
 garbage collection, 240–42
 pointers, 236–40
 security, 236
`unsafe` keyword, 223–24, 237
unsigned numeric types, 68–69
user-defined value types, 91–94
`using` keyword, 50
`using` statement, 168–70, 172
utilities, 8
 ILDASM, 62–65
 private constructors, 181
 set-up, 39
 TLBIMP, 230–31, 234–35, 245

`ValueType` objects, 75
value types, 80–94, 101, 169
 boxing/unboxing, 88–91
 comparing, 86–88
 converting between types, 88–89
 copying, 83–84
 destruction, 84–85
 explicit casting, 78–80
 narrowing conversions, 78–80
 `ref` keyword, 186–87
 scope, 84–85
 structures, 201, 209–11
 `System.ValueType` object, 91
 type declaration, 81–82
 user-defined, 91–94
 `ValueType` objects, 91
 visibility, 84–85
variable declaration, 76–78
variable ranges, 77–78
variable types, 13, 26
verbatim string literal, 77
`virtual` keyword, 193–95, 200–201
Virtual Machine technology (VM), 6
visibility, 84–85, 175
 inheritance, 200
 interfaces, 202
Visual Basic.NET, 8–9, 13–14
 data types, 45
 IntelliSense, 57
 logical operators, 98
Visual Inheritance, 20
Visual Perl, 8
Visual Studio .NET (VS.NET), 7–8,
  19–20, 27–30
 assemblies, 59–65
 Base Class Library, 53–55
 Command Prompt, 39
 COM support, 233–34
 IntelliSense, 57, 65
 namespaces, 54–55
 preferences, 27
 Web Forms Designer, 12
 Windows Forms, 30–32, 53
`volatile` keyword, 188

web resources
 Code Notes, x
 Infusion Development Corp., x
web services, 22–23, 35
Web Services Description Language
  (WSDL), 22
`while`/`do while` constructs,
  103–4
`WhoAmI` application, 64–65
Win32DLLs, 56, 134, 222, 224–30
 unsafe code, 236–37
Windows Component Update, 36–38
Windows Forms application, 19–20,
  30–32, 51–53
Windows OS, 4, 17–19, 35–36
 COM+, 19, 35–36
 COM (Component Object Model),
  18–19
 Graphics Device Interface (GDI),
  20
 Win32 API (Applications
  Programming Interface), 17–18

XML (Extensible Markup Language),
  6, 15
 comments, 74
 data exchange, 21
 `SoapFormatter` class, 138
 Visual Studio.NET, 29
 web servies, 22–23